THE LEAGUE OF NATIONS

Perspectives from the Present

THE LEAGUE OF NATIONS

Perspectives from the Present

Editors: Haakon A. Ikonomou and Karen Gram-Skjoldager

CONTENTS

Part 2 The League in Context

The League between Nation States and Empires

The League, Economy and Expertise

Part 3 The League – Projections and Presence

Narrating the League

The League's Material Existence

Concluding Essay

FOREWORD

By Michael Møller

United Nations Under-Secretary-General
Director-General of the United Nations Office at Geneva

FOREWORD

The League of Nations Perspectives from the Present

It gives me great pleasure to pen this foreword for *The League of Nations – Perspectives from the Present*, a book of such importance and timeliness for multilateral diplomacy. A book researched in the Archives of UN Geneva, where I serve as Director-General, and issued by the University of Aarhus, where I commenced my journey to become an international civil servant. A book that recalls the origins of multilateralism and the legacies of the League of Nations, the organisation which Lord Robert Cecil called "the great experiment... [without which] the United Nations could never have come into existence".

Its publication coincides with the centenary of the Versailles Peace Treaty, when the League of Nations Covenant was first signed by the future members of the organisation. We take this same milestone, the anniversary of the Covenant, for our own celebrations of "100 Years of Multilateralism in Geneva". Over a period of nearly two years spanning from June 2019 to November 2020, we will be celebrating the achievements of the League and the continuous development of multilateral diplomacy over the past century.

A pioneering organisation, the League not only passed to the United Nations the iconic building that hosts the UN Geneva and which is currently being renovated to ensure it remains a centre for multilateral diplomacy for many years to come. Rather than just this physical property, we inherited so much more from the League, including the "Spirit of Geneva", described by Robert de Traz in his eponymous essay and inspiring us to this day.

If today we can say that every person on the planet, in any 24-hour period, is somehow impacted by the work of the UN and the other international entities in Geneva, this is precisely because of the first steps taken by the League, including on issues such as refugee protection, health and other social issues, economic assistance, labour regulation, communications, knowledge exchange and multilingualism.

Having an innovative and ambitious vision for international relations, the League's founders and members believed, as we do today and as our predecessors did when they were establishing the United Nations, that peace and prosperity can only be secured through co-operation at the global level.

We all need to live without fear of aggression and violence. We all need strong economies, plentiful resources, safe dwellings and education. We all need human rights and human dignity. We all need our planet to be a secure and welcoming home.

These needs, which all nations share, are enshrined in the 2030 Agenda for Sustainable Development Goals adopted in 2015 by the General Assembly of the United Nations. These seventeen Global Goals can be considered a culmination of the hundred years of work of the League of Nations and the United Nations. To achieve them, we need multilateralism now more than ever. No single country can respond to these challenges alone, as they go far beyond national borders.

Understanding the past can help us to respond to these challenges. It is still common to see the League of Nations as a failure. However, as Sean Lester, its last Secretary-General, recognised in 1946: "It was not the League which failed. It was not its principles which were found wanting. It was the nations which neglected it. It was the Governments which abandoned it". Historians can help us identify the mistakes which were made at that time, but they also are helping us to unveil the multiple successes on which we can continue to build, joining forces and uniting our strengths to preserve the limited and dwindling resources of our planet for future generations.

In this regard, *The League of Nations – Perspectives from the Present* is a very welcome read. Largely based on research conducted in the League of Nations Archives, a UNESCO Memory of the World collection of which the UN Geneva is the proud custodian, this book offers us a much-needed perspective on our shared history. I am glad the UN Geneva was able to assist the tremendous research that was needed for it to come to fruition.

The ongoing digitisation of the complete archival collection of the League of Nations will allow us to make, by 2022, 15 million pages of exceptional knowledge on international relations during the interwar era freely available to the public worldwide. I look forward to the UN Geneva's future not only as a facilitator of collaboration between nations, but also as a much-needed centre of research on the history of multilateralism, to which I consider this book to be a significant contribution.

INTRODUCTION

"The history of the League of Nations is brief, thrilling and tragic. The first attempt to gather the nations of the world to cooperate peacefully – and the direct forerunner of the United Nations – has a history and legacy that is both complex and of immense importance to our understanding of the contemporary world".

MOGENS LYKKETOFT
Former President of the United Nations General Assembly

Haakon A. Ikonomou and
Karen Gram-Skjoldager

THE LEAGUE OF NATIONS

Perspectives from the Present

In the decade since the international financial crisis, the interwar period has crept into political and public discourse, acquiring a renewed contemporary significance. Today, bookshelves are full of publications warning us that we are about to re-learn the lessons of the interwar years the hard way: Madeleine Albright and prominent historians Timothy Snyder, Richard J. Evans, Harold James and Jan-Werner Müller, are just a few of those who have drawn the comparison. The former Greek Minister of Finance, Yanis Varoufakis, in his review of Adam Tooze's book on the 2008 financial crisis, wrote that he feared we had reached "a 1930s moment". Even those arguing that this is not the case – like David Runciman – must first battle visions of a return to the interwar years as a central "trope of our public life". The return of the interwar period to contemporary political discourse has tapped into and boosted a scholarly revisiting of the League of Nations, the first global organisation with a permanent secretariat created to oversee the peace and prosperity of the world. Interestingly this scholarship does not only – or even primarily – study the League as a failure in the face of economic crisis and the rise of nationalism and totalitarianism, but approaches it as a laboratory of early global governance, with legacies reaching up to the present.

Indeed, in recent years the League of Nations has attracted vast scholarly interest; a landslide of research has been produced on the organisation and its role and significance in interwar European history, as well as twentieth-century international and global history more broadly. The League serves, it seems, as a canvas on which historians re-animate, interpret and seek to understand the challenges of the contemporary world – a frame of reference for our troubled times. One of the central aims of this edited volume is to weave some of these long historical threads, connecting the multifarious research on the League with present political and cultural debates and concerns. It is not an alarmist account; nor is it an attempt to peddle a unified interpretation of the relationship between then and now. Rather, we have organised a wealth of exciting new research on the League into five broad frameworks – *Inside the League*, *The League between Nation States and Empires*, *The League, Economy and Expertise*, *Narrating the League* and *Materialising the League* – to offer the curious reader some avenues through which she can engage with the topics and relate them to the contemporary world. Hopefully, this will prompt many new questions – the buds of future research.

The League of Nations as an object of study has also become an 'academic site', where International History has re-invented itself by integrating new, innovative approaches from social, cultural and media history. Far from perceiving the League solely as an arena for Great Power politics, as used to be the case, the historiography of the League has been a driver of innovations in International History: by directing our attention to the League's technical, economic and cultural work, by considering how the League as a new form of international governance shifted notions of sovereignty and political legitimacy, and by exploring the social world of the League and the political and cultural characteristics of the first transnational technocratic and administrative elite. The second aim of this edited volume, then, is to show not only that the League was a laboratory of global governance at the time, but also that it is – as a research object – a laboratory for international historians today. Thus, while our first aim is analytical, our second aim is historiographical, as we display a broad palette of innovative research on the League and bring to the fore subjects and approaches we anticipate will play a significant part in the years to come. The introductions to the book's three main sections offer further elaborations of this point.

Both aims are natural products of the fact that this publication started out as a research blog. Three years ago (2016), Karen Gram-Skjoldager initiated the research project *The Invention of International Bureaucracy – The League of Nations and the Creation of International Public Administration, c. 1920-1960*. As one of her postdocs, Haakon A. Ikonomou was tasked with editing a small research blog on the project and relevant research conducted elsewhere. The blog soon became a lively site for all types of research on the League, and since we welcomed small pieces on ongoing research, it developed into a fine tool for sensing new trends and currents within the field. Having gathered, curated and published nearly 30 excellent blogs – cutting-edge research delivered in an accessible and poignant manner – we decided to develop a selection of these into a broad, easy-access outreach book to showcase recent approaches to and findings in League of Nations research. The format of the edited volume allows us to place the contributions in their historiographical, methodological and current political contexts.

This book is published on the 100th anniversary of the signing of the Treaty of Versailles, which also marked the birth of the League of Nations. It is our own small contribution to the centennial celebration of the creation of the League. In a time of international political crisis and disintegration, it seems fitting to foreground the many ways the first global international organisation shaped its times and continues to shape our world – and the many ways historians have used this complex international creation to re-shape International History as an academic discipline.

BIBLIOGRAPHY

Published material

Albright, Madeleine: *Fascism: A Warning*, Harper, 2018.

Evans, Richard J.: *The Third Reich in History and Memory*, Little, Brown Book Group, 2015.

Müller, Jan Werner: *What is Populism?*, University of Pennsylvania Press, 2016.

Snyder, Timothy: *On Tyranny: Twenty Lessons from the Twentieth Century*, Bodley Head, 2017.

Online sources

James, Harold: 'America's Neville Chamberlain', 01.08.2018, project-syndicate.org.

Runciman, David: 'How Democracy Ends', Lecture recorded at Churchill College as part of the CSAR lecture series, 07.12.2017, talkingpolitics-podcast.com.

Varoufakis, Yanis: 'Crashed: How a Decade of Financial Crises Changed the World – review', 12.08.2018, theguardian.com.

PART 1

INSIDE THE LEAGUE

THE boom in historical scholarship on the League of Nations in recent years has been closely tied to the transnational turn in history. The majority of researchers working on the League have focused on particular aspects of the League's work – such as economy, health, trafficking or refugees – and used the organisation as an analytical entry point to access and map the networks of individuals, associations and ideas that came to shape perceptions and policies on these issues across borders and continents. Patricia Clavin aptly captures this approach in her seminal study of the League's economic and financial policy, *Securing the World Economy. The Reinvention of the League of Nations 1920-1946* (Oxford: Oxford University Press), when she describes the organisation as "a site where a plurality of views about global and regional coordination and cooperation were generated" (7). In Part 2 of this book, we present a selection of studies that practice and develop this approach.

In Part 1, by contrast, we address one of the underexplored dimensions in recent transnational historiography on the League. Often studies within the transnational tradition have shown only limited interest in the institutional infrastructure of the organisation, approaching it as they do from a perspective of networks and ideas rather than institutions. In 'Inside the League', we present some of the insights that can be gained by viewing the League of Nations not only as an arena and a 'dot-connector' for various new transnational forms of expertise and policy-making, but also as an object of study in its own right.

In other words, venturing 'Inside the League' means taking it seriously as an institution with its own distinct set of professional norms, procedures and practices that can and should be explored as constituting a distinct social and political world. Going 'Inside the League' also means shifting the analytical gaze from ideas and policy agendas towards *practice*. The five contributions in this section are in tune with the recent 'practice turn' in International Relations Theory, brought forth by among others Emanuel Adler and Victor Pouliot ("International practices", *International Theory* 3 (1), 2011, 1-36), since they focus on the everyday administrative procedures and professional routines that structured, reproduced and gradually transformed the League as an institutional entity. Finally, looking 'Inside the League' involves a change of analytical scale. The chapters in this section do not focus on the major political turning point decisions that set out the parameters of the League's work; neither do they address the long-term shifts in political agendas and global governance structures that played out in and around the League. Instead, they adopt a micro-scale approach that investigates the everyday practices through which different actors 'did' international organisations – be they politicians, leading members of the Secretariat, female staff or translators and interpreters.

Karen Gram-Skjoldager

Torsten Kahlert and
Karen Gram-Skjoldager

THE MEN BEHIND THE MAN

Canvassing the Directorship of the League of Nations Secretariat

When Kofi Annan passed away on 18 August 2018, it was a global news story. Newspapers, TV and radio around the world reported on Annan's passing, and commentators discussed and assessed his achievements and shortcomings as UN Secretary-General from 1997 to 2006. This massive media response is telling of the importance we ascribe to Secretaries-General as symbolic representatives of the international organisations they head and for international order and cooperation more broadly.

However, Secretaries-General do not run international organisations alone. The current UN Secretary-General António Guterres, like his predecessors, has the help of dozens of Division Heads that hold the day-to-day responsibilities for the UN Secretariat's many tasks, ranging from disarmament and public information to social and economic affairs. In much the same way, the League of Nation's first Secretary-General, Sir Eric Drummond, ensured that a group of Directors was put in charge of the League's many different policy areas from the very beginning.

In this chapter, we scrutinize this small administrative elite and ask: who were these 'men behind the man'? What were their social, professional and national characteristics, how did they end up in these leading roles and how did the Secretariat leadership evolve over time? In asking these questions, we adopt an approach that is becoming increasingly popular in the study of international organisations, namely to move past the formal structures and procedures and focus on the people populating the organisation, either through biographical or – as in this case – prosopographical studies.[1] As we will demonstrate, mapping central group characteristics such as education, nationality and age for an influential group of people over time can offer fruitful analytical insights into the defining social and political qualities of an organisation and how they evolved over time.[2]

THREE GENERATIONS

The Secretariat of the League of Nations existed from 1919 to 1946. Seen from today, these 27 years may seem like a short life span, but the Secretariat was not a static unit. Starting out with a mere three employees when Drummond set up his first small office in London, the Secretariat went through a rapid process of expansion, professionalisation and differentiation. The League's personnel peaked in 1931 with around 650 people working in the Secretariat and 115 higher officials, including 12 Directors running the large bureaucratic operation. During the 1930s, economic depression, political conflicts and setbacks together with the withdrawal of several member states and the relatively disastrous Secretary-Generalship of Joseph Avenol led to a steady decline in the size of the League Secretariat.[3] This was followed by a dramatic scaling down of the organisation with the onset of the Second World War.

We will show that three different 'generations' of Directors led the Secretariat – each with distinct characteristics in terms of age, national and professional backgrounds, career trajectories and gender.[4] The changing norms for the kind of people who were able to land these positions in the higher echelons of the Secretariat mirrored both the professionalisation of the administration and the changing powers of, and limits on, the Secretariat defined by member states. By way of conclusion, we will offer a few examples of the types of careers that the League Directors had after their service in the League, thereby reflecting on the role of this group in postwar multilateralism.

A children's tea party in an East End Street in London, celebrating the Treaty of Versailles in 1919. While the First World War had ended in 1918, the official peace celebrations took place after the Treaty of Versailles had been signed on 28 June 1919. This kind of children's celebration was held all over the British dominions, marking the end of the global war on a global scale.

THE DIRECTORS IN THE INSTITUTIONAL SETUP OF THE SECRETARIAT

The Secretariat was organised around a basic structure of 9 to 12 functionally defined Sections and three hierarchical Divisions.[5] The Directors belonged to the top division in this tiered hierarchy. The Sections were the most important units of the Secretariat, each charged with managing a particular policy area – be it Health, Economy and Finance, Mandates or Minorities. Each section included officials from all three divisions.

(1930)

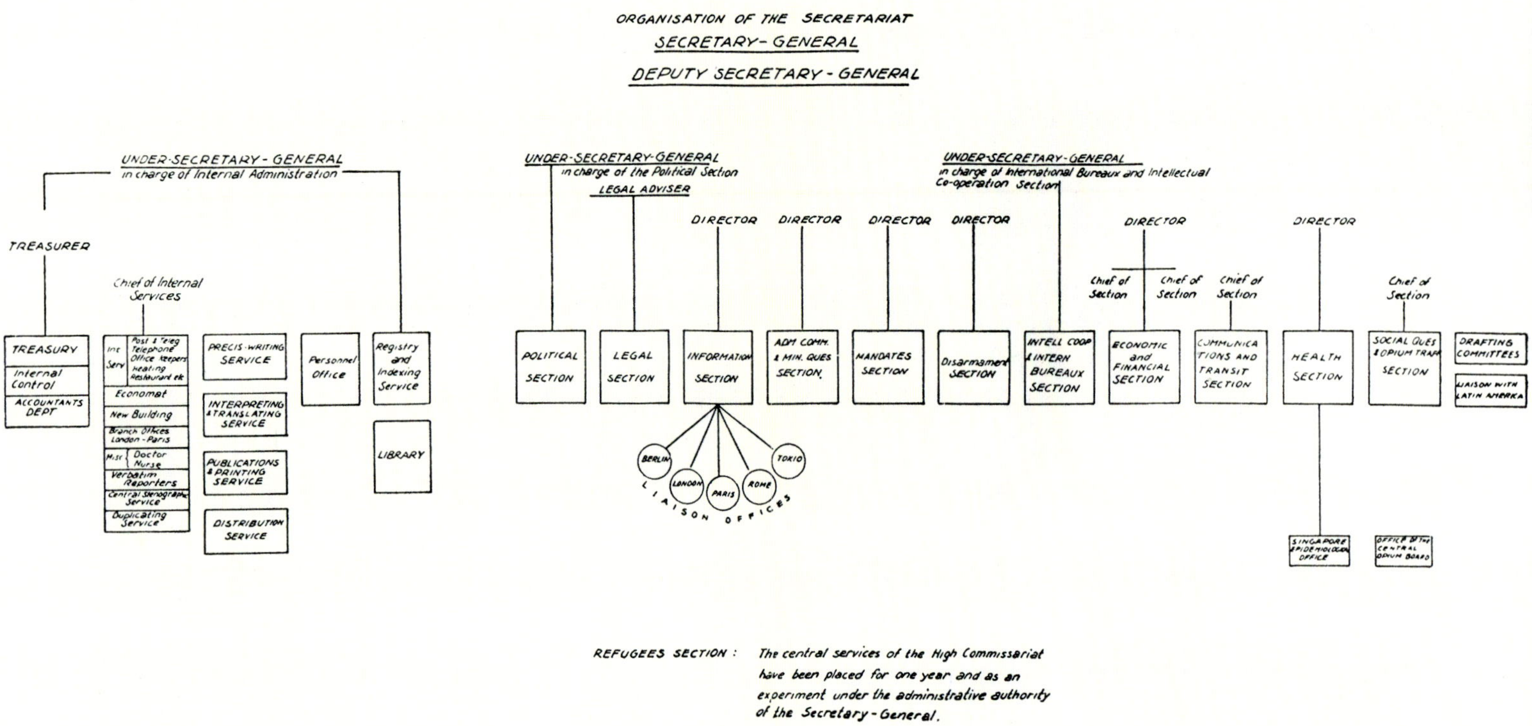

Directorships in the League of Nations Secretariat were hard-won, prestigious positions. Together with the Secretary-General and the Deputy- and Under-Secretaries-General, the Directors made up the Secretariat's leadership and were decisive in shaping the rules and practices of the new administrative body, while also defining the image of the international civil servant through their practices.

Directorships were supposed to be temporary and over the course of the League's existence, the Secretariat's Directorship counted 31 Directors from 15 different countries. None of the Directors held the position for the entire lifespan of the Secretariat (1919-1946), though some had long careers; a striking example of this is Ludwik Rajchman, the Director of the Health Section from 1921 to 1939.

The organisational chart is taken from Egon Ranshofen-Wertheimer's book on the Secretariat of the League of Nations from 1945. The chart represents the Secretariat's organisational form around 1930 and showcases the functional work's division into sections. It also highlights how the League developed the basic structure of international administration as we know it today.

FOUNDING FATHERS – THE FIRST GENERATION (1920-1927)

After his appointment as the first Secretary-General, Sir Eric Drummond made two decisions that came to shape the Secretariat's work throughout the interwar period. The first was to build the Secretariat along functional rather than national lines, as described above. The second was to organise the administration as an international civil service in which, in theory, a person of any nationality could fill any position. At least on paper, meritocracy was the ideal.

According to the Covenant, the League's constitution, all decision-making power in terms of staffing lay exclusively with the Secretary-General. This was crucial, especially for the first, founding generation of Directors. After his appointment in the spring of 1919, Drummond was working on a very strict time schedule; the Council and the Assembly were supposed to meet for the first time in the autumn of that year. As Ikonomou argues in chapter 11, the first group of leading personnel was therefore recruited in an informal and improvised manner, through Drummond's personal networks and connections to various foreign services. These pioneers, moreover, were left to recruit their own Section staff, with relatively little meddling from the Secretary-General, before the Secretariat settled its bureaucratic practices.

The result was a relatively heterogeneous group in terms of education and professional backgrounds, ranging from diplomats, like the Norwegian Eric Colban or the Italian Bernardo Attolico, to the French journalist Pierre Comert, the Dutch lawyer Joost van Hamel, the British economist Arthus Salter and the French historian Paul Mantoux. The early Secretariat leadership also included one woman: Dame Rachel Crowdy, who led the Social Questions and Opium Traffic Section. Though professionally diverse, the early Secretariat leadership had a strong *esprit de corps* based on their recent war experience. Several of the Directors had worked in the Inter-Allied War Councils, and many had been involved in the negotiations at the Paris Peace Conference.

In terms of national background, the early Directors were less diverse. In an international organisation, nationality is a potential resource and source of legitimacy. With two British and two French directors, and one each from Italy and Japan, Drummond had given a dominant position to the Great Powers that created the organisation. Following the American decision not to join the League, Drummond believed that keeping the major member states well represented was pivotal.[6] Apart from this privileged position of the major member states, there was also a strong North European dominance in the Secretariat; the other Directors came from Allied or neutral countries such as the Netherlands, Norway, Switzerland and Poland. This composition of the Secretariat Directorship persisted throughout the first half of the 1920s, shaping the Secretariat's administrative rules and practices as the new organisation was moulded on British Foreign Office principles and procedures.

The composition of the Directorship became an object of criticism almost immediately. During the Second General Assembly, Drummond received harsh criticism from smaller and non-European countries for the British/French dominance of the Secretariat and the Directors and Under-Secretaries-General in particular. During the 1920s a gradual internationalisation of the Secretariat's recruitment practices took place.[7]

THE INSIDERS – THE SECOND GENERATION (1928-1932)

Between 1927 and 1932, all Directors apart from Rajchman in the Health Section were replaced and a second generation of Directors with a slightly different profile took over the leadership of the Secretariat. The second generation had a more homogenous professional background, with university degrees in law and professional experience from the diplomatic services.[8] More importantly, most of them were older (three years on average) and promoted from *within* the Secretariat to their Director positions, rather than appointed from the outside. This was a reflection both of the professionalisation of the Secretariat as a bureaucratic administration and of the gradual recognition that international administration required a particular international professional skillset that was being developed and acknowledged in the organisation.

The importance of qualifications obtained inside the organisation had already been acknowledged in the first set of Staff Regulations in 1922, which states that higher positions in the Secretariat should "as far as possible be filled by the promotion of officials already serving Secretariat" (article 16).[9] Likewise, discussions in the so-called Appointments Committee, a deliberative internal body headed by Drummond in which all major decisions regarding recruitment and promotions were debated, reveal how hiring someone from the 'outside', particularly for higher positions, was considered a distinct risk.[10]

However, the focus on internal promotions to the Directorships was also a conservative rule that benefited League officials from member states that were already strongly represented inside the organisation. It is therefore unsurprising that, with the second generation of Directors, the national composition diversified only slightly. Most remarkably, the first South American – Juan Antonio Buero – entered the Directorship, as head of the Legal Section. Likewise, the Greek Thanassis Aghnides became the first Director from the Balkan region, heading the Disarmament Section. Simultaneously, however, the minimal gender diversity that the Secretariat could boast in its higher echelons in its early years disappeared, as Dame Rachel Crowdy's contract was not extended – triggering widespread criticism from female employees and women's organisations alike.[11]

The homogenisation and professionalisation that characterised the second generation of Directors was supported at the political level by the so-called Committee of Thirteen, which issued a report in 1930 that recommended that the career of an international civil servant be made as similar to that of a national civil servant as possible by strengthening their workers' rights and developing a proper pensions scheme. However, a minority report was also issued. This report, promoted by Germany and Italy, argued that the Secretariat be reorganised into a system of national delegations of bureaucrats seconded to Geneva for shorter periods of time in order to secure stronger membership control over the new and independent political institution.[12] While this was a minority viewpoint, it was a telling indication that support for the League was waning and conflicts around the Secretariat were escalating.

THE THIRD GENERATION (1933-1946)

The third generation (1933-1946) was very similar to the generation before it. The new Directors had a slightly higher average age but the majority were still trained diplomats and there was a predominance of internal promotions, all indicating a continued professionalisation of the League's recruitment and promotion practices.

At first glance, the national diversity of the group did not change significantly. However, one shift did take place; among the ten Directors recruited from 1933, six were from small European countries. Adrianus Pelt, who became Director of the Information Section in 1934, was Dutch, while and Edouard Rodolpho de Haller, who headed the Mandates Section from 1935, was Swiss. During this period, no British Directors were appointed. This shift can be seen as a reflection of the rising influence of the Assembly, with its large and diverse membership, on the Secretariat's personnel policy and the growing relative weight of small/neutral states, especially from Europe, towards the end of the League's existence.[13] It is also reasonable to assume that it was a reflection of the League's waning political status and influence by the mid-1930s.

Finally, it should be pointed out that across all three generations of Directors, there was one notable absence: the defeated powers in the First World War were systematically excluded. Germany entered the League in 1926 and while there were as many German Members of Section as British ones during the following two years, no Germans ever landed a Director's position. Germany was represented among the Under-Secretaries-General. However, though this was a higher-ranking post, it was a less hands-on position within the Secretariat, with a certain ambassadorial streak to it. The only time Drummond offered a Director's post to a German, it was part of a larger trade-off scheme: Drummond offered the politically uncontentious position of Director of Social Questions and Opium Traffic Section to the German Dr. Gertrud Bäumer in order to position a Briton as head of the Disarmament Section. The deal fell through though, and the Swede Erik Ekstrand was appointed to head the Social Section.[14]

1

2

3

CONCLUSION AND PERSPECTIVES – AFTERLIVES

Where did the Directors go when they left the Secretariat and the newly invented profession of international civil servant? Though a lot more research is needed here, we know that many Directors (re)joined their national foreign services and became ambassadors in major capitals. Eric Drummond's career was in this sense typical, as he became ambassador to Rome following his 13-year stint as Secretary-General. While he considered this post a demotion – he would have preferred the post as Ambassador in Washington[15] – for others, such as the Norwegian Erik Colban, who left the Directorship of the Disarmament Section to become minister of the Norwegian Embassy in Paris, their ensuing diplomatic careers were considered prestigious and successful.[16] Others, particularly Directors from the small and neutral countries, went on to work for the UN after the Second World War. Examples include the Dutch head of the Information Section Adriaan Pelt and the Greek Director of the Disarmament Section Thanassis Aghnides. A third and smaller group that included the British Director of the Financial Section & Economic Intelligence Service Alexander Loveday, and the Spaniard Salvador de Madariaga, took up posts in academia.[17]

However, much still remains to be understood about the characteristics, professional practices and career trajectories of the League Directors. Historians have only recently begun to uncover the broader patterns and significance of these 'men behind the man'. As the earlier monographs on Secretaries-General are steadily complemented by in-depth studies of the officials surrounding them, a more nuanced, balanced and not least interesting picture will emerge. The brief survey of the Directorship of the League of Nations presented here should prepare the ground.

The second generation of Directors:
❶ Pablo de Azcárate (1890-1971), Spain ❷ Thanassis Aghnides (1889-1984), Greece ❸ Pietro Angelo Stoppani (1879-1968), Italy ❹ Vito Catastini (1879-?), Italy ❺ Erik Ekstrand (1880-1958), Sweden ❻ Salvador de Madariaga (1886-1978), Spain.

NOTES

1 See for example Mourlon-Druol: 'Less than a Permanent Secretariat'; Tollardo: *Fascist Italy*; Auberer: 'The Ultimate Backroom-Boy', 76-99; Fröhlich and Williams (eds): *The UN Secretary-General*; Kahlert: 'Pioneers'.

2 For a general introduction to prosopography, see Keats-Rohan (ed.): *Prosopography*.

3 For more on his specific brand of internationalism, see Moraes' blog: 'Multiple Internationalisms'.

4 The findings in this chapter draw on a larger prosopographical analysis conducted by one of the authors (Kahlert: 'Pioneers in international administration') and on the so-called LONSEA database. This database, which can be accessed at www.lonsea.de, was developed in the framework of the research cluster "Asia and Europe in a Global Context", which is directed by Madeleine Herren and based at the University of Heidelberg. It has been publicly available since 2010.

5 Ranshofen-Wertheimer: *The International Secretariat*.

6 Gram-Skjoldager and Ikonomou: 'The Construction of the League'.

7 Gram-Skjoldager and Ikonomou: 'The Construction of the League', 9-11, 17-18.

8 Kahlert: 'Pioneers'.

9 LoNA R1460 – Staff Regulations 1st Edition, Geneva, 1 June 1922.

10 LoNA – S956 – File 1. This was the case, for example, when Salvador de Madariaga left the Secretariat in 1927, and a new Director of the Disarmament Section had to be found. The choice eventually fell on Erik Colban, previously Director of the Minority Section.

11 LoNA – S749. Personnel file Dame Rachel Crowdy, private file, part II, letters from various organisations concerning length of contract.

12 Ranshofen-Wertheimer: 'The International Secretariat', 28-31.

13 For an analysis of the relative increase of Scandinavian officials within the League Secretariat in the late 1930s and early 1940s, see Gram-Skjoldager, Ikonomou and Kahlert: 'Scandinavians' (forthcoming, 2019).

14 LoNA – S957 File 1 – *Minutes of the Seventh Meeting of the Appointments Committee held on the 16th May, 1930*.

15 For a brief overview of Eric Drummond's life and career, see Gram-Skjoldager: 'Drummond'.

16 Colban: *Femti år*.

17 Kahlert: 'Pioneers'.

BIBLIOGRAPHY

Unpublished material

League of Nations Archives (LoNA) S749 – Personnel file Dame Rachel Crowdy.

League of Nations Archives (LoNA) S956-7 – Appointments Committee files.

League of Nations Archives (LoNA) R1460 – Staff Regulations 1st Edition, Geneva, 1 June 1922.

Published material

Auberer, Benjamin: '"The Ultimate Backroom-Boy": The Border-Crossing Career of Joseph Vivian Wilson in the League of Nations Secretariat', *Comparativ* 23 (6), 2013, 76-99.

Colban, Erik: *Femti år*, Oslo: H. Aschehoug, 1952.

Fröhlich, Manuel and Abiodun Williams (eds): *The UN Secretary-General and the Security Council: A Dynamic Relationship*, Oxford: Oxford University Press, 2018.

Gram-Skjoldager, Karen: 'Drummond, Sir James Eric'. In Bob Reinalda, Kent Kille and Jaci Eisbenberg (eds): *Biographical Dictionary of Secretaries-General of International Organizations*, 2016. (06.02.2019).

Gram-Skjoldager, Karen, Haakon A. Ikonomou and Torsten Kahlert: 'Scandinavians and the League of Nations Secretariat, 1919-1946', *Scandinavian Journal of History* (e-pub ahead of print, January, 2019).

Gram-Skjoldager, Karen and Haakon A. Ikonomou: 'The Construction of the League of Nations Secretariat. Formative Practices of Autonomy and Legitimacy in International Organizations', *International History Review*, 2017.

Kahlert, Torsten: 'Pioneers in International Administration. A Prosopography of the Directors of the League of Nations Secretariat' (forthcoming).

Keats-Rohan, Katharine S.B. (ed.): *Prosopography Approaches and Applications: A Handbook*, *Prosopographica et Genealogica Vol. 13*, Oxford: P&G, Prosopographica et Genealogica, 2007.

Moraes, Marco: 'Multiple Internationalisms at the League of Nations Secretariat, 1933-1940'. http://projects.au.dk/inventingbureaucracy/blog/show/artikel/multiple-internationalisms-at-the-league-of-nations-secretariat-1933-1940/ (08.01.2019).

Mourlon-Druol, Emmanuel: 'Less than a Permanent Secretariat, More than an Ad Hoc Preparatory Group: A Prosopography of the Personal Representatives of the G7 Summits (1975–1991)'. In Emmanuel Mourlon-Druol and Federico Romero (eds): *International Summitry and Global Governance: The Rise of the G7 and the European Council, 1974-1991*, London: Routledge, 2014, 64-98.

Ranshofen-Wertheimer, Egon: *The International Secretariat: A Great Experiment in International Administration, Studies in the Administration of International Law and Organization Vol. 3*, Washington: Carnegie Endowment for International Peace, 1945.

Sluga, Glenda and Patricia Clavin (eds): *Internationalisms: A Twentieth-Century History*, Cambridge: Cambridge University Press, 2017.

Tollardo, Elisabetta: *Fascist Italy and the League of Nations, 1922-1935*, London: Palgrave Macmillan, 2016.

Haakon A. Ikonomou

AN INTERNATIONAL LANGUAGE

The Translation and Interpretation Service

"I wonder if you could tell me the meaning of an obscure Finnish word I've got here? I think it's perhaps something to do with fishing tackle", goes one of the lines in the infomercial "The League at Work", produced by the League in the late 1930s.[1] This movie, which introduces viewers to all the aspects of the Secretariat, starts with the Translation and Interpretation Service. And no wonder: it was one of the peculiarities of the Secretariat – indeed, one of the features that made it *international* in all its doings.

In the last decade or so research on the League has turned its attention to the expertise privileged and produced by the League, as well as the specific modes of governance this created and their lasting effect into the postwar years.[2] Recently, historians have taken a specific interest in the long history of media relations and public diplomacy in and around international organisations, as a distinctive expertise, and particularly in the League's information and propaganda efforts.[3] However, there has been comparatively little exploration of the particular kind of expertise that went into ensuring continuous communication within the organisation, and which enabled the League's Information Section to reach political elites and populations – spanning many languages – across the world.[4]

A new 'bottom-up' history of international administrations is currently being written, tied into research about women in international organisations,[5] who often work in the internal and clerical services, and about the bureaucratic practices of the League more generally.[6] This chapter is a small contribution to this body of work: it seeks to understand both the practical and symbolic significance of the translation and interpretation service.

SO MUCH TO DO!

The Interpreters and Translators Service was one of the earliest functioning elements of the League Secretariat. It was necessary, not only because the League employed two official languages – French and English – but also because the Secretariat communicated with and between member states in a multitude of languages, particularly during the annual Assemblies, which gathered delegates from all over the world. "As the business of the League will be conducted in the French and English languages", Secretary-General Eric Drummond made clear upon the organisation's creation, "it is essential for the efficiency of the organisation that the members of the 'material' side of the organisation should be drawn from French- and English-speaking nations".[7] And so they were. From June to October 1919 a single Service was set up with a small number of French and English translators and interpreters, under the direction of the Swiss Dr. Parodi.

The Service soon split into two distinct sub-sections – interpreters (oral) and translators (written) – and the original five employees were joined by new staff in the course of 1920. The division between interpretation and translation was made after the First Assembly in the late fall of 1920. Translators and interpreters did very different things, the Secretariat discovered, and the translation sub-section was strengthened with two chief translators, ensuring that all official and public documents produced by the Assembly, Council or Secretariat were of the best quality possible.

With the expansion of the Secretariat and the move from the temporary seat in London to the permanent seat in Geneva, the workload grew explosively. In the two last months of 1919, the Service worked with 300 documents; in all of 1920 they handled 2200 documents; in the three first months of 1921 they had already handled 1200 documents. This development required a slight expansion of the Service, and by early 1921, it consisted of one Director, two Chief Translators, fourteen Translators, four Interpreters and two Assistant Secretaries. Its workload would continue to grow: in 1928, the Eighth Assembly reported that the amount of translation had doubled, and the amount of verbal interpreting had increased by about five times since 1921.[8]

The Service dealt with almost all written material and all speeches produced in Geneva. The translators not only worked with documents drawn up by the various sections of the Secretariat, but also translated communications of every kind received by the League of Nations. The interpreters worked in a rather spasmodic fashion, having much to do in connection with Assemblies, Conferences and meetings of Commissions or Committees. Between such events, they would help the translators. Both sub-sections had to deal with a wide range of languages, necessitating fluency in both French and English, and covering most other Member State languages with the help of specific employees specialised in a region or language group (German, Spanish, Nordic languages, Slavic languages etc.).

The rhythm of Geneva, the fact that work was created by events entirely out of the Secretariat's hands, meant that the interpreters and translators worked strange and long hours. As the Director reported in 1921, it often "called for great devotion to duty on the part of its members; during Conferences [...] and during the Assembly night work was always necessary". The unique environment and tasks in Geneva also meant that the Service acquired, with time, a distinct way of doing things – making the multilingual organisation hum as if it had just one language.[9]

The translation and interpretatio service was dominated by native speakers of French and English, and many local Swiss nationals held prominent positions. One such was the Geneva-born Humbert-Denis Parodi (1878-1953 Recruited to the Secretariat as it set up shop in London in 1919, he directed the service for several years and stayed on with the Secretariat until his retirement in 1938.

TOWARDS A GENEVA LANGUAGE

Being a translator for the League required a thorough knowledge of general political questions, alongside a feel for complicated technical subjects. As one of the first League chroniclers, Howard-Ellis writes that by 1928 the Eight Assembly estimated that about three-quarters

of all the translation work was "highly technical". The translator's work involved "specialized knowledge of such subjects as medicine, serology, epidemiology, transport, military and naval matters, aviation, economics, chemistry, public finance, international and commercial law".[10] Accordingly, the translation and interpretation service developed highly specialised language skills. Moreover, as many national administrations were rather less proficient and skilled in writing up official texts in English or French, the translators preferred to receive material in the original language – translating themselves from the writer's native tongue.

In time, therefore, the Service created a *lingua franca* suited to the technical terminology of the League, allowing for smooth translation from French to English (or vice versa) and taking diplomatic tact into consideration. As Egon Ranshofen-Wertheimer notes:

> Out of trial and error grew slowly a terminology and technical language which gave League documents that special style so often criticized by language purists who were unaware of the difficulties involved. This terminology and style may have been involved and may have smacked of bureaucratic pedantry but its adoption was the only way out of difficulties which otherwise would have been quite insurmountable.[11]

It could be said that this Geneva language was constructed for the League to function as the optimal instrument of understanding between the different Member States, even if it meant having to forego 'proper' English and French. The practical significance of the translation and interpretation service, then, could hardly be underestimated – but their symbolic role was of equal importance.

TRANSLATION AND INTERPRETATION AS HEROIC INTERNATIONALISM

The translators and interpreters – one of the peculiarities of the internal administrative services, setting them apart from national public administrations – and their development of a distinctly international bureaucratic language facilitated equality of terms and understanding. It was, as former staff members would maintain, the international language of the League, and thus also a crucial part of the League's diplomatic function as a political arena.[12]

For die-hard internationalists like Ranshofen-Wertheimer, a former member of the Information Section of the League, the Translation and Interpreting Service symbolised the purest form of internationalism. The degree of coordination, he mused in his book on the Secretariat, was "reflected in the clockwork precision with which documents were supplied [...] one of the glories of the Geneva administration",

Miss Maria Luisa Aruajo, a UN Interpreter, at work in a booth overlooking a meeting room. In the mid-1960s, some fifty interpreters serviced delegates from 114 nations, presenting their views in one of the five official languages or their native tongue. Technological advances, more suitable workspaces and a bigger staff removed the average translator somewhat from the action 'on the floor'.

indeed, "one of the most efficient administrations the world has ever seen".[13]

This internationalism went beyond the bureaucratic set-up of the Service:

> In the final count it was the human element [...] not the administrative patterns and techniques, which accounted for the efficiency with which the technical tasks were dispatched [...] A staff whose high skill and readiness to work at all hours of the day and the night presented to the outside world a picture of flawless teamwork. [...] The routine and traditions established in the first years triumphed over all the obstacles – those coming from outside as well as those created by developments within the administration.[14]

The nostalgia of those first-generation chroniclers of the League experiment, often writing during the Second World War, tended to enhance the heroic internationalism, indeed martyrdom, of the Secretariat, defying the cruelties of the world to the very end.[15] One could say, tongue-in-cheek, that as the political significance of the League had long been forgotten, what remained was the importance of expertise and bureaucracy.

Consider this story, recalled by Ranshofen-Wertheimer:

This writer remembers many instances in which interpreters performed seemingly impossible feats. Sir John Simon once put the French interpreter deliberately to a dramatic test during the involved deliberations of the Disarmament Conference. He concluded a long and difficult speech with a quotation from Shelley, obviously to challenge the skill of the French interpreter, Monsieur M. The latter interpreted the speech as usual with hardly any recourse to notes, as was his habit, and, incidentally, the habit of nearly all top interpreters. To the amazement of the listeners he rendered the Shelley quotation in French verse, thus reaching a peak which will never be surpassed in the history of this art.[16]

Less pioneering 'heroism' and more smooth machinery? This is the reference centre (Documents Control Division) on the 15th floor of the Secretariat building at the UN Headquarters (May 1954). Documents kept here were stored and ordered for the use of the translators. Though the UN was and is under constant budgetary scrutiny, the facilities of the early days were extraordinary compared to the material circumstances the League officials worked under.

The choice of Sir John Simon as the interpreter's nemesis cannot have been coincidental. He was, after all, known for his lack of love for the League's method of solving international problems. In this tale, therefore, the bureaucrat of the Secretariat is the true internationalist – as he would be in many memoirs and histories produced by former League staff.

A NEW DIPLOMACY – THE SYMBOLIC SIGNIFICANCE OF TRANSLATION AND INTERPRETATION

Ranshofen-Wertheimer's writings, amongst others, suppress the challenges translators and interpreters met within the Secretariat. Carolyn N. Biltoft refers how an official of the service complained in 1921 that the staff was wholly unequipped to handle the many languages of the Assemblies. In the early years of the League, officials were only qualified in English and French translation and interpretation. By the Second Assembly, the official complained, "difficult documents in other languages were continuously being sent to his department for translation [and] his department was continually being asked to translate from — German, Italian, Spanish, Dutch, Swedish, Danish, Norwegian and in a pinch Flemish, Rumanian, Portuguese, Catalan and certain Eastern languages". Indeed, the Secretariat refused to hire translators trained in languages other than French or English. As Biltoft argues, "the Secretariat thought it would set a dangerous precedent that would undermine the League's official stance on the language question".[17] Hardly condoning polyglot cosmopolitanism, then, which begs the question: why was this the narrative that later became emphasised?

Two tentative observations can be made here, in addition to the fact that the League's political significance had dwindled by this point. First, as political scientist and anthropologist Iver B. Neumann has noted, in diplomacy there is a certain heroism embedded in the ideal of being a self-effacing medium of understanding between two parties.[18] Thus, the translator – creating real-time "sense" between politicians under challenging circumstances – becomes the symbol not only of diplomacy itself, but also the self-proclaimed role of the League.

This ties in with the second observation. The League spent, in the words of Biltoft, "innumerable hours securing better acoustic arrangements, circulating information to the delegates and *above all providing translation and interpretation services* for the vast array of speeches and documents produced" (my italics), because this was the bureaucratic underpinning of the new, open diplomacy. In line with the belief that language could shape politics; that public opinion could discipline governments; and that, following the Wilsonian ideal, "the word would replace the swords in organizing international relations", translation and interpretation was seen to have a transformative effect in the transition from old to new diplomacy.[19]

Strange, that such grandiose interpretations could come from such tedious tasks as translating a Finnish word for a kind of fishing tackle.

NOTES

1 See the chapter by Helle Strandgaard Jensen, Nikolai Schulz and Emil Eiby Seidenfaden in this edited volume.

2 A frontrunner: Clavin: *Securing the World Economy*. See in this volume: Tomoko Akami, Søren Friis and Hagen Schulz-Forberg's chapters.

3 Brendebach, Herzer and Tworek: *International Organizations and the Media*. See also Seidenfaden's and Akami's contributions in this edited volume.

4 For some interesting endeavours in this sub-field, see Roland: *Interpreters as Diplomats*; Biltoft: 'Speaking the Peace'.

5 See Piguet's contribution to this edited volume.

6 Gram-Skjoldager and A. Ikonomou: 'The Construction of the League of Nations Secretariat'.

7 League of Nations Archives (hereafter, LoNA), Geneva, R1455, 09.07.1919, Draft Resolution for submission to the Organisation Committee, at meeting to be held in July.

8 Howard-Ellis: *The Origin, Structure and Working of the League of Nations*, 193.

9 This section builds extensively on LoNA, C.E./1-27-1921, Report on the Organisation, Work, and Personnel of the Interpreters and Translators Section.

10 Howard-Ellis: *The Origin, Structure and Working of the League of Nations*, 193.

11 Ranshofen-Wertheimer: *The International Secretariat*, 139.

12 Shenton: *Cosmopolitan Conversation*.

13 Ranshofen-Wertheimer: *The International Secretariat*, 150-151.

14 Ranshofen-Wertheimer: *The International Secretariat*, 151.

15 Gram-Skjoldager and Ikonomou: 'Making Sense of the League of Nations'.

16 Ranshofen-Wertheimer: *The International Secretariat*, 140-141.

17 LoNA, R1457 File 2353, Folder 9836, 09.08.1921, Memorandum by Mr. Dennis, Circular Letter to the Secretariat; from Biltoft: 'Speaking the Peace', 47-48.

18 Neumann: *At Home with the Diplomats*.

19 Biltoft: 'Speaking the Peace', 46.

BIBLIOGRAPHY

Biltoft, Carolyn N.: 'Speaking the Peace: Language, World Politics and the League of Nations, 1918-1935' (PhD Dissertation), Princeton, NJ: Princeton University, 2010.

Brendebach, Jonas, Martin Herzer and Heidi J. S. Tworek: *International Organizations and the Media in the Nineteenth and Twentieth Centuries. Exorbitant Expectations*, London: Routledge, 2018.

Clavin, Patricia: *Securing the World Economy. The Reinvention of the League of Nations, 1920-1946*, Oxford: Oxford University Press, 2013.

Gram-Skjoldager, Karen and Haakon A. Ikonomou: 'The Construction of the League of Nations Secretariat. Formative Practices of Autonomy and Legitimacy in International Organizations', *International History Review*, 2017.

Gram-Skjoldager, Karen and Haakon A. Ikonomou: 'Making Sense of the League of Nations – Historiographical and Conceptual Reflections on early International Public Administration', *European History Quarterly* (accepted).

Howard-Ellis, Charles: *The Origin, Structure and Working of the League of Nations*, London: George Allen & Unwin, 1928.

Neumann, Iver B.: *At Home with the Diplomats: Inside a European Foreign Ministry*, Ithaca, NY: Cornell University Press, 2012.

Ranshofen-Wertheimer, Egon F.: *The International Secretariat. A Great Experiment in International Administration*, Washington: Carnegie Endowment for International Peace, 1945.

Roland, Ruth A.: *Interpreters as Diplomats a Diplomatic History of the Role of Interpreters in World Politics*, Ottawa, Ont.: University of Ottawa Press, 1999.

Shenton, Herbert Newhard: *Cosmopolitan Conversation; the Language Problems of International Conferences*, New York: Columbia University Press, 1933.

Karen Gram-Skjoldager

TAMING THE BUREAUCRATS

The Supervisory Commission and Political Control of the Secretariat

In the run-up to the 2016 Brexit referendum, a key criticism of the EU raised by many supporters of the Leave campaign was the dominant position of opaque, powerful 'unelected bureaucrats' in Brussels. The problem of transparency and accountability in international organisations is as old as international organisations themselves, and one that politicians have grappled with since the creation of the League of Nations. There are good reasons for this; while a national administration is part of the executive branch of government and under permanent control of the legislative branch, an international administration such as the League Secretariat is *the only* permanent element in an international organisation.[1] It therefore has more room for manoeuvre and is subject to less rigorous and direct parliamentary scrutiny than national executives.

This chapter will explore how the problem of managing and supervising international administrative power was dealt with when it first appeared, with the League. A key aspect of this is the function and role of the so-called Supervisory Commission (initially called the Control Commission), a body set up by the member states in 1921 to keep the Secretariat in check. The analysis will show that while the Commission was set up to exert member state control over the new, independent, international executive, it also became the battle ground for other, broader political conflicts and struggles – between different League bodies, different member states and conflicting ideologies. In doing so, the potential of taking a microscale approach to international organisations is demonstrated; looking at the League through the day-to-day practices of building and managing power balances around the Secretariat enables us to connect the Secretariat to broader stories of national interests, ideological trends and transformations in international politics.

THE POWER OF THE PURSE

When the Secretariat was created in 1919, hardly any thought was given to the questions of political oversight and economic auditing of its activities. However, by 1921, the League Assembly had become concerned with the Secretariat's rapidly growing expenses and recommended that the League Council appoint a 'Control Commission' (from 1922 called the Supervisory Commission) to audit the Secretariat's economy.[2]

The members of the Commission were a mix of prominent politicians and financial experts. Besides supervising the Secretariat they were also authorised to control the finances of the International Labour Organisation (ILO) and the International Court of Justice. During its first year, the Commission established a practice of meticulously reviewing all aspects of the Secretariat's income and expenses, probing into everything from rules for gifts and donations to travel expenses and money spent on publications and telephone calls.[3] Formally, the Commission had no policy-shaping functions, but it developed a practice of reviewing the Secretariat's draft budget for the upcoming year as members enthusiastically scrutinised the Secretariat's planned activities, from mandates and minorities to economic and financial co-operation, weeding out any expenses they considered unnecessary or wasteful.[4] During the 1920s, this work took an increasingly political turn. It got into the position of not only considering the question of how a given piece of work could be most economically done, but also whether it should be done at all or should be done in preference to another matter.[5]

A telling example of the Supervisory Commission's influence can be found in 1931, when the League Assembly decided that in view of the expanding world economic crisis, additional cuts had to be made to the already reduced budget for the Secretariat. This task was left squarely with the Supervisory Commission, without any guidelines, and resulted in a systematic reduction of the Secretariat's outreach activities; substantial cuts were made to publications, meetings, conferences and subsistence allowances to attendees at League events.[6] These reductions were hardly controversial but they nonetheless showed the substantial space for decision-making the Supervisory Commission had carved out for itself between the Assembly and the Secretariat.

The Supervisory Commission was created at the 1921 League Assembly. In its early years, the Assembly was mainly a diplomatic body with delegations made up of diplomats and technical and legal experts. Gradually, however, delegations came to include parliamentarians and government ministers of increasing political prominence. As a consequence, the Assembly insisted on having a larger say in relation to the League Council as well as the League Secretariat.

THE SUPERVISORY COMMISSION AND THE INSTITUTIONAL BALANCES OF THE LEAGUE

The Supervisory Commission also became a site for renegotiating the broader institutional balances between the Secretariat, the Council and the Assembly. Originally, the Commission was set up by and reported back to the League Assembly's Fourth Committee. From the outset, it was therefore seen as a tool not only for controlling the activities of the Secretariat but also for asserting the Assembly's competence over the Council in budgetary affairs.[7] However, the authority to appoint the Commission had been placed with the Council and this did not suit Carl J. Hambro, a Norwegian conservative politician and Assembly delegate, who later became Chairman of the Commission. In the 1928 League Assembly, Hambro suggested that the authority to appoint the Commission should be transferred to the Assembly, as he believed that full control of expenditures should be given to the body in which all states that contributed financially were directly represented.[8] His suggestion was passed unanimously but the Council responded by transferring the authority to the *Presidency* of the Assembly – which was dominated by the same great powers that dominated the Council. Once again, Hambro objected and in 1930 he succeeded in placing the appointment of Commission members with the Assembly's Fourth Committee. While this might seem (and indeed was) a minor procedural adjustment, for

Hambro it marked a critical symbolic turning point in the League's development; it was the first time a body had been created that was exclusively accountable to and appointed by a League body (in the form of an Assembly Committee), and not to the member states. For Hambro this was vital if the new international organisation was to develop into an international federation along the lines of the US federal system, which he hoped it would.[9]

THE SUPERVISORY COMMISSION AND THE RISE OF THE SMALL STATES

Hambro's push to increase the Assembly's authority in relation to the Supervisory Commission was part of a broader agenda to strengthen the position of the smaller member states in the League. During the 1920s, objections to the great powers' domination of the Secretariat grew; in particular, the posts of Under-Secretaries-General were criticised. These generously paid top jobs in the League administration had originally been created as 'ambassadorial posts' that gave the great powers oversight of, and influence on, the Secretariat's work. There were no clearly defined tasks or organisational responsibilities attached to these posts and by the late 1920s they were still the exclusive territory of the major European states and Japan. This caused discontent and the 1928 Assembly gave the Supervisory Commission the task of setting up a sub-committee to look into the staff situation in the Secretariat.[10] As work in the sub-committee was delayed, the Supervisory Commission was sidetracked in this discussion by the so-called Committee of Thirteen, set up in 1930 to conduct a larger evaluation of the Secretariat's work.[11] However, the Commission and Committee had one thing in common: Hambro, who, irrespective of the arena, pushed for the abolishment of the Under-Secretary-Generalships, better and more permanent forms of employment in the Secretariat that could secure a more neutral and politically detached bureaucracy and broader representation from all the League's members in the administration.[12] When it came to tipping the balance between small and large member states, the Supervisory Commission did not play an independent institutional role but was merely one of many showgrounds for Hambro's small-state agenda.

Carl Joachim Hambro (1885-1964) was one of the most ardent defenders of the League Assembly's institutional interests. This mirrored his position in Norwegian politics; a Member of Parliament from 1919 to 1957 and its President for 17 years, he had a keen eye for the importance and role of Parliament. Today, Hambro is mainly known for his role after the German attack on Norway in 1940, when he drew up the so-called *Elverumsfullmakt*, which created the constitutional foundation for Norway's exile government.

WAR AND THE PROBLEM OF AVENOL

During the Second World War, the Supervisory Commission became the only functioning League body, apart from the Secretariat. After the outbreak of the war, the Council and the Assembly ceased to function and in accordance with a 1939 Assembly emergency decision, the

Commission was given wide political powers, including the financial and administrative competences of the Council.[13] As it was immediately evident that it would be difficult for the Commission to convene during the war, Hambro, who had now become the Chairman of the Commission, was authorised to make decisions on its behalf after written consultation with the other Commission members.[14]

Hambro's first challenge was the strange and unexpected behaviour of the French Secretary-General, Joseph Avenol, over the summer of 1940. Avenol, a long-time League official, had been Secretary-General since 1933. He held deep anti-British and anti-American sentiments and in response to the German invasion of France in May 1940, he claimed that the only viable option for the League now was to turn into an exclusively 'European' League that should "work hand in hand with Hitler in order to achieve the unity of Europe".[15] Avenol's plans were rushed and vague and nothing became of them. Nonetheless, they triggered an intense power struggle within the Secretariat over the summer of 1940, as he tried to fire British staff and ship important League files to France.[16]

It is unclear to what degree Hambro and the Commission was kept informed of the internal developments in the Secretariat. We do know that he only intervened in one of its secondary aspects: the possible transfer of the League's economic and social activities to the US. In June 1940, Avenol received an invitation from Princeton University, who offered to host the Secretariat's economic and social work. Given his aversions to all things Anglo-American, it was unsurprising that he refused

the offer. This gave Hambro the prerogative, who, together with British and American diplomats, sought to encourage, persuade and pressure Avenol to accept the invitation.[17] The efforts proved unsuccessful and it was only when Avenol had been replaced by the Irish Deputy Secretary-General, Seán Lester, in late August 1940 that the move took place. Still, Hambro's actions were a clear indication that he viewed the League as part of the Anglo-American political sphere and that he believed the Supervisory Commission still had a role to play in the more political aspects of the League Secretariat's affairs.

BETWEEN MONTREAL AND GENEVA

In 1941, Hambro implemented major budget cuts to the Secretariat, as member states redirected all available resources to the war effort.[18] To Seán Lester, these budget cuts represented a major threat to the League – not only because it was, in his words, "quite impossible" to make the cuts "without cutting into the living wood more deeply than

The empty Council building in the Palais des Nations. After the outbreak of war in 1939, the Secretary-General had to lay off the majority of the League's staff and the Council and Assembly ceased to function. Left in the enormous building was Seán Lester with a staff of around 100 people who were practically cut off from the outside world – as well as their political masters.

I am prepared to be responsible for",[19] but because the ILO, which had relocated to Montreal at the beginning of the war, was not met with similar budgetary cutbacks.[20] Lester took this as an indication that the ILO Secretary-General, his compatriot Edward J. Phelan, "could do as he pleased" with the Supervisory Commission,[21] and feared that Phelan aimed to "take over the best and most useful work of the Secretariat, which was – (and perhaps is) – regarded as a decayed and disintegrated organization". "If limits of competence are not defined," Lester noted exasperatedly, "there is no reason why the ILO should stop anywhere".[22] The frustration and exaggeration in Lester's reflections are tangible, but his fundamental observation that the institutional centre of gravity for international organisation was shifting away from Geneva to America and from legal and political towards social and economic affairs was accurate. With America's entrance into the war and a growing political belief that economic and social reconstruction would have to lie at the heart of the postwar order, the Secretariat in Geneva rapidly lost what little authority it had left.[23]

Seemingly unaware of Lester's frustrations with the role of the ILO and the Supervisory Commission in this process, in the autumn of 1941 Hambro floated the idea with Lester that the Supervisory Commission could serve as an institutional centre for the discussion of postwar reconstruction plans and should appoint a committee to consider the issue. Lester and the Foreign Office agreed that this was a bad idea. In two letters to Lester, Roger Makins made it clear that he believed that such a committee fell outside of the special powers that had been granted to the Supervisory Commission and that Hambro's initiative would be most "inopportune". He therefore asked Lester to "gently discourage" the proposal.[24] Lester was more than happy to comply and in his response to Hambro he made sure to point out that when the time was ripe for discussing the postwar order, "the foundations will quite definitely have to be the present League and the present Covenant".[25] As we know, this was not the case; difficult as it was for Lester to accept, the League was too tainted by the failures of the 1930s to play any such role and the US and USSR made it quite clear that they wanted to start the organisation of the postwar world order with a clean slate.

CONCLUSION AND PERSPECTIVES – PREPARING FOR PEACE

Since its creation in 1921, the Supervisory Commission's status and role had steadily grown and expanded. While originally intended as an auditing body set up to control the Secretariat's expenses, it quickly expanded its influence by establishing a practice of approving future budget items. In the late 1920s, it also increased its institutional autonomy as the Assembly's struggle to assert authority over the Council lead to appointments of members to the Commission being transferred from the Council to an autonomous Assembly committee. The Commission's influence peaked after the outbreak of the war, when the Council and the Assembly accorded it extensive political powers. However, as the Supervisory Commission's authority grew, the League's political power shrunk and crumbled; the blow to the League's moral authority dealt by the outbreak of the war and Avenol's actions in the summer of 1940, and the subsequent budget collapse, was merely the culmination of a decline in political status that had been happening for a decade. By 1944, Hambro had realised that the organisation had outplayed its role. That year he used the Commission Report to argue for the importance and relevance of the idea of the Supervisory Commission itself in the emerging postwar organisations. In the report, he envisioned a world where many different international organisations would exist side-by-side, and argued that one central Supervisory Commission that reached across these organisations would be needed. If such a body was not set up, he argued:

> The danger that a number of independent international authorities with unrestricted power to fix emoluments and conditions of employment might compete with one another for the services of particular individuals, is a real one. If it is considered desirable that the salaries and terms of service of international officials should be suitably ordered and correlated, the work can be most satisfactorily done by the co-ordination of a central financial authority.[26]

Unsurprisingly, League officials did not see things the same way. At a meeting in Washington in 1943, former League officials met to discuss the lessons learned from the Secretariat, and one of the participants, evaluating the increasingly political role that the Supervisory Commission had gained during the previous two decades, stated that "it was one of the great defects of the organisation that such a body should ever have got into this position".[27]

NOTES

1 Ranshofen-Wertheimer: *The International Secretariat*, 9.

2 'First Report of the Commission of Control', A.7.1922.X, League of Nations Archives, Geneva.

3 For the first prominent example of this, see 'Supervisory Commission. Second Annual Report', A.2.1923.X.

4 'Supervisory Commission. Second Annual Report', A.2.1923.X.

5 'Proceedings of the Conference on Experience in International Administration Held at Washington on January 30, 1943, under the Auspices of the Carnegie Endowment for International Peace', here cited from Ranshofen-Wertheimer: *The International Secretariat*, 23.

6 'Report by the Supervisory Commission to the Fourth Committee', C.646.M.260.1931.X, League of Nations Archive, Geneva, 1-7.

7 'Folkeforbundets Sekretariat. En kritisk gennemgaaelse av C.J. Hambro', *Morgenbladet* (Oslo), 17.05.1930, cf. also Hambro: *Folkeforbundet og dets arbeide*, 57.

8 Ranshofen-Wertheimer: *The International Secretariat*, 22.

9 Hambro: *Folkeforbundet og dets arbeide*, 55-56.

10 'Folkeforbundets Sekretariat'.

11 'Folkeforbundets Sekretariat'.

12 'Folkeforbundets Sekretariat'.

13 'Report of the Supervisory Commission for the Year 1940', C.152.M.139.1940.X, League of Nations Archives, Geneva, 1; 'Supervisory Commission: General Summarised Report on its Work during the Period of Emergency, 1940-1946', A.5.1946.X, League of Nations Archives, Geneva, 1.

14 'Supervisory Commission: General Summarised Report on its Work during the Period of Emergency, 1940-1946', A.5.1946.X, League of Nations Archives, Geneva, 3.

15 Barros: *Betrayal*, 238.

16 Barros: *Betrayal*, 214-258.

17 Barros: *Betrayal*, 224-240.

18 'Supervisory Commission: General Summarised Report on its Work during the Period of Emergency, 1940-1946', A.5.1946.X, League of Nations Archives, Geneva.

19 Lester to Loveday [no date, probably October 1941], P203/48, Seán Lester's Papers, University College Dublin Archives.

20 Lester to Makins 6 October 1941, P203/48, Seán Lester's Papers, University College Dublin Archives. According to a comparison of the ILO and League Secretariat budgets drawn up by Lester and sent to Hambro in early 1942, the main problem was not the differences in budget reductions (from 1938 to 1942 the ILO's budget was reduced by 62%

compared to 69% for the Secretariat), but that the ILO had systematically exceeded their budget – in 1940 by as much as 30%. Norwegian National Archives, Hambro's private papers, RA/PA-0260/F/L0011/0012, Societé des Nations, Geneva, 19 February 1942, Lester to Hambro.

21 Lester to Jacklin [no date, probably October 1941], P203/48, Seán Lester's Papers, University College Dublin Archives.

22 Lester to Makins, 6 October 1941, P203/48, Seán Lester's Papers, University College Dublin Archives.

23 Clavin: *Securing the World Economy*, 267ff.

24 Telegrams from Makins to Lester, 5 September (quote) and 27 September 1941, P230/48, Seán Lester's Papers, University College Dublin Archives.

25 Lester to Hambro, 24 October 1941, P203/48, Seán Lester's Papers, University College Dublin Archives (quote); Lester to Makins, 3 November, P203/48, Seán Lester's Papers, University College Dublin Archives.

26 'First Report of the Supervisory Commission for the Year 1944', C.27M27.1944.X, League of Nations Archives, Geneva, 3.

27 'Proceedings', here cited from Ranshofen-Wertheimer: *The International Secretariat*, 23.

BIBLIOGRAPHY

Unpublished material

League of Nations Archives, Geneva:

First Report of the Commission of Control, A.7.1922.X.

First Report of the Supervisory Commission for the Year 1944, C.27M27.1944.X.

Report of the Supervisory Commission for the Year 1940, C.152.M.139.1940.X.

Report by the Supervisory Commission to the Fourth Committee, C.646.M.260.1931.X.

Supervisory Commission. Second Annual Report, A.2.1923.X.

Supervisory Commission: General Summarised Report on its Work during the Period of Emergency, 1940-1946, A.5.1946.X.

Norwegian National Archives, Hambro's private papers, RA/PA-0260/F/L0011/0012: Societé des Nations, Geneva.

University College Dublin: Seán Lester's Papers, P203/48.

Published material

Barros, James: *Betrayal from within. Joseph Avenol, Secretary-General of the League of Nations, 1933-1940*, New Haven: Yale University Press, 1969.

Clavin, Patricia: *Securing the World Economy. The Reinvention of the League of Nations 1920-1946*, Oxford: Oxford University Press, 2013.

Hambro, Carl J.: 'Folkeforbundets Sekretariat. En kritisk gennemgaaelse av C.J. Hambro', *Morgenbladet* (Oslo), 17 May 1930.

Hambro, Carl J.: *Folkeforbundet og dets arbeide*, Oslo: H. Aschehoug, 1931.

Ranshofen-Wertheimer, Egon: *The International Secretariat: A Great Experiment in International Administration, Studies in the Administration of International Law and Organization Vol. 3*, Washington: Carnegie Endowment for International Peace, 1945.

Marco Moraes

COMPETING INTERNATIONALISMS AT THE LEAGUE OF NATIONS SECRETARIAT, 1933-1940

The Secretariat of the League of Nations was founded in 1919 as the first fully international civil service in history. Just what that word 'international' meant, however, remained a source of tension throughout its existence. The multiplicity of internationalisms in the interwar period is evident in the 1933-1940 administration of the League's second Secretary-General, Joseph Avenol. Most of the existing literature assesses Avenol as an inept and misconceived official, an arch-appeaser who undermined the League's principles.[1] However, if we assess his political actions alongside his administrative measures and in light of recent studies of alternative internationalisms at the time, particularly fascist internationalism, we can paint a much more complex, and darker, picture of the practice of internationalism then. Such a picture reminds us that there is not just one interpretation of 'internationalism', and that international organisation can take many forms – a valuable lesson for today.

BEFORE AVENOL

The League's first Secretary-General, Eric Drummond, outlined the international civil service model at the Paris peace conference,[2] reaffirming it in memos to the League's Preparatory Commission in 1919[3] and the Council in 1920: "[t]he Members of the Secretariat act, during their period of office, in an international capacity, and are not in any way representatives of their own country".[4] This became an institutional principle through the 1920 *Balfour Report*[5] and the 1921 *Noblemaire Report*,[6] and was subsequently adopted into the League's first *Staff Regulations*,[7] remaining there for the course of its existence.[8] As Ole Jacob Sending put it, "[t]he Secretariat was to represent and manage the international as a space distinct from the sum total of member states' interests, this distinctiveness being anchored in rules established to regulate state interaction".[9]

From the start, this was a source of debate. During the Drummond administration (1919-1933), the tension peaked in the 1930 Report of the Committee of Thirteen,[10] when a small but vocal minority, led by Germany and Italy, argued that "[s]o long as there is no Super-State, and therefore no 'international man', an international spirit can only be assured through the cooperation of men of different nationalities who represent the public opinion of their respective nationalities".[11] In practice, too, the Secretariat had often been divided over the meaning of internationalism: for all his creative efforts, Drummond was always concerned with ensuring that his office's initiative did not stray too far from the Council. Early on, Jean Monnet had criticised this tendency of Drummond's,[12] and the head of the Mandates Section, William Rappard, complained that Drummond was too worried about keeping the British and the French happy, instead arguing that the Covenant provided enough authority for the Secretariat to act on its own initiative.[13] Despite his caution, however, Drummond ultimately did not curtail his more independent officials with any great show of power; Avenol's approach would be very different.

All too often we conflate 'internationalism' with liberal internationalism. Joseph Avenol's leadership of the League contrasted markedly with Drummond's, and as the 1930s progressed his pro-appeasement and supposedly apolitical stance came to subvert many of the values the League had been founded upon. His actions, however, were not anti-internationalist: rather, they show how internationalism is a process that can serve different, even nationalist, political ends.

JOSEPH AVENOL, SECRETARY-GENERAL (1933-1940)[14]

Avenol was initially seen as an apolitical technocrat. A French economist, he had succeeded Monnet as Drummond's deputy and was recognised as an able administrator, if an inept political operative. That Avenol was neither interested nor well-informed about politics was no

secret: he believed international organisation should be a technical-socio-economic affair, without independent political initiative.[15]

As Secretary-General, Avenol quickly showed that his 'apolitical' stance was anything but. In the key crises of the 1930s, his ostensibly technical focus belied a marked political stance. In Manchuria, he immediately decreased the League's diplomatic activities, even pressuring the more technical sections to avoid any work that might upset Japan. In Ethiopia, it gradually became clear he was using behind-the-scenes negotiations to obtain confidential information for Italy rather than as an impartial mediator,[16] and by summer 1935, he was openly advocating an Italian mandate for Ethiopia. Rather than upholding the Covenant, he sought to (a) leave open the possibility of Japan and Italy (and Germany) returning to the League, avoiding anything which might offend them, and (b) avoid crossing France and Britain, then in appeasement mode. This resulted in a 'neutrality' policy in which he avoided any mention of aggression and cut League programmes with potential political influence.

The underlying politics became explicit with the 1939 Soviet invasion of Finland. Avenol was determined to have the USSR expelled, even though "[t]he Finns themselves had no particular wish to see Russia expelled" (they wanted to stop the war and obtain assistance).[17] A fervent anti-communist, Avenol believed that "so long as the Soviet Union is a member of the League it would be impossible for the League to function".[18] He now worked the League machinery masterfully to enforce the Covenant: immediately seizing on a breach, trying unorthodox routes to bring it to the League's attention and lobbying extensively to secure the vote. Unfortunately, he did all this when the League could no longer play a decisive role, and the entire affair confirmed the impression of bias.[19]

From this Avenol may seem merely like a conservative French nationalist pursuing appeasement, as so many others did – shameful in retrospect, but not exceptional. This is the traditional view in the literature, that he "wished to represent what he viewed as correct French foreign policy".[20] However, if we also analyse Avenol's internal administrative measures, his behaviour in the crucial months of early 1940 and

his own views of international organisation, we obtain a more nuanced view of his 'internationalism'.

Administratively, Avenol changed the Secretariat's management from the British civil service's style of decentralised, bottom-up dynamics to a French *cabinet* style – a more hierarchical and highly centralised structure that "discourage[d] the spirit of initiative so important for any administrative body as the most vital check against bureaucratization".[21] The change also gave Avenol direct control of all League matters, making him "virtually immune, at least within the Secretariat, to any questioning of his actions".[22] A centralised system can have advantages, but it requires dedicated leadership from a hands-on Secretary-General, and frequent boosts to staff morale. Neither were present.[23] Thus "[p]oorly led, many Secretariat sections lost their capacity

In 1945 the great powers were eager to portray the founding of the UN as a fresh start, ostensibly sidelining the League and snubbing the few League officials in San Francisco. Behind the scenes, however, League Secretary-General Seán Lester oversaw an enormous transfer of assets, projects, personnel and – crucially – bureaucratic templates to the UN. The new international secretariat was largely modelled on the League's, albeit with important lessons learnt about the character of internationalism.

for independent behind-the-scenes activism".[24] Avenol's reform aimed at de-emphasising political initiative by Secretariat officials. Additionally, in the late 1930s he began to make drastic staff cuts – partly as a necessary cost-cutting measure, and partly as a way of purging anti-appeasers, such as France's Marcel Hoden, Poland's Ludwik Rajchman and Britain's Koni Zilliacus.[25]

This complemented his move away from political-diplomatic action (conflict resolution) and toward 'technical' work (socio-economic, scientific and humanitarian). As the League's political influence decreased, this proposal's appeal increased. It peaked with the *Bruce Report* of August 1939,[26] which recommended creating a Central Committee for Economic and Social Questions, steered by Member States' ministers of finance, health, transport etc., which would oversee technical bodies researching and proposing solutions to common problems.[27] The proposal "closely followed the views and opinions of the Secretary-General [...marking] the high point of Avenol's endeavour to turn the League into an organisation for economic and social cooperation in which political activities would be either eliminated entirely or reduced drastically".[28] Avenol's goal was to preserve what he saw as the League's business, which did not include its legal principles. In January 1939, he commented that "practically the entire world was engaged in [...] a demi-guerre in which the ordinary principles of order and international law were suspended", so that the political side of the League should "remain dormant".[29]

APOLITICAL TECHNOCRACY OR FASCIST INTERNATIONALISM?

In examining how Avenol's policies fitted with alternative internationalist movements of the time, recent literature on fascist internationalism proves particularly helpful.

From Madeleine Herren to Mark Mazower, historians have recently explored the wide variety of Nazi and fascist planned and actual international institutions, from the International Chamber of Law to the Deutsche Kongress Zentrale ("DKZ"), showing that, far from being antagonistic to international organisation, fascist regimes actually had rather developed plans for international order – only with very different 'internationalist' principles and concepts from the League and other post-1919 organisations.[30]

Particularly relevant are studies of fascist plans for corporatist international organisation, like Jens Steffeck's recent study[31] of Giuseppe de Michelis's 1934 *World Reorganisation on Corporative Lines*,[32] one of the earliest and more influential works promoting such ideas. This was a branch of fascism bent on organising the world along rationalist lines, "exporting Italy's socio-economic model of 'corporativism' to the rest of the world".[33] The starting point was that "[t]he interdependencies in the global market required international cooperation to address the uneven distribution of labour, natural resources and capital across the globe. Only sustained international efforts at triangulation could bring these three resources fruitfully together".[34] This 'triangulation' would occur between European powers and colonial territories under the auspices of a technocratic, economics-minded international organisation not unlike a League of Nations stripped of its legalistic (or, in the fascist view, hypocritically moralistic) dimension.

As Steffek notes, the parallels between this corporatist view and David Mitrany's functionalist model of international organisation are striking: the belief in modern technocracy and systematic rationalisation, the primary focus on functionalism rather than legalism, the scientificism of a supposedly 'apolitical' bureaucracy. Avenol's project came quite close to this, especially towards the late 1930s, when his conservativism and appeasement coalesced into a systemic view of international order. *The Bruce Report*, Avenol's brainchild, was a model blueprint for corporatist international organisation. It was not necessarily a fascist plan (although Bruce was a notable appeaser, even during the 'phoney war' of 1940), but a perfectly functionalist one prioritising 'technical' socio-economic cooperation over legal or political structures. It was, in fact, realised after 1945 with ECOSOC – the crucial difference, however, is that ECOSOC was born alongside the very legalist (and political) structure of the UN, whereas Avenol's conception involved substituting the League altogether with this kind of technical organisation.

Stanley Bruce shared Avenol's enthusiasm for the League's technical dimension, and in 1939 led a committee to propose reforms to the League. Published shortly before the outbreak of war, the *Bruce Report* (inspired and largely guided by Avenol) advocated a technocratic socio-economic organisation along functionalist lines. It was not a fascist plan, but it highlights many of the similarities of liberal functionalist internationalism with fascist internationalist plans for world corporatism.

Here Avenol's behaviour in 1940, after the outbreak of war, becomes clearer. He planned to remake the League into a pan-European technocratic organisation serving the Axis,[35] hoping that "[t]he increasing tension between England and its former ally France, and the tightening Nazi grip on Europe would assist in its execution".[36] He grew convinced that the Axis would win the war, telling colleagues that the League "should work together with the Germans to expel the English from Europe",[37] and that

> except for the Germans and Italians who have a program, a doctrine, and a method, no one seems to me to have one. [Their programmes] must not be rejected wholesale; they contain things which one can no longer reject [...] 1941 will remain the starting point of a historic era; it is the end of the world of the 19th century. We are at the beginning of a great revolution.[38]

In July 1940 Avenol tried to approach the German Consul in Geneva to discuss these plans.[39] He enthused to one colleague that there would soon be "a new France, which was to be given a new soul to work in collaboration with Germany and Italy and keep the British out of Europe".[40] To another he said that "Germany would militarily dominate Europe; he was not sure if Hitler wanted a League but fairly sure that Mussolini would, to form a certain balance";[41] the idea seemed to be that a (fascistic) League with France and Italy could provide a measure of equilibrium with Germany.

In mid-July 1940 Avenol wrote to the new Vichy regime pledging his support. The administration replied telling him to resign (Pétain was wary of appearing close to the League).[42] After several convoluted attempts to prevent his deputy Seán Lester (who he considered disloyal due to his anti-appeasement stance) from succeeding him, Avenol tried to shut down the League by refusing to renew its budget. When that failed, in August 1940, he gave effect to his resignation and left for a week-long trip to Vichy (unsuccessfully seeking a job in the new regime), leaving Lester to head the organisation. Lester would be the League's final Secretary-General, seeing it through the war and transferring its work to the UN.

Towards the end of the war, Avenol published a book, *L'Europe Silencieuse* (*Silent Europe*),[43] in which he outlines his views on postwar international organisation – a fascinating document, as much for what it does not say as for what it does. He writes at length on the need for economic cooperation, rational management structures and the '*élan vital*' of Europe. He obsessively categorises states by their economic power and demographic 'energy'. Few are the discussions of international law, rights and – not least – international service.

CONCLUSION

Considering the multiplicity of internationalisms, the similarities between fascist internationalism and liberal functionalism, and the fate of other institutions at the time, we can see that Avenol's plans were not as far-fetched as is often thought. Many other international organisations, voluntarily or not, did align themselves with fascism before or during the war. As Sandrine Kott observed, once the war started several "technical bodies like the International Bureau of Education or the Bank for International Settlements were collaborating with the Nazis".[44] The International Criminal Police Commission (later Interpol) effectively became a Nazi organisation during the war, moving its headquarters to Berlin and having as its Presidents SS generals, including Reinhard Heydrich and Ernst Kaltenbrunner.

The question then becomes not 'how could Avenol behave thus?', which is what is usually asked, but rather 'why did the League *not* suffer the same fate as those other institutions?'. Mazower suggests that the League "was altogether a bigger and ideologically vastly more loaded proposition, and Avenol, who did put out feelers to Pétain, completely misjudged the situation".[45] The key is what constituted that 'loaded' proposition. Part of it was the inherent legalism of the League's brand of internationalism, which provoked such hatred from fascists and Nazis, from Carl Schmitt onwards, who wanted to "expose the League's internationalism for the sham it really was".[46] Thus, studying Avenol's tenure, by showing alternative ways that League official could act internationally, reinforces Karen Gram-Skjoldager's point that the Secretariat "serves as a prism through which we can grasp the broader ecosystem of social and political systems of the time".[47]

Studying the Avenol years helps us reassess the typical dichotomies we use for the study of international organisations and the interwar period – political/technical, internationalist/nationalist, collaboration/resistance – forcing us to refine our theoretical and methodological lenses. Many of the answers are difficult to find – as they were then – but it is important that we at least get the questions right.

NOTES

1 E.g. Rovine: *The First 50 Years*; Barros: *Betrayal from Within*.

2 'Organisation of the League of Nations' (31.05.1919), TNA FO 608/242.

3 'Organisation of the League of Nations', LoNA 29/749/38.

4 'Staff and Organisation of the Secretariat' (5/1920), LoNA 29/6890/1083, 4.

5 'Balfour Report' (19.05.1920), LoNA 29/4434/1083, 3.

6 'Report of the Committee of Experts (Noblemaire Report)' (07.05.1921), *LNOJ – Records of the Second Assembly*, Fourth Committee Minutes.

7 'Statutes for the Personnel of the Secretariat' (1922), LoNA 30/11713, 4.

8 'Staff Regulations – 1945', LoNA 18A/2892/563, 4. For a study of the establishment of the staff regulations and early recruitment patterns as a way of balancing legitimacy and autonomy, see: Gram-Skjoldager and Ikonomou: 'The Construction of the League of Nations Secretariat'.

9 Sending: 'The International Civil Servant', 338-339.

10 'Report of the Committee of Enquiry on the Organisation of the Secretariat, the International Labour Office, and the Registry of the Permanent Court of International Justice (The Committee of Thirteen)', *Records of the Eleventh Assembly*, Fourth Committee Minutes, LoNA S.929, 8.

11 'Report of the Committee of Enquiry on the Organisation of the Secretariat, the International Labour Office, and the Registry of the Permanent Court of International Justice (The Committee of Thirteen)', *Records of the Eleventh Assembly*, Fourth Committee Minutes, LoNA S.929, 8.

12 Pedersen: 'The League of Nations Secretariat'.

13 Pedersen: *The Guardians*, 54-59.

14 A note on sources: while for succinctness the notes in this section draw mostly on secondary sources, a more detailed examination of this topic, drawing mainly on primary material from the League of Nations Archives (especially the Avenol Papers, the Lester Papers and the Directors' Meetings Minutes), can be found in the doctoral thesis I am writing at the University of Oxford.

15 League of Nations Directors' Meeting Minutes no.74 (28.02.1923), quoted in Pedersen: *The Guardians*, 45.

16 Barros: *Betrayal from Within*, 57, 77.

17 Walters: *A History of the League of Nations*, 807.

18 Quoted in Barros: *Betrayal from Within*, 198.

19 Bendiner: *A Time of Angels*, 397.

20 Rovine: *The First 50 Years*, 137.

21 Rovine: *The First 50 Years*, 155.

22 Barros: *Betrayal from Within*, 23.

23 Pedersen: 'The League of Nations Secretariat'.

24 Pedersen: *The Guardians*, 294.

25 Barros: *Betrayal from Within*, 173-175.

26 'The Development of International Cooperation in Economic and Social Affairs' (22.08.1939), LoNA A.23.1939.

27 Walters: *A History*, 762.

28 Barros: *Betrayal from Within*, 195-196.

29 Barros: *Betrayal from Within*, 189.

30 See, e.g. Herren: 'Fascist Internationalism'; Martin: *The Nazi-Fascist World Order*; Mazower: *Governing*.

31 Steffek: 'Fascist Internationalism'.

32 Michelis: *World Reorganisation*.

33 Steffek: 'Fascist Internationalism', 4.

34 Steffek: 'Fascist Internationalism', 9.

35 Gageby: *The Last Secretary-General*, 192.

36 Barros: *Betrayal from Within*, 233.

37 Rovine: *The First 50 Years*, 160.

38 Quoted in Rovine: *The First 50 Years*, 160.

39 Gageby: *The Last Secretary-General*, 190.

40 Quoted in Barros: *Betrayal from Within*, 233.

41 Quoted in Gageby: *The Last Secretary-General*, 192.

42 Rovine: *The First 50 Years*, 159.

43 Avenol: *L'Europe Silencieuse*.

44 Kott: 'Fighting the War', 366.

45 Mazower: *Governing*, 192.

46 Mazower: *Governing*, 181.

47 Gram-Skjoldager: 'Between Internationalism and National Socialism'.

BIBLIOGRAPHY

Primary Sources

League of Nations Archives (LoNA) – UN, Geneva:

'Balfour Report' (19.05.1920), LoNA 29/4434/1083, 3.

'Organisation of the League of Nations', LoNA 29/749/38.

'Report of the Committee of Enquiry on the Organisation of the Secretariat, the International Labour Office, and the Registry of the Permanent Court of International Justice (The Committee of Thirteen)', *Records of the Eleventh Assembly*, Fourth Committee Minutes, LoNA S.929, 8.

'Report of the Committee of Experts (Noblemaire Report)' (07.05.1921), *LNOJ – Records of the Second Assembly*, Fourth Committee Minutes.

'Staff and Organisation of the Secretariat' (5/1920), LoNA 29/6890/1083, 4.

'Staff Regulations – 1945', LoNA 18A/2892/563, 4.

'Statutes for the Personnel of the Secretariat' (1922), LoNA 30/11713, 4.

'The Development of International Cooperation in Economic and Social Affairs' (22.08.1939), LoNA A.23.1939.

The National Archives (TNA) – Kew, London

'Organisation of the League of Nations' (31.05.1919), TNA FO 608/242.

Secondary Sources

Avenol, Joseph: *L'Europe Silencieuse*, Neuchatel: Editions de la Baconniere, 1944.

Barros, James: *Betrayal from Within – Joseph Avenol, Secretary-General of the League of Nations, 1933-1940*, New Haven: Yale University Press, 1969.

Bendiner, Elmer: *A Time of Angels – The Tragicomic History of the League of Nations*, New York: Knopf, 1975.

Gageby, Douglas: *The Last Secretary-General: Sean Lester and the League of Nations*, London: Town House, 1999.

Gram-Skjoldager, Karen: 'Between Internationalism and National Socialism - Helmer Rosting in the League of Nations Secretariat', entry in the blog *The Invention of International Bureaucracy* (11.03.2016).

Gram-Skjoldager, Karen and Haakon A. Ikonomou: 'The Construction of the League of Nations Secretariat. Formative Practices of Autonomy and Legitimacy in International Organizations', *International History Review*, 2017.

Herren, Madeleine: 'Fascist Internationalism'. In Glenda Sluga and Patricia Clavin (eds): *Internationalisms: A Twentieth-Century History*, Cambridge: Cambridge University Press, 2017, 191-212.

Kott, Sandrine: 'Fighting the War or Preparing for Peace? The ILO during the Second World War', *Journal of Modern European History* 12 (3), 2014, 359-376.

Martin, Benjamin: *The Nazi-Fascist World Order for European Culture*, London: Harvard University Press, 2016.

Mazower, Mark: *Governing the World – The History of an Idea*, London: Allen Lane, 2012.

Michelis, Giuseppe de: *World Reorganisation on Corporative Lines*, London: G. Allen & Unwin, 1935.

Pedersen, Susan: *The Guardians – The League of Nations and the crisis of empire*, Oxford: Oxford University Press, 2015.

Pedersen, Susan: 'The League of Nations Secretariat as a Site of Political Imagination', Annual Nicolai Rubinstein Lecture in Intellectual History and the History of Political Thought, Queen Mary University of London (15 March 2017).

Rovine, Arthur: *The First 50 Years: the Secretary-General in World Politics*, Leiden: A.W. Sijthoff, 1970.

Sending, Ole: 'The International Civil Servant', *International Political Sociology* 8 (3), 2014, 338-340.

Steffek, Jens: 'Fascist Internationalism', *Millennium*, 44 (1), 2015, 3-22.

Walters, Francis: *A History of the League of Nations*, Oxford: Oxford University Press, 1960.

Myriam Piguet

GENDER DISTRIBUTION IN THE LEAGUE OF NATIONS

The Start of a Revolution?

The Covenant, the founding document of the League of Nations, formally opened the hiring practices of the organisation to women. Today, historians refer to the League and its Secretariat as pioneers of gender equality in interwar international diplomacy. But while the League was the first diplomatic organisation to recognise equal employment in its principles, its practices were a different story.

During its first decade of existence, the Secretariat of the League of Nations respected gender equality as regards proportions in its appointments: among a total of 488 working at the Secretariat in 1925, 245 were women.[1] Princess Gabrielle Radziwill was one of them, holding the grade of Senior Assistant in the Information Section. But her 1922 letter to Sir Eric Drummond – Secretary-General of the League of Nations – shows that behind the numbers lay complex discrepancies and power structures:

> While in no way protesting against my contract, I would like [...] to renew once more the protest I made [...] against the status of a certain number of women members in the Secretariat, whose work is akin to that of Member of Section, and who are grouped under the name of Senior Assistant [...] They are treated in a manner which seems to me to be out of proportion to their work when compared with that of other grades in the Secretariat.[2]

These words resonate with the experiences of women today, many of whom hit the 'glass ceiling' when trying to reach a position with responsibilities in the private or public sector. In the interwar period, however, such a statement marked something entirely new, as most European diplomatic administrations withheld all higher positions from women.[3] This chapter sheds light on the first generation of female international civil servants while exposing some structural barriers they faced as employees of the Secretariat of the League of Nations.

A UNIQUE STEP TOWARDS GENDER EQUALITY

From the outset, the League of Nations chose an innovative and distinct path, allowing women to be considered on an equal footing with their male counterparts in terms of positions. Officially, no difference was made between men and women regarding hiring, promotions or dismissals. This decision, taken by the peacemakers gathered in Paris, owed much to the lobbying of women's international organisations.

On 10 April 1919, a joint deputation consisting of *The International Council of Women* and the *Conference of Women Suffragists in the Allied Countries and the United States* – affectionately referred to as "*Mothers of the World*" by Woodrow Wilson[4] – was received by the League of Nations Commission at the Paris Peace Conference.[5] The two organisations demanded that women should be able to take up positions in the League on similar terms as men. After the meeting, the following sentence was added to Article 7 of the League of Nations' Covenant: "All positions under or in connection with the League, including the Secretariat, shall be open equally to men and women".[6]

Article 7 was an important victory for the international feminists, and – so they hoped – represented the beginning of the end of the gendered bourgeois diplomatic practices, in place since the institutionalisation of the profession in the nineteenth century.[7] However, the activism of the international feminist movements was not the only driver behind Article 7;[8] it was also influenced by deep ideological and economic forces. Ideological, because considering internationalism without

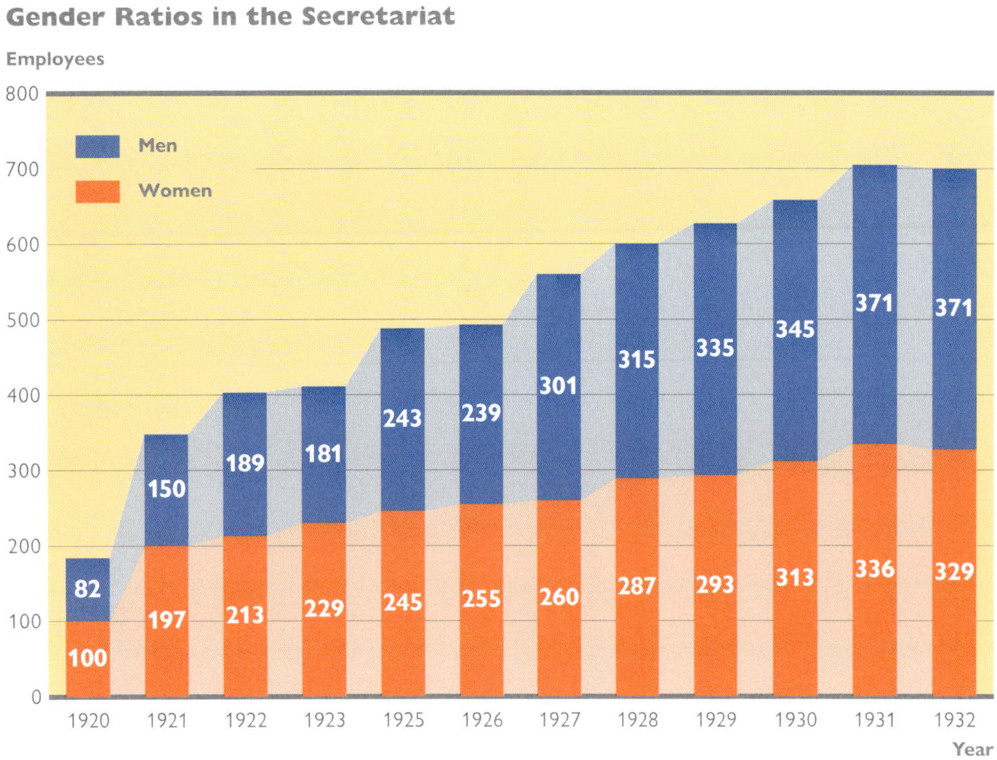

Table 1[12]

women's rights had become difficult: women had been actively engaged in non-governmental peace movements and movements fronting internationalism since the late nineteenth century. Following the First World War, they were increasingly drawn into the formal political sphere and allowing them into the bureaucratic machinery of the League seemed a logical next step.[9] At the same time, the women of the League also served to strengthen its progressive internationalist image, as they participated in the creation and communication of a fresh and accessible aesthetic of international diplomacy.[10] Economic, because the utility of women at work had been well proven during the First World War: the bureaucratic revolution of national (and international) administrations that took place in the interwar period required a large number of feminine hands to tackle the associated humdrum secretarial work.[11]

Consequently, throughout Sir Eric Drummond's Secretary-Generalship, women constituted half of the League's employees. At first glance, then, the League Secretariat appears to be an institution where parity between genders was protected and respected.

A GAP TO BE UNCOVERED

In a recent book, the British historian Helen McCarthy tells the story of women's entry into and presence in the UK diplomatic service, using an innovative and inspiring methodology drawing on both quantitative and qualitative sources.[13] Her theme and approach resonates with current shifts in International History, towards more sociological enquiries,[14] and particularly works focusing on the role of gender and the influence of women in both international organisations and global governance. However, many aspects of women's contribution to international diplomacy remain to be uncovered – among them, their entry into and role in international administrations. Inspired by McCarthy's work, I approached the League of Nations archives with the idea of collecting both data and biographical information, to relate the experience of women workers inside the Secretariat of the League. Rather unsurprisingly, my results show that the League of Nations was not as gender equal as its Covenant proclaimed.

THE BUREAUCRATIC REVOLUTION THAT FAVOURED THE EMERGENCE OF WOMEN IN INTERNATIONAL ADMINISTRATION

In the Secretariat of the League, women were numerous but largely confined to low and middle status – often exclusively feminine – job functions, such as shorthand typist, copyist or secretary. The prominence of these jobs in the Secretariat was a consequence of the institutionalisation and automation of administration in the context of the industrial revolution, which resulted in the outsourcing of certain types of semi-mechanised routine tasks to women.[15] In the League, women were mainly assigned to the Internal Administration Services and thus were central to the development of its highly organised bureaucracy.[16] The Stenographic Service – or Pool – and the Dactylo Service were the largest departments in the Secretariat; both were overwhelmingly feminine and led by women, respectively Grace Isabelle Day and Julienne Piachaud.

THE CHICAGO DAILY TRIBUNE: TUESDAY, APRIL 29, 1919.

They Got Equality for Women in the League of Nations

Representatives of Various Countries Who Appeared Before the Peace Conference at Paris.

PHOTO—TRIBUNE FOREIGN SERVICE

Standing, left to right: Miss Constance Drexel and Mrs. Juliet Barrett Rublee, United States; Dr. Girard Mangin, Mme. Grinberg, Mme. Maria Veronne, France; Mrs. Corbett Ashby, Great Britain; Mme. Brunschwig, France; Mme. Schievoni, Italy; Mrs. Fern Andrews, United States. Seated, left to right: Mme. d'Amelio Tivoli, Italy; Mme. Avril de Sainte Croix, France; Mme. Jules Siegfried, France; the Marchioness of Aberdeen and Temaire, Great Britain; Mme. de Witt Schlumberger, France.

The decision to allow women inside the League's machinery was received enthusiastically by the press, especially in the United States. Numerous articles can be found about the women of the League in local and international newspapers, such as this piece from the *Chicago Daily Tribune*. The picture shows the representatives of the women's organisations that took part in the Versailles Conference and pushed for equality in the League.

The position of shorthand typist within the League Secretariat was attractive to European women during the interwar period. Well paid, it also provided appealing opportunities of promotion within the institution. Many women benefited from this opening, pursuing successful careers in the Secretariat. For instance, Piachaud, who was initially hired to the Pool of shorthand typist in 1920, became Chief of the Service within two years.[17]

However, shortly after her promotion in 1922, she complained to Sir Eric Drummond about not being considered equal to her male counterparts from the Roneo (stencil duplication) and Distribution Services.[18] Seven years later, in 1929, her salary was still 16,250 Swiss francs, while her colleague Willem Van Asch van Wijck, who held the same position as Chief of Service in the Distribution Service, received a salary of 19,000 Swiss francs.

From 1922 to 1931, Dame Rachel Crowdy was the Head of the Social and Opium Section of the Secretariat and the only female Chief of Section. In 1929, looking to recruit a new Member for her Section, she advised and convinced the Appointment Committee to add a paragraph into all calls for applications for the job of Member of Section specifying that the post was open to women and men alike. This measure was quite extraordinary and innovative for the inter-war period.

IN PRACTICE, GENDER INEQUALITY REMAINED

Piachaud was granted a lower salary than her male colleague because of an inequality located in her position's ranking. League of Nations employees were classified into three divisions: the second and the third corresponded to clerical and supporting staff, whereas the first was reserved for executive officials carrying diplomatic and technical duties. Both Piachaud and her colleague carried the job title Chief of Service, but his was part of the first division whereas hers was ranked at the top of the second division – the so-called intermediate class.[19] These kinds of imbalances emerge as a repetitive pattern in the Secretariat's administration, resulting in women generally being paid less than men for the same type of work. Some women at the top of the second division were actually carrying out independent diplomatic work, such as Radziwill, who was in charge of the League's relations with international women organisations; others had technical roles, like Florence Wilson, who was the Head of the League's library. As for the only woman at the directory level: Dame Rachel Crowdy, who ran the Opium and Social Section, never reached the grade of Director of Section. One prominent exception was the Head of the English Translation Service, Lady Mary Blennerhasset, as she and her male equivalent from the French Service were considered equals, in both grade and salary.

Female employees' median salary reflects this inequality: 9,934 Swiss francs in 1925,[20] way below the 12,000 Swiss francs of a so-called Member of Section – the entry level of the first division.[21] This observation is an illustration, of course, of the high number of clerical positions, but we reach the exact same conclusion if we only consider the high officials, such as Blennerhasset or Crowdy: their median salary was 25,667 Swiss francs,[22] while a typical Chief of Section's started at 28,000 Swiss francs.[23]

To advance their careers and reach the executive ranks, female employees had first to face a glass ceiling. Women remained vastly outnumbered by men in the first division. Though some of them had the same kind of duties as their first division colleagues, they generally had to complain to attain the same recognition and very few women were assigned to the first division's entry-level position – Member of Section. Yet one positive development can be noted: in the first years of the Secretariat's existence, there was only one female Member of Section; by 1931, this number had grown to six, the largest number under Drummond's Secretary-Generalship.[24]

Employees of the stenographic service. The service was the biggest in the Secretariat with more than 50 employees in 1932 – all essential to its functioning. The date of this picture is unknown, but we can spot Julienne Piachaud, Head of Service between 1922 and 1940, sitting at the centre wearing a white shirt.

Table 2[25]

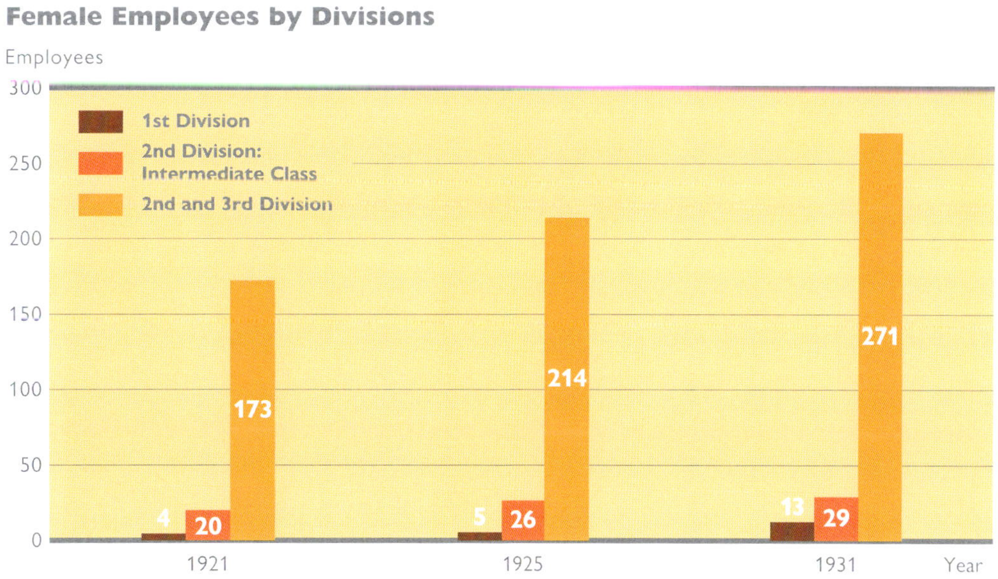

THE GENDERED DIVISION OF LABOUR

Another form of gender inequality is found in the gender distribution across the different policy areas of the Secretariat. The idea that specific roles were suitable for women remained throughout Sir Eric Drummond's Secretary-Generalship. Of the six female Members of Section in 1931, three were assigned to the Social and Opium Section,[26] a small but overwhelmingly feminine section, and the only one led by a woman. With rare exceptions, women were bound to roles for which they had recognised 'specific qualifications' in line with their gender and complementary to the ones of the men. Women of the first division were assigned jobs that let them practise their 'natural' propensity for nurturing and caretaking, noticeably articulated around what would later be called 'humanitarian aid', and especially matters addressed specifically by the Opium and Social Section, related to women and children's health.[27] In the second division, women were bound to the positions of short-typist and secretary, which were almost never tackled by male employees. Both observations show that the old bourgeois vision of women – naturally organised, kind, attentive and pacifist – was still very much in fashion.

A QUESTION OF EDUCATION

These imbalances were not only – perhaps not even primarily – outcomes of the Secretariat leadership's decisions, but just as much a reflection of the structural social conditions surrounding the Secretariat. The minutes of the Appointments Committee, which was in charge of staff recruitment and promotions, are very revealing in this regard; finding suitable women was a rather difficult task for a number of positions because of the low level of women's education worldwide.[28] Despite every post being equally open to both genders, female applicants often had insufficient or the wrong kind of education for the position. Consequently, women had a hard time competing with their male counterparts, and those who landed higher posts often had rather atypical former work experience. For instance, Henriette Schlesser, the private secretary of Deputy Secretary-General Joseph Avenol, was previously the Assistant Director at *l'Ecole de Haut Enseignement Commercial pour Jeunes Filles* in Paris.[29] This former line of work, despite being far from her role of private secretary, represents one of the highest levels of authority a woman could reach in the early twentieth century.

Because of the attractive working conditions, women tended to stay in the Secretariat longer than their male counterparts, building their careers once inside the institution. Of the six female Members of Section in 1931, half had climbed the ladders from the second division, and one, Nancy Williams – who was in charge of typing the minutes of the Appointment Committee and was the only woman to take part in these meetings – had started her career in the Pool of short-hand typists.

Both Williams and Piachaud attest to the fact that the League was seeking qualified women and provided them with opportunities to climb the career ladder once inside the Secretariat. Perhaps even more remarkably, the criticisms of the women themselves – such as Radziwill – were, to some extent, heard. However, women's opportunities remained limited and controlled by a gendered perception of employment. Ultimately, the outcomes of Article 7 were far from the spill-over effect hoped for by women's international organisations at the signing of the Covenant.

CONCLUSION

Sir Eric Drummond's Secretary-Generalship marked the zenith of the League of Nations' journey towards greater gender equality. With his departure in 1933, the escalating international tensions of the 1930s and the eroding status of the League, the number of employees decreased steadily, and in the first division, men replaced the departing women.[30] Often, these successors were welcomed with superior grades and salaries, whereas the achievements of women such as Wilson and Crowdy – who had built their sections from scratch – fell into oblivion.

Still, most social evolution is slow and characterised by ups and downs. Article 7 was not without effect: it opened the League's doors to qualified women, and offered a generation of female professionals who pushed to join men at work and serve in the international field a chance to take part in the establishment and development of the world's first international administration. Whilst it might appear a modest gesture, it was a first decisive step towards greater female representation on the formal international scene, and a revolution for women's labour rights.

NOTES

1 The prosopographical work presented in this chapter relies on the Permanent Staff List of the Secretariat for the years 1920 to 1932 – with the exception of the year 1924, which is missing in the archives – hereafter mentioned as: Permanent Staff Lists of the Secretariat, 1920-1932 (incomplete). League of Nations Archives (hereafter LoNA), 1185 and S.696-7.

2 Letter from Miss Radziwill to Sir Eric Drummond, 02.02.1922. LoNA, Section files, Personnel files, box s. 861, file 2950-2967, Sta.B.65/Shelf 56, file 2955.

3 James and Sluga (eds): 'Introduction', 1-9.

4 Miller: *Lobbying the League*, 20-21.

5 Miller: *Lobbying the League*, 20-21.

6 Ranshofen-Wertheimer: *The International Secretariat*, 366.

7 Mori: 'How Women Make Diplomacy', 138-139.

8 Mori: 'How Women Make Diplomacy', 366.

9 Mori: 'How Women Make Diplomacy', 365.

10 Herren: 'Gender and International Relations', 186.

11 'Pour la plupart des contemporains, il est clair que la technique dactylographique, comparable à la pratique du piano, convient particulièrement aux jeunes filles instruites de la petite bourgeoisie, que la situation de leur famille contraint à travailler.' Gardey: *La dactylographe et l'expéditionnaire*, 83.

12 Permanent Staff Lists of the Secretariat, 1920-1932 (incomplete). LoNA, 1185 and S.696-7.

13 McCarthy: *Women of the World*.

14 Knudsen and Gram-Skjoldager (eds): 'Introduction', 16.

15 D. Gardey: *La dactylographe et l'expéditionnaire*, 66-67.

16 58% of the total of women employees in 1925 were assigned to the Internal Administration Services.

17 Letter from Sir Eric Drummond to Mme Piachaud, 1st November 1922. LoNA, Section files, Personnel files, Box s. 854bis, file 2813-2826, Sta. B. 65 / Shelf 56, file 2825.

18 Letter from Mme Piachaud to Sir Eric Drummond, 21st February 1924. LoNA, Section files, Personnel files, Box s. 854bis, file 2813-2826, Sta. B. 65 / Shelf 56, file 2825.

19 Historians of University of Heidelberg, *LONSEA database* (10.10.2018).

20 Permanent Staff Lists of the Secretariat, 1920-1932 (incomplete). LoNA, 1185 and S.696-7.

21 Ranshofen-Wertheimer: *The International Secretariat*, 295.

22 Permanent Staff Lists of the Secretariat, 1920-1932 (incomplete). LoNA, 1185 and S.696-7.

23 Permanent Staff Lists of the Secretariat, 1920-1932 (incomplete). LoNA, 1185 and S.696-7.

24 Permanent Staff Lists of the Secretariat, 1920-1932 (incomplete). LoNA, 1185 and S.696-7.

25 Permanent Staff Lists of the Secretariat, 1920-1932 (incomplete). LoNA, 1185 and S.696-7. Miller: *Lobbying the League*, 97, Table 1.1 and 1.2.

26 Staff List of the Secretariat, September 1931. LoNA, S.697, C.399.M.161, Geneva.

27 Miller: *Lobbying the League*, 277-278.

28 Minute of Appointment Committee, Section files, LoNA, S.-954-957.

29 Notice Individuelle, 30.10.1926. LoNA, Section files, Personnel files, box S.876, file 3142-3163 Sta. B. 65 / Shelf 56, file 3154.

30 Ranshofen-Wertheimer: *The International Secretariat*, 369.

BIBLIOGRAPHY

Unpublished material

League of Nations Archives (LoNA), Staff Lists of the Secretariat, 1920-1932. 1185 and S.696-7.

LoNA, Section files, Personnel files, Box s. 854bis, file 2813-2826, Sta. B. 65/Shelf 56, file 2825, Letter from Sir Eric Drummond to Mme Piachaud, 01.11.1922.

LoNA, Section files, S.-954-957, Minutes of Appointment Committee, 1920-1932.

LoNA, Section files, Personnel files, box S.876, file 3142-3163, Sta. B. 65. Shelf 56, file 3154, Notice Individuelle, 30.10.1926.

LoNA, Section files, Personnel files, box s. 861, file 2950-2967, Sta.B.65/Shelf 56, file 2955, Letter from Miss Radziwill to Sir Eric Drummond, 02.02.1922.

Published material

Gardey, Delphine: *La dactylographe et l'expéditionnaire: histoire des employés de bureau, 1890-1930*, Paris: Belin, 2001.

Herren, Madeleine: 'Gender and international Relations through the lenses of the League of Nations (1919-1945)'. In C. James and G. Sluga (eds): *Women, diplomacy and international politics since 1500*, Abingdon: Routledge, 2016, 182-201.

Historians of University of Heidelberg, *LONSEA database* (10.10.2018).

James, Carolyn and Glenda Sluga: 'Introduction: The long international History of women and Diplomacy'. In C. James and G. Sluga (eds): *Women, diplomacy and international politics since 1500*, Abingdon: Routledge, 2016, 1-12.

Knudsen, Ann Christina Lauring and Karen Gram-Skjoldager: 'Introduction'. In A.C.L. Knudsen and K. Gram-Skjoldager (eds): *Living Political Biography: Narrating 20th Century European Lives*, Aarhus: Aarhus University Press, 2012, 1-19.

McCarthy, Helen: *Women of the World: the Rise of the Female Diplomat*, London: Bloomsbury, 2014.

Miller, Carol: *Lobbying the League: Women's international organisations and the League of Nations*, D.Phil. Thesis, University of Oxford, 1992.

Mori, Jennifer: 'How Women Make Diplomacy: The British Embassy in Paris, 1815-1841', *Journal of Women's History* 4, 2015, 137-159.

Ranshofen-Wertheimer, Egon: *The international Secretariat: A Great Experiment in International Administration*, Washington: Carnegie Endowment for International Peace, 1945.

PART 2

THE LEAGUE IN CONTEXT

EVER since Susan Pedersen encouraged historians to go "back to the League of Nations", in her 2007 article in the *American History Review* (112(4), 1091-1117), and ask how it functioned and what it did, rather than why it failed, a stream of game-changing publications have re-cast the organisation from being an 'failure' to being a 'father' (or 'mother') of many subsequent modalities of global governance. Of particular interest are two glacial and profound transformations of the social, political and economic world that were organised and accelerated by the Geneva system. The first is the transformation from a world of empires to a world of nation states. Under this rubric falls the distribution and League administration of German colonies and the Ottoman Empire, the so-called Mandates System, explored in Susan Pedersen's *The Guardians. The League of Nations and the Crisis of Empire* (Oxford: Oxford University Press, 2015), and the Minorities Regime monitored from Geneva, which treaty-bound the newly created Eastern European states to secure the rights of its minority populations. The most complete study of the latter subject remains Carole Fink's: *Defending the Rights of Others: The Great Powers, the Jews, and International Minority Protection, 1878-1938* (Cambridge: Cambridge University Press, 2004). The second transformation was underpinned by the incessant productivity of experts within an increasingly diverse array of sciences, which in the interwar period had Geneva as their hub and focal point. These experts produced and standardised scientific rules, norms and practices on a global scale – a (sometimes) common language to measure and govern the world. These processes are open-ended and still ongoing, and we would do well to keep in mind that there is nothing linear or inevitable about their trajectories from the interwar period onwards (as many of the contributions of this section will show). They were then, as they are now, complex, multidirectional and riddled with conflict and contestation.

Putting the 'League in Context' means placing it within these transformative processes in new ways. The first section of Part 2 takes a closer look at the first internationalised regimes of 'sovereignty governance'. Its first three contributions do this from 'the ground up', starting with the middle-men, practitioners, narrators and tinkerers of these new regimes in order to rethink, and perhaps complicate, the relationship between the imperial and the national. These chapters show that the micro-historical and biographical approach enables the historian to move within the 'black box' of international organisations and – to paraphrase Oscar Handlin in *Truth in History* (Cambridge, Mass.: Harvard University Press, 1979, 276) – use the personal to inform the societal (and vice versa).

The second section looks at the many shades of expertise within, and around, the League. The League was no island; rather it was a spider in a vast web, or a "dot-connector", as one of the authors says. This made its powers far-reaching but diffuse, transformative but scattered. Historians have only begun to connect these dots, and what emerges is not a monolithic ‘norm entrepreneur’. Rather, the League was a custodian of multiple ‘laboratories’, where experts and scholars helped define the economic, social and political parameters of our contemporary world. The first two chapters of *The League, Economy and Expertise* explore two such laboratories; the next two explore what expertise meant in practice, and how historians should go about studying it as situated and practised. The last chapter shows how some knowledge produced by the League (in the field of health) was relatively directly transposed into policy formation in the postwar era.

Haakon A. Ikonomou

Florian Wagner

NATURISM, THE PERMANENT MANDATES COMMISSION, AND THE DENIAL OF THE VIOLENT NATURE OF COLONIALISM

After the First World War, Belgium designated one of its most outstanding colonial experts, Pierre Orts, as a member of the new League of Nations' Permanent Mandate Commission (PMC), which administered colonial territories conquered by the allies during the war. Taking up this position in 1921, Orts made it clear that he would also use the PMC to ward off German claims to have their colonial empire restituted:

> She [Germany] is incapable of colonization and has shown herself unworthy of fulfilling her civilizing mission. Concerning this matter, a formidable dossier of accusations has been put together. We can add a few pieces to that dossier ourselves, especially a photography [*sic*] that our colonial officers found in German East Africa, on which one can see a considerable number of German colonists in a state of complete nudity.[1]

Pierre Orts' proof of German immorality was as amusing as it was cynical. He considered nudity a deplorable sign of a specific German colonial barbarism that brought Germans near to the "natives". In evoking nudism to question Germany's civilising ability, he obscured the fact that Africans had suffered from German colonisation as much as they had under Belgian, British and French rule. More importantly, by scandalising nudity, Orts relativised the structural violence that shaped German rule in East Africa, which had manifested itself in arbitrary justice, compulsory expropriation, forced labour, corporal punishment, racial discrimination and the devastating war against the population labelled 'Maji-Maji', which caused a famine and the deaths of 100,000 East Africans.[2]

To make sense of Orts' perverted moralising, I will argue in this essay that it stood for a more general tendency in the PMC to address colonial scandals, without challenging the colonial system as such. Although making isolated colonial scandals public (such as the nudity of the Europeans), the PMC and its members concealed structural colonial violence instead of revealing it.

This argument is in line with Susan Pedersen's eminent study that unveils the generic colonial character of the PMC. It also follows her reading of the PMC, claiming that it introduced a public culture of "international talk" about colonial scandals. However, it disagrees with her argument that publicising scandals gave colonialism a bad name.[3] On the contrary, by singling out isolated affairs and shaming them on an international scale, the PMC purported the idea that colonialism could be "reformable" and "liberal" – without shaking its foundations at all.[4]

The nudity scandal is perhaps a particularly absurd case. Yet it captures the underlying belief of PMC members like Orts in a racist world order, and the civilisational deficits of the colonised peoples. By repeating such ideas and spreading them as an 'officialized' basis of an internationalist and allegedly liberal colonialism, the PMC perpetuated and reinvigorated them. Orts represents this marriage of racism and the PMC's policy: he was its longest-standing member and attended all its meetings from 1921 to 1939.

THE PMC: A CIVILISING INSTITUTION

It is well known that the PMC emerged from Article 22 of the Covenant of the League of Nations, and was meant to assume the tutelage of the peoples "not yet able to stand by themselves". It was charged with watching over their "well-being and development" as a "sacred trust of civilization". In practice, it internationalised the former territories of the Ottoman Empire and the German colonial empire and "entrusted" them "to advanced nations", who were mostly colonising powers. Their task was to develop the territories and to "civilize" its inhabitants. If those inhabitants saw their own well-being at risk, they could send petitions to the PMC in Geneva, who in turn could theoretically urge the mandatory power concerned to alter its policy.[5] This procedure did not give the inhabitants of the mandates a right to petitioning in the legal sense, nor was the PMC a court whose verdict was legally binding. As Susan Pedersen has argued, the petitions were not legal documents and it was up to the mandatory power to change the law of the colony according to the PMC's recommendations. Consequently, the PMC rarely took action to improve the lot of the colonised. It did have the merit, however, of making their concerns public.[6]

Orts personified much of what made the PMC, with regard both to its ideology and to its actual policy. On the one hand, he represented a small nation that was a big empire overseas and wanted to use the PMC to assert itself and its interests. On the other hand, he was a convinced internationalist who believed in the solidarity of the civilised Christian nations (excluding Germany after the First World War), which he opposed to the non-Europeans who were backward and had to be civilised. Thus, he was a devoted PMC member who did not hold back from criticising his own country if it ignored the PMC's guidelines. Orts will be our protagonist, insofar as he illustrates the PMC's policy in the interwar period.[7]

USING THE EARLY LEAGUE TO INFLUENCE THE "INTERNATIONAL TALK" TO BELGIUM'S ADVANTAGE

What was the purpose of Orts' initiative to add nudity to the "formidable dossier of accusations" against the Germans? The "dossier" referred to a blue book the British government had published after the First World War to prove that the Germans were unable to fulfil the civilising mission and argue that their colonies should be redistributed among the other colonial powers. At first glance, it seems likely that Orts, who represented Belgium and its colonial interests at the Peace Conference of 1919, wanted to secure a portion of the German colonies for Belgium. In the course of the war, Belgian colonial troops from the Congo had conquered parts of German East Africa, specifically Ruanda-Urundi and the fertile region around Tabora. However, the archives tell a different story. Instead of claiming these Eastern African territories at the Peace Conference, the Belgian negotiator asked for territory in Western Congo to secure the estuary of the Congo River.[8] For a long time the Belgians insisted on extending their territory in the West, at the expense of Portugal. Only after the diplomats at the Peace Conference refused to concede Portuguese territory did the Belgian government agree to administer Ruanda-Urundi as a League mandate. Orts and the British envoy Lord Milner sealed this deal in the Orts-Milner accords in 1919.[9]

What other reasons could Orts have had for creating a scandal of German immorality, apart from in revenge for German aggression against Belgium in Europe during the war? He may well have been attempting to distract attention from Belgium's own very violent colonial history: ever since the mass killings in the Congo under Leopold II in the early twentieth century, the more potent colonial powers had questioned Belgium's ability to govern and civilise such a vast territory as the Congo. At the Peace Conference, Milner seemed to raise the same issue claiming that Belgian troops in Africa had not contributed much to the defeat of the Germans.[10]

That was hardly true, but Orts was cautious not to go into details about the conquest of German East Africa. The Belgian colonial army had plundered local resources to supply their troops and consequently caused a famine among East Africans. Belgian officers had officially allowed their troops to kidnap local women and to rape them. The ferocity of Congolese troops long haunted the memory of East Africans.[11] Regardless of this cruelty, Orts was successful in portraying Belgium as a victim of German aggression during the war, not only in Europe, but also in the Congo.[12] Consequently, the League of Nations entrusted the Belgian state with the mandate over Ruanda-Urundi.

Becoming a member of the PMC finally enabled Belgium to put

pressure on the big powers. Theoretically, Orts could even penalise the British and the French if they did not govern their mandates according to the rules. He did not do that, to avoid retaliation. The PMC established a new balance of mutual whitewashing.

COLONIAL INTERNATIONALISM AND THE "NEUTRALITY" OF THE PMC

Solidarity among colonisers had many origins and was nothing new. Before the First World War, Europeans competed for colonies but avoided military conflicts through diplomatic congresses, be it during the partition of Sub-Saharan Africa (1884/5) or of Morocco (1911). Diplomats continued to uphold this system of checks and balances while the era of conquest gave way to the period of colonial development. Faced with issues of practical administration after their conquests, colonial officers developed a strong sense for competitive emulation, as they tried to emulate strategies of ruling and exploitation from the more profitable colonies.

Taking up the idea of mutual learning, administrators established the International Colonial Institute (ICI) at Brussels in 1893. It brought together international colonial experts at annual meetings to exchange strategies of efficient administration and develop a colonial science. Its members, who came from twelve colonising countries, styled themselves as "neutral" experts who also took indigenous interests into account. However, the ultimate goal of the ICI was to legitimise colonialism by minimising its excesses, and it did so way into the interwar period.[13] For example, the ICI officially endorsed forced labour in the colonies, at the very moment when the International Labour Organisation (ILO) wanted to ban it worldwide in 1928.[14] The PMC built on these pre-existing networks and recruited its own members among those of the ICI.[15] Two thirds of all PMC members were also ICI members, among them Orts and the famous *spiritus rector* of British colonialism, Lord Lugard. They brought with them the idea that imperialism was more than an expression of nationalism. They shared the purpose of giving colonialism a good name. Against this background, Orts' concern about

While Europeans did not want to see other Europeans naked in the tropics, they took thousands of pictures of naked Africans to prove their allegedly uncivilised and childish behaviour. The rare picture of naked Germans, seen here, was taken in German South-West Africa but is not the photograph Orts described. However, a similarly banal photo caused the scandal that Orts popularised.

Germans "going native" in the colony was also a real concern about the reputation of colonialism as such. What is more, Orts had also been part of internationalist Catholic networks, which might explain why he considered the naked Germans a sort of original sin that might pose a threat to the (Christian) civilising mission. In this regard, he was very much in line with the social Catholicism that influenced the colonial policies of the 1930s.[16] Obviously, the PMC had also declared the civilising mission its main purpose and the members took it seriously.

There was no doubt about Orts' loyalty to colonial internationalism. Like him, most PMC members saw themselves as neutral experts who did not represent the interests of their countries of origin. Belief in internationalism went as far as readmitting German delegates to the PMC in 1926. While Orts despised them as a Belgian citizen, he accepted working with them in the PMC. In retrospect, his reproach of immoral nudity turned out to be a compliment rather than a critique, given that it relativised the violent rule of the Germans. Other colonial internationalists also quickly glossed over German atrocities. British officials who had used the blue book to delegitimise the German colonial empire during the war stopped printing it and withdrew it from sale in the 1920s.[17]

"NEUTRALITY" AS SOLIDARITY AMONG COLONISERS

Such "neutrality" meant that the members of the PMC did not blame each other for the violence inherent to colonialism as such. As Susan Pedersen has shown, the PMC ignored most petitions coming from the inhabitants of the mandates, especially under Pierre Orts' chairmanship (1936-1940). Even in its early days, Orts defended the PMC against progressive ideas. In 1923, he went as far as betraying the League's guiding principles. Although its mission was to support the native population in the mandates, he turned down a proposal to force South Africa to value natives over white settlers in its South West African mandate. The PMC dropped the plan.

On another occasion, Orts bitterly attacked the British Anti-Slavery Society, whose members had rightly accused France of turning all land it deemed vacant in its Cameroonian and Togolese mandates into state property. As late as 1932, he publicly refuted the British Colonial Office's plan to grant independence to the Iraq mandate, even though this was only nominally. In this case, however, Orts failed to assert himself and Iraq became independent.[18] Ironically, the British Colonial Office seemed to be less colonial than the PMC under Orts' influence; Orts held the view that the peoples of the Levant might look back on an "ancient civilization" but were nevertheless "not able to govern themselves".[19] The colonial internationalist Orts, and with him a part of the PMC, seemed to be less progressive than the colonial powers who administered the mandates.

SCANDALS AND REFORM INITIATIVES

As PMC members did not have the right to visit the mandates or to speak personally to its non-European inhabitants, they received their complaints in the form of petitions, via colonial administrators, who

The enduring legacy of the mandates is remarkable. They outlived the League of Nations, the institution that was responsible for the initial success but also the ultimate failure of the mandate system. In 1945, when the United Nations took over, it renamed the former mandates "trusteeships". Instead of the Permanent Mandates Commission, a Trusteeship Council watched over the gradual education of the populations in the territories as they became independent nations. The Council existed until 1994.

annotated them. As we have seen, the petitions were not legal documents and the PMC's rare recommendations to eschew colonial scandals were not legally binding. The PMC's reluctance to react to the petitions did not prevent its members from uncovering colonial scandals.

In 1928, when the International Labour Organisation pushed for a ban on forced labour in the colonies, Orts travelled to British East Africa and the Belgian Congo (but avoided mandate territories). Curiously, he found fault only with the Belgian Congo, where Catholic missionaries informed him that the Belgian authorities encouraged forced labour in colonial companies.[20] He inspected an official labour recruitment camp and found 600 men in a desperate state, haunted by fever and without any medical assistance. Half of the prisoners – among them children and old people – were not in a shape to work at all.[21] Once they started working in the copper industries in Katanga, Orts complained, mortality reached up to 144 per every thousand.[22] Orts showed little empathy with the Congolese, but feared that such recruitment practices and the considerable mortality rates would lead to the exhaustion of the Congo's workforce.

When he approached the Belgian colonial ministry on the matter, he felt he was treated as if he were "a tourist who had superficially visited only a part of the colony and jumped to conclusions too quickly".[23] Consequently, he published several articles, invoking his expertise as a PMC member and threatening that he would engulf Belgium in a crisis that equalled the campaign against Leopold's rubber scandals before the First World War.[24]

LEGITIMISING COLONIALISM THROUGH REFORM

Orts' campaign against abuses of Congolese workers certainly risked discrediting the country's colonial project. Yet he thought of his criticism as a way to save the colonial project from abuses, rather than to bring it down. In his pamphlets, he explained that the entire world admired the Belgians for their colonial achievements and that the great colonial powers had all reformed their colonial policy at some point.

Great Britain, for example, had sent three commissions of inquiry to East Africa, India and Palestine in the previous two years to deal with "serious difficulties" in the colonial administrations. These commissions, Orts concluded, "have in no way damaged the British reputation". On the contrary, they showed its progressive attitude.[25]

Seven years in the PMC had made Orts confident that correcting colonial methods did not threaten colonialism as a whole. Indeed, the PMC had contributed to stabilising, colonialism. It had warded off criticism by claiming that colonial rule could be improved, and was not a problem in itself. After all, Orts' 1928 campaign coincided with the ILO's debate about the legitimacy of forced labour in the colonies. The debate on forced labour did not delegitimise colonial rule as such, although mandate powers like France steadfastly refused to ban forced labour both from their mandates and from their colonial territory.[26]

The tone in Europe and in the colonies had changed by that time:

as rising violence and scandals seemed to become an integral part of European society in the late 1920s, it became possible to relativise the structural repressive system of colonialism and label its excesses as situational misbehaviour of individual colonisers. The PMC had played its part in normalising violence by merely registering cases of misbehaviour in the colonies without eliminating them. PMC members claimed that they were able to uncover and control abuses through the petitions that the inhabitants of the mandate territories could send to Geneva if they felt a disadvantage or saw their rights violated (though the accused mandatory power could read and annotate the petitions before they reached the PMC). In reality, the PMC widely ignored the petitions and rarely compelled the mandatory powers to change their policy.[27] The consequences of this development became clear when Mussolini's Italy attacked Ethiopia and the League failed to sanction the brutal conquest. Orts, then the chairman of the PMC, also failed to take a clear stand against Italy's crimes against humanity.[28]

The last trusteeship territory was Palau. Originally a part of the German Empire, it became a Japanese mandate in 1919, and a US trusteeship after 1945. The population of Palau was well aware that the US used its trusteeships for nuclear testing and dumping nuclear waste in the Pacific. As early as 1979, Palau had written its own constitution, which contained a nuclear-free clause. However, it did not become officially independent until 1994, when the UN stopped the trusteeship system.

CONCLUSION

Orts and the PMC represented both continuity and change in interwar colonialism. Orts stuck to his values, considering nakedness a less civilised act than colonial violence. So did the PMC, which failed to veto colonial crimes and continued to believe in the colonial mission as a legitimate means to bring about progress. Accepting open colonial violence as an integral part of the civilising mission of so-called progressive colonialism seemed to come to an end in 1919, when the allies excluded Germany from the international community for having committed such crimes. However, the condemnation of specifically 'German' colonial crimes served the purpose of concealing the violent nature of colonialism as such. With the return of German delegates to the PMC after 1926, the failure to ban forced labour in the late 1920s and the continuation of aggressive colonial wars, open and public colonial violence became widely accepted as a means to induce "progress". The PMC occasionally criticised colonial violence but never penalised it. Like most Europeans, its members continued to deny the structural violence of colonialism. Pierre Orts took the lead in defending this colonialism.

NOTES

1 Archives Générales du Royaume Belge (AGRB), Orts Papers, 439 Orts: Souvenirs de ma carrière, ouvrages, annexe, 124.

2 Becker: *Der Maji-Maji-Krieg*.

3 Pedersen: *The Guardians*, 4.

4 Ribi Forclaz: *Humanitarian Imperialism*.

5 http://avalon.law.yale.edu/20th_century/leagcov.asp#art22 (10.01.2019).

6 Pedersen: 'Samoa', 235.

7 Susan Pedersen's comprehensive study addressed the correspondence in Orts' archive that related directly to the PMC. I will add a few sources, such as material from the League of Nations and ILO archives and especially Orts' memoirs, to understand his personal background and the origins of his moral and political attitudes. Most of the sources used here are personal documents and reflect Orts' point of view.

8 AGRB, Orts Papers, I 184 Carton 389 Orts: Souvenirs de ma carrière, 148-150.

9 AGRB, Orts Papers 434, Accords Orts Milner 1919, revision de celui-ci 1923: Mémoires Orts: Entrevue avec Lord Milner à l'Hostel Majestic le 20 Mars 1919, 2-4.

10 AGRB, Orts Papers 434, Accords Orts Milner 1919, revision de celui-ci 1923: Memoires Orts: Entrevue avec Lord Milner. l'Hostel Majestic le 20 Mars 1919, 2-4.

11 Pesek: *Das Ende eines Kolonialreiches*, 249-250.

12 See Horne: *German Atrocities*.

13 Wagner: 'Private Colonialism'.

14 ILO Archives CAT-6C-13-1: J.Goudal 'Rapport sur ma mission à Bruxelles (XX session de l'ICI 24-29.06.1929)', cited in Daele: 'Industrial States and the Transnational Exchanges', 209. See also Wagner: 'Private Colonialism', 202.

15 For the close relation between the League of Nations, the PMC and the ICI, see the extensive correspondence in The League of Nations Archives and Wagner: *Colonial Internationalism* (forthcoming).

16 Cooper: *Decolonization*, 291.

17 Silvester and Gewald (eds): *Words Cannot be Found*.

18 Pedersen: *The Guardians*, 124-125, 139, and 266.

19 AGRB, Orts Papers, I 184, Carton 389 Orts: Souvenirs de ma carrière, 190.

20 They also published their accusations in Belgium, see 'Les abus du recrutement de la main d'oeuvre au Congo. Protestation des chefs religieux catholiques de la Colonie', *La Libre Belgique*, 20.01.1929.

21 'Le Congo en 1928'. In AGRB, Orts Papers, Carton 439 Orts: Souvenirs de ma carrière, ouvrages, 13.

22 'Le Congo en 1928'. In AGRB, Orts Papers, Carton 439 Orts: Souvenirs de ma carrière, ouvrages, 11-12.

23 'Le Congo en 1928'. In AGRB, Orts Papers, Carton 439 Orts: Souvenirs de ma carrière, ouvrages, 8.

24 For example in *Le Flambeau* 2 (February 1929) and 'Le Congo en 1928'. In AGRB, Orts Papers, Carton 439 Orts: Souvenirs de ma carrière, ouvrages, 11.

25 'Le Congo en 1928'. In AGRB, Orts Papers, Carton 439 Orts: Souvenirs de ma carrière, ouvrages, 3.

26 For an overview, see Maul: 'The International Labour Organization'.

27 Pedersen: *Guardians*, 77-95.

28 Pedersen: *Guardians*, 292.

BIBLIOGRAPHY

Becker, Felicitas and Jigal Beez (eds): *Der Maji-Maji-Krieg in Deutsch-Ostafrika 1905-1907*, Berlin: Links, 2005.

Cooper, Frederick: *Decolonization and African Society. The Labor Question in French and British Africa*, Cambridge: Cambridge University Press, 1996.

Daele, Jasmien van: 'Industrial States and the Transnational Exchanges of Social Policies: Belgium and the ILO in the Interwar Period'. In Sandrine Kott and Joëlle Droux (eds): *Globalizing Social Rights: The International Labour Organization and Beyond*, ILO Century Series, Houndmills: Palgrave Macmillan, 2013.

Horne, John and Alan Kramer: *German Atrocities, 1914. A History of Denial*, New Haven: Yale University Press, 2002.

Maul, Daniel Roger: 'The International Labour Organization and the Struggle against Forced Labour from 1919 to the Present', *Labor History* 48 (4), 2007, 477-500.

Pedersen, Susan: *The Guardians. The League of Nations and the Crisis of Empire*, Oxford: Oxford University Press, 2015.

Pesek, Michael: *Das Ende eines Kolonialreiches: Ostafrika im Ersten Weltkrieg*, Frankfurt and New York: Campus, 2010.

Ribi Forclaz, Amalia: *Humanitarian Imperialism. The politics of anti-slavery activism, 1880-1940*, Oxford: Oxford University Press, 2015.

Silvester, Jeremy and Jan-Bart Gewald (eds): *Words cannot be found: German colonial rule in Namibia an annotated reprint of the 1918 Blue Book*, Boston, MA: Brill, 2003.

Wagner, Florian: *Colonial Internationalism. How Cooperation Among Experts Reshaped Colonialism (1880s-1950s)*, forthcoming 2019.

Wagner, Florian: 'Private Colonialism and International Co-operation in Europe, 1870-1914'. In Roland Cvetkovski and Volker Barth (eds): *Imperial Co-operation and Transfer, 1870-1930: Empires and Encounters*, London: Bloomsbury, 2015.

Laura Almagor

ISRAEL ZANGWILL ON NATIONALITY AND 'THE LEAGUE OF DAMNATIONS'

Never in fact in human history has anything been so written about and so little thought out as the League of Nations.[1]

Harsh words, penned in 1920 by the Anglo-Jewish fiction writer, political actor and commentator Israel Zangwill (1864-1926). The literary gentleman had much more to say, and often in even more damning terms, about the Versailles Peace Treaty, President Woodrow Wilson and what he termed the "League of Damnations". But a critic may very well also be an idealist, and there was a lot in the underlying ideals of the League that appealed to Zangwill. However, rapidly unfulfilled hopes in connection to the new organisation made him lament the disappointing realities of world politics at the war's end.

The publications most extensively portraying Zangwill's opinions on the League were *The Principle of Nationalities*, which served as the 1917 Conway Memorial Lecture, and *The Voice of Jerusalem* (1920), a critical reflection on universalist Jewish values and postwar world order, as well as on Zangwill's own publication record on these topics. In the following, an in-depth analysis of these texts will take centre stage. Thus far, the Anglo-Jewish author's biographers and other scholars interested in "Zangwilliana" have not exactly ignored these seminal publications, but an exploration of the *political* significance of the rapid

Israel Zangwill, circa 1905. In 1905 novelist and Zionist Zangwill (1864-1926) left the Zionist Movement to establish the so-called Jewish Territorialist Organisation (ITO). For the following two decades the ITO unsuccessfully laboured to find territories within existing colonial empires, but outside Palestine on which to create Jewish settlements. After Zangwill disbanded the ITO in 1925, the movement was reestablished in 1934 and continued its activities well into the post-1945 period.

change in outlook that these texts display, especially vis-à-vis the League of Nations, has yet to be undertaken. It is in this realm that the current contribution breaks new ground.[2] What do we stand to gain from investigating the opinions of this remarkable, albeit nowadays largely forgotten figure?

First of all, Zangwill's views render him an intellectual 'connector' between the history of the League of Nations and Jewish history and politico-religious thought. The historical pivotal points in this story are the British issuing of the Balfour Declaration in 1917 – which promised a Jewish National Home to the Zionist Movement in the soon-to-be British Mandate of Palestine – and subsequent reneging on this promise, culminating in the 1922 Churchill White Paper. Secondly, the Anglo-Jewish writer demonstrated a sharp eye for the cynical realities behind the seemingly universalistic ideals underlying the League's inception, and his publications on the topic reveal a foresighted and exceptionally eloquent realist. Often straying from the mainstream political path, he was nevertheless a representative of the generally pro-British Anglo-Jewish elite, and an important opinion-maker in both the Jewish and non-Jewish British and American public spheres.

ISRAEL ZANGWILL

For those not well-versed in either Zionist history or Victorian-era literature, the name Israel Zangwill may not ring all that familiar. However, the erstwhile literary giant's eventual obscurity would have been surprising to his educated contemporaries. Once termed the "Dickens of the Ghetto" and compared to Leo Tolstoy, Heinrich Heine, Thomas Hardy,

Henry James, George Bernard Shaw and Rudyard Kipling, Zangwill was a household name in both Anglo-Jewish and gentile circles, and a much-respected political activist and commentator. Besides authoring literary classics such as *Children of the Ghetto* (1892) and the play *The Melting Pot* (1908) – popularising that term to refer to American multiculturalism – the London-born Zangwill was an avid agitator on behalf of suffragism. He was also a highly sought-after publicist and public speaker on a wide variety of other issues, ranging from minority rights (first and foremost, but certainly not exclusively, for the Jews) to biting commentaries-turned-polemics with famous anti-Semites, and even with the Ku Klux Klan. Zangwill was also one of the most important early Zionists. In 1905, he seceded from the Zionist movement to head the so-called Jewish Territorialist Organisation (ITO), until its dissolution in 1925. In that capacity, Zangwill negotiated with numerous international government representatives in his attempt to find territories for Jewish settlement.[3]

For several decades Zangwill was thus an international celebrity. Despite the occasional rediscovery of his literary writings, as well as the recent resurfacing of his name in several studies that attempt to recover the "Lost Atlantis" of non-Zionist Jewish politics,[4] Zangwill is now a largely forgotten figure. The reasons for this may be summarised by the inscription on Zangwill's columbarium in London's Liberal Jewish cemetery, undoubtedly penned by the writer himself before his death: "A Man of Letters and a Fighter of Unpopular Causes".[5]

Several of Zangwill's "unpopular causes", however, have gained in topicality during the more than 90 years that have passed since his death. Lingering gender inequality suggests that the accomplishments of the suffragist movement have not consolidated what its proponents set out to achieve. Moreover, disgruntled leftist Israeli youth asked some years ago: "Lama lo Uganda?" ("Why not Uganda?"),[6] referring to the 1903 British offer to the Zionists of a part of the British African possessions. The rejection of this proposal spurred Zangwill to establish the ITO in 1905. When one dives into Zangwill's extensive political writings, one finds that he demonstrated deep insights into a wide range of political developments. For instance, he heavily criticised the British and Zionist activities in the Middle East in the face of the opposition posed by the existing Arab population of Palestine. Particularly insightful are his reflections on the League of Nations during its early years. As a committed pacifist, the notion of a supranational body governing world peace surely spoke to Zangwill, but as a cynical realist he also scrutinised the League, which he quickly deemed a failure.

Cover of Theatre Programme for Israel Zangwill's play "The Melting Pot" (1908), 1916. Paradoxically, while Zangwill argued against the merits of the nation-state, as a Jewish activist he was simultaneously seeking some form of Jewish political or cultural autonomy. He observed that European Jews lived under constant threat, a realisation that also underpinned his famous play *The Melting Pot*. The play opened in Washington D.C. in 1908 and its premiere was attended by none other than US President Theodore Roosevelt.

'NATIONALITY'

As the First World War was approaching its end, the concept of the 'nation' came to stand at the centre of the discussions as to the exact makeup of the postwar world. Not coincidentally, it was precisely the word 'nation' that was to become one of the constitutive elements of a League of *Nations*. What was this "principle of nationalities", Zangwill asked, for which so many men had lost their lives and were likely to die in the future? The writer considered this "master-principle" in ominous terms: "When States and Kingdoms talk of truth and justice, 'Earth,' said Wordsworth, 'is sick and Heaven is weary'."[7] And in the light of the recent atrocities, Zangwill did not harbour much faith in the moral strength of mankind.[8]

Whatever the future held, the term 'nationality' was not going to be of much practical value. Neither wolves nor oxen are self-conscious about their belonging to a pack or a herd; "is it necessary for some gifted ox-tongue to proclaim their bovi-nationality?"[9] Useful or not, the concept did need to be defined once and for all. Formulating such a definition was not a simple task. Fixing "nationality" based on geographical realities made no sense. "Indeed, if the early races [*sic*.] had been scattered by Miltonic or Teutonic archangels, with or without Zeppelins, they could scarcely have been more mixed today." 'Nationality',

Zangwill concluded, was therefore nothing other than "a state of mind corresponding to a political fact".[10]

TWO MEN, ONE BROTHER

This constructivist (in contrast to primordial) understanding of nationality meant that as political facts changed nationalities were also not fixed: "The notion that Nationalities are immortal is obscurantist."[11] The changeability of the concept made it a dangerous thing: "Nationality, deep as life, but narrow as the grave, is closing in on us." What made this situation even more perilous was the fact that religion was giving way to "nationality" (by which Zangwill here in fact meant "nationalism") as a permanent placeholder for cohesive shared experiences, especially in times of violent crisis. "[T]he Lord God Patrie was a jealous god", leaving no space for other, more benign forms of group identity.[12]

Despite its demise, Zangwill nonetheless distinguished a continued role for religion in the universalistic ambitions connected to the League of Nations. He cherished a lifelong interest in the Jewish roots of Christianity and was well-versed in Jewish tradition. The famed author made a point of showing the Jewish underpinnings of the spirit guiding the Wilsonian project. Judaism's messianic streaks had always been based on the notion of a Jewish mission for the betterment of mankind. In that vein, Zangwill urged for an investment in the universalisation of Jewish-inspired tribalism. In effect, "the brotherhood of peoples" would be strengthened: "It takes two men to make one brother."[13]

The price for such an unavoidable investment in the strengthening of smaller national units would be to relinquish the notion of a powerful "World-League". Unity only arises in opposition to an external adversary, or so Zangwill claimed: "World-Nationality would arrive tomorrow if only the Martians would invade us." He did offer a solution to this conundrum for the future League of Nations: the supranational body should do away with "nationality" and sovereign states, and invest in different kinds of class-based, religious, artistic or scientific "brotherhoods". Zangwill conceded the unlikeliness of this scenario, and therefore he proposed a true investment in a moral system of nationalities, based on "Reason and Love", aimed at freedom from oppression.[14]

Anti-Zionist demonstration at Damascus Gate, Jerusalem, March 1920. Zangwill gained historical notoriety as a supposed early proponent of the expulsion of the Arab population from Palestine. In reality, the Anglo-Jewish writer rather believed that the Arabs' departure was a necessary precondition for the Jewish state-building project to work. However, as the Arabs were not willing to leave, instead of resorting to forcible removal, the Zionist conclusion was that Palestine constituted an unfeasible home for the Jews.

THE LEAGUE OF DAMNATIONS

Three years after this in-depth exploration of nations and nationalities (despite his call not to conflate them, even Zangwill himself used the terms interchangeably), *The Voice of Jerusalem* was able to reflect on the newly operational League of Nations. In a 1917 speech given on the occasion of the issuing of the Balfour Declaration, Zangwill had still praised the developing League, without which, he said, "the whole world will perish". By 1920, though, his verdict was damning: the endeavour had become a "fiasco".[15]

Zangwill solemnly concluded that the fact that "humanity standing at the crossroads of history should have failed to take the turning to the right, is the saddest episode in all man's long tragic adventure". It was not, he lamented, "a League of Nations that has been brought forth, but a League of Damnations". Instead of a "League of Love", the organisation had in fact become a perpetuation of the bad old world order, an attempt to end "'the war against war' by a Peace against Peace" that would never allow true peace.[16]

The main culprit of this epic failure was President Woodrow Wilson, who had so disastrously designed the League. Interestingly, Wilson largely shared Zangwill's liberal values, which in fact underpinned the American president's desire to present the Treaty of Versailles and the League as a "readjustment of those great injustices which underlie the whole structure of European and Asiatic society". The system of bilateral agreements between individual (European) states had failed, but now, under the League's guidance, states and sovereigns with their imperialistic ambitions were no longer to rule the world; the new ruler was "the power of the united moral forces of the world, and in the Covenant of the League of Nations the moral forces of the world are mobilized".[17] Even if such universalistic language would have certainly appealed to Zangwill, he shared with several other commentators the opinion that Wilson had nonetheless shown himself not just incompetent, but also arrogant, sporting a sense of "papal infallibility". Instead of acknowledging his own defeat in the negotiation process, Wilson had "triumphantly waved scraps of paper from which the Fourteen Points have been practically erased".[18]

A JEWISH MORAL VANGUARD

Much of Zangwill's discontent with the League had to do with his own long-standing (albeit problematic) engagement with the Zionist project in Palestine. The 1917 Balfour Declaration had quickly revealed itself as a pipe dream, and the subsequent mandate system, in which several areas, including Palestine, Syria and Iraq, were placed under Great Power tutelage until they "matured" enough to gain independence, turned out to be an obscured system of dividing the spoils of war between the victorious powers. Zangwill criticised the Zionists for having failed to grasp that they had been used as a pawn, and for not having

Sir Herbert Samuel, first High Commissioner for Mandate Palestine, walking into Jaffa, 1920. After having experienced a brief bout of enthusiasm for the 1917 Balfour Declaration, Zangwill quickly changed his views again and started complaining that because of the Zionist inability to solve the Arab Question, the Declaration "was like offering a home of his own to a tramp in a crowded lodging-house". The famed author remained critical of the British mandate in Palestine until his death in 1926.

acted upon opportunities when they presented themselves. The most striking missed opportunity for both the Zionists and the international community, Zangwill argued, was the failure to stimulate the Palestinian Arabs to migrate to the newly established Arab states in the region to make place for Jewish settlers from Europe. "Race redistribution in the interests of the general world-happiness is, I take it, one of the functions of the League of Nations".[19]

The mandates were thus a scam, a "new-fangled hypocrisy", meant to cover up the lust for new colonies on the part of the Great Powers.

"How European statesmen are able to [...] keep from winking when talking to us of these moral 'Mandates,' which so mysteriously correspond with their secret treaties and ambitions, is a standing marvel. They must assuredly assume in us a *sancta simplicitas* beyond the sucking babe's." Whereas officially the mandate system was supposed to safeguard some form of justice in the governed areas, in Africa, most of which was nominally outside of the system, "the white man is allowed to batten upon the negro [...] unrestrained by international control".[20]

Surprisingly, most of this rant against the League served to support the mildly hopeful message that Zangwill had already set out to convey in *The Principle of Nationalities*: true universalistic morality did exist in the millennia-old Jewish messianic tradition. After all, it was the "vision of our [the Jews'] own Isaiah: 'They shall beat their swords into plough-shares and their spears into pruning hooks; nation shall not lift sword against nation, neither shall there be war anymore'". This moral imperative constituted the "Voice of Jerusalem" and could be extrapolated to guide a real and sound League of Nations project. If different peoples and creeds would invest in their own betterment with this "Voice" in mind, without "that crude and cynical view of nationality which regards every nation as necessarily the enemy of every other", the "brotherhood of man" would be achieved.[21]

In practical terms, and anticipating the era of decolonisation, Zangwill therefore suggested replacing the "discredited" Hague Peace Palace with a Temple of Peace in Jerusalem. With large parts of Asia and Africa still practically undeveloped and with a growing westward gaze on the part of the biggest non-western players, India and Japan, Jerusalem could have an important role to play. "In the Holy City of three great religions even diplomatists might find cynicism difficult, and our poor battered humanity might take a fresh upward impulse of faith and hope." Such a Jerusalem-based institution might counteract the evils of nations. Individuals may have good intentions, but "in our corporate capacity we are demoniac".[22]

CONCLUSION: AGAINST THE GRAIN

Zangwill's writings on nationality and the League of Nations provide insights into the dark perspectives of a well-known Jewish political and cultural figure at the time of the birth of the world organisation. Even before most other liberal intellectuals abandoned their "near-millennial expectations" of world peace that Wilson had inspired, Zangwill's reflections anticipated later criticism of the overall project. His publications also bring together the respective histories of the League and of one of the most visible minorities in twentieth-century political history. It may have been his membership of this Jewish minority group that led Zangwill to profess a disillusionment in the League's capacities, since it resembled the growing disappointment experienced by the colonised nations throughout 1919. For a brief period, these dependent peoples had hoped the "Wilsonian Moment" would enable them to obtain some form of self-determination through a transformation of the world order. That hope now proven idle – even Wilson himself had never been interested in breaking up the western colonial empires – colonial leaders started faring a generally less peaceful course towards independence in the ostensibly only workable shape of the nation-state.[23]

In an era when such statehood was becoming ever more the accepted norm, despite the lofty universalistic ideals that seemed to constitute the League's official rationale, Zangwill went against the grain by arguing against the merits of the nation-state. At the same time, he never fully gave up on the League's future. On the contrary, he was convinced that if state and bureaucratic borders between peoples could finally be overcome, if the "mania for 'sovereign rights'" of both western and non-western peoples could be brought to an end, then the ideals of a world community could also be met.[24]

NOTES

1 Zangwill: *The Voice of Jerusalem*, 120-121.

2 This article therefore focuses on a small selection of *published* sources. For the most extensive collection of primary sources related to Israel Zangwill, I refer the reader to the writer's personal archives (collection number A120), as well as the archives of the ITO (collection number A36), both held at the Central Zionist Archives in Jerusalem.

3 For the best recent biography on Zangwill, see Rochelson: *A Jew in the Public Arena*. For more on Zangwill's activities as a Territorialist, see Alroey: *Zionism without Zion* and Rovner: *In the Shadow of Zion*, as well as my doctoral dissertation: Almagor: 'Forgotten Alternatives'.

4 Myers: 'Rethinking Sovereignty and Autonomy', 48, 50. Scholars who in recent years have contributed to this broader Jewish political narrative include, amongst others, Noam Pianko, Joshua Karlip, Kenneth B. Moss, Kalman Weiser, James Loeffler, Dmitry Shumsky, Adam Rovner, David E. Fishman, Jeffrey Shandler, Stefan Vogt, Joshua Shanes and Simon Rabinovitch.

5 Rovner: *In the Shadow of Zion*, 114.

6 See, for instance, a somewhat ludicrous videoclip, in which three Israeli comedians pose this same question: https://www.youtube.com/watch?v=Sgcdo2Ovjok (09.01.2019).

7 Zangwill: *The Principle of Nationalities*, 13-15.

8 Zangwill: *The Principle of Nationalities*, 26.

9 Zangwill: *The Principle of Nationalities*, 29-30, 33.

10 Zangwill: *The Principle of Nationalities*, 37, 46.

11 Zangwill: *The Principle of Nationalities*, 67. See also Zangwill: *The Voice of Jerusalem*, 12.

12 Zangwill: *The Principle of Nationalities*, 79, 84-85.

13 Zangwill: *The Principle of Nationalities*, 91-92, 96, 98-99.

14 Zangwill: *The Principle of Nationalities*, 96, 99-100, 107.

15 Zangwill: *The Voice of Jerusalem*, 85, 115, 120.

16 Zangwill: *The Voice of Jerusalem*, 120, 122-123, 127-128.

17 Wilson: 'League of Nations'.

18 Zangwill: *The Voice of Jerusalem*, 120-121. French Prime Minister Georges Clemenceau famously complained about Wilson's supposed over-zealous arrogance when he exclaimed: "Mr. Wilson bores me with his Fourteen Points; why, God Almighty has only Ten!", quoted in Wecter: *The Hero in America*, 402.

19 Zangwill: *The Voice of Jerusalem*, 105. The Englishman's short-lived promotion of such a population exchange scheme, however much in line with dominant geopolitical convictions that lasted well into the post-1945 period – as Mads Drange's contribution to this volume also shows – was to gain him the not entirely deserved reputation of a hardliner regarding the Arab Question in Palestine. See, a.o., Rochelson: *A Jew in the Public Arena*, 166, and Almagor: 'Forgotten Alternatives', 113-115.

20 Zangwill: *The Voice of Jerusalem*, 101, 115, 125. Erez Manela also extensively argues that the "Wilsonian moment" in fact served to help perpetuate the existing imperial system: *The Wilsonian Moment*.

21 Zangwill: *The Voice of Jerusalem*, 85.

22 Zangwill: *The Voice of Jerusalem*, 100, 125.

23 Manela: *The Wilsonian Moment*, 5, 9, 13.

24 Zangwill: *The Voice of Jerusalem*, 130, 132.

BIBLIOGRAPHY

Published material

Almagor, Laura: *Forgotten Alternatives. Jewish Territorialism as a Movement of Political Action and Ideology, 1905-1965*, PhD Dissertation, Florence: European University Institute, 2015.

Alroey, Gur: *Zionism Without Zion. The Jewish Territorial Organization and its Conflict with the Zionist Organization*, Detroit: Wayne State University Press, 2016.

Manela, Erez: *The Wilsonian Moment. Self-Determination and the International Origins of Anticolonial Nationalism*, Oxford: Oxford University Press, 2007.

Myers, David N.: 'Rethinking Sovereignty and Autonomy: New Currents in the History of Jewish Nationalism', *Transversal* 13 (1), 2015, 44-51.

Rochelson, Meri-Jane: *A Jew in the Public Arena: The Career of Israel Zangwill*, Detroit: Wayne State University Press, 2008.

Rovner, Adam: *In the Shadow of Zion: Promised Lands before Israel*, New York: NYU Press, 2014.

Wecter, Dixon: *The Hero in America: A Chronicle of Hero-worship*, New York: C. Scribner's Sons, 1941.

Wilson, Woodrow: 'League of Nations' [also known as the 'Pueblo Speech']. 25.09.1919. http://www.presidency.ucsb.edu/ws/index.php?pid=117400 (09.01.2019).

Zangwill, Israel: *The Principle of Nationalities*, New York: The Macmillan Company, 1917.

Zangwill, Israel: *The Voice of Jerusalem*, New York: The Macmillan Company, 1921.

Online sources

YouTube, 'Ma Kashur – Lama Lo Uganda (Why not Uganda – English Sub'. (09.01.2019).

Mads Drange

THE UNTOLD STORY OF ERIC COLBAN AND THE GRECO-TURKISH POPULATION EXCHANGE

On 17 November 1923, Erik Colban and Huntington Gilchrist, from the Minority Section of the League of Nations, met with Secretary-General Eric Drummond in his office in Palais Wilson to discuss a matter of great urgency. The Secretary-General had recently received a letter from the Turkish Minister of Foreign Affairs about alleged Greek violations of the Greco-Turkish Population Exchange Agreement, urging him to take action. According to Turkish reports, Muslim farmers in Macedonia had been forced to leave their farms to make room for Greek refugees before they had been able to sell or gather together their property. With winter approaching, they were now stuck on the Macedonian plateau without food and shelter, waiting to be transported to Turkey.[1] The Turkish minister wrote to Drummond because, according to him, the international Mixed Commission, which was responsible for the execution of the agreement, was not doing its job: "The impotence to which this organization [the Mixed Commission] is being reduced by Greece is unquestionably likely to impair the prestige enjoyed by the League of Nations in the eyes of the world, and to put confidence in the League to a severe test".[2]

Why did a minister from a country that was not even member of the League complain to the Secretary-General about the execution of a bilateral agreement neither sanctioned nor supported by the League? And what did this matter have to do with the world's confidence in the

League? The answers to these questions are found in the wide scope of the League's work in the early interwar years, and its influence over Europe in a time of transition, when empires were becoming nation states.

THE MINORITY SECTION OF THE LEAGUE OF NATIONS

The transformation of Central and Eastern Europe from a region of multi-ethnic empires to one of new nation states, following World War One, was the result of numerous compromises between the allies during the Paris Peace Conference in 1919, and the powerful allure of the Wilsonian idea of national self-determination. However, the patchwork of different ethnic and religious groups meant it was impossible to cater to all national interests; the territorial make-up of the new nation states also created new minorities. To ensure the rights of these minorities, a number of protective treaties were signed between the Allied and the new states, covering more than 50 minorities and more than 30 million people.[3] To make sure that these treaties were respected, a Minority Section was established at the League of Nations secretariat, led by the Norwegian theologian Eric Colban. He organised his section into two units. The first, led by the American Huntington Gilchrist, dealt with Administrative Commissions such as the Saar and Danzig commissions. The second, run by the Danish diplomat Helmer Rosting, was responsible for minority questions.

The minority system of the League was based upon investigations of petitions sent to the League by anyone claiming to have witnessed or experienced breaches of the Treaties. This system of petitions was confined by a number of legal restrictions, but required the Great Powers of the League to review and respond to the complaints.[4] Consequently, minorities and even individuals could challenge national or imperial interests, as the only requirements were that the petitions had to relate to the Treaty in question, that they could not come from an anonymous source and that they could not contain "violent language".[5] The League Council was responsible for the Minority Treaties, and when a petition was received, an *ad hoc* panel of three Council representatives was formed to investigate whether the complaints had merit or not. However, prior to this, the Minority Section carried out a preliminary review of the complaints, determining their "receivability".[6] This gave Colban and his colleagues real influence over minority questions. With time, Colban developed his own procedures, which involved secret discussions between his Section and the parties involved, and problems were often solved without the involvement of the Council.[7] According to Colban himself, the success in safeguarding the rights of minorities in the 1920s was "due not so much to the official action by the Council of the League of Nations as to unofficial negotiations with the Governments concerned on the one hand and the leaders of the minorities on the other".[8]

Minority questions were among the most contentious political topics in the Balkans and Eastern Europe in the years following the Paris Peace Conference, and the Minority Section thus became an important part of the League bureaucracy. The ideas behind the minority protection regime are well described by scholars such as Carol Fink, and the actual enforcement of the system has also received attention from historians.[9] What is less documented, however, is the ways in which the autonomy of the Minority Section, taken or given, allowed Colban to involve himself in matters beyond the scope of his Section. One example is the execution of the Greco-Turkish Population Exchange Agreement, a controversial minority agreement not sanctioned by the League of Nations, and often referred to as a state-sponsored ethnic cleansing.

THE GRECO-TURKISH POPULATION EXCHANGE AGREEMENT

The Greco-Turkish population exchange was part of the Lausanne Treaty, which replaced the former Peace Treaty between the Allies and the Ottoman Empire, the Sèvres Treaty, following the Greco-Turkish war and the establishment of the Turkish Republic. A bilateral agreement between Turkey and Greece, the Population Exchange Agreement stated that: "As from 1st of March, 1923, there shall take place a compulsory exchange of Turkish nationals of the Greek Orthodox religion estab-

Campaign poster for the American Committee for Relief in the Near East. This was one of the oldest American humanitarian organisations, founded in 1915 as a response to the Armenian genocide and the famine in the Levant. The suffering of the Christian minorities in the region got extensive coverage in American media, and at its peak, the organisation managed to raise more than 110 million dollars, feeding hundreds of thousands of refugees.

lished in Turkish territory, and of Greek nationals of the Muslem [*sic*] religion established in Greek territory."[10] The agreement was negotiated by Fridtjof Nansen between the Greek Prime Minister Eleftherios Venizelos and the new President of the Turkish Republic, Mustapha Kemal (Ataturk), who shared the desire for ethnically and religiously homogenous nation states.[11] Nansen saw the agreement as a pragmatic attempt to solve the problem of more than a million Greek Orthodox refugees who had fled the Aegean Coast of Turkey during the war, and were now living in refugee camps in Greece. To him, swapping populations seemed like the lesser of two evils, as the Greek Muslims could take over the farms of the Turkish Christians on the west coast of Turkey, and vice versa.[12]

While Nansen worked for the League of Nations, the League itself had no formal role in the execution of the agreement, and it was not part of the mandate of the Minority Section. Quite the opposite: many of the Allied nations were sceptical about the agreement and the idea of a forced population exchange based upon religion.[13] The only responsibility the League accepted in respect to the agreement was the appointment of neutral members to a Mixed Commission, including Turkish and Greek representatives, which was to supervise and facilitate the population exchange, and carry out the liquidation of movable and immovable property according to the terms agreed upon.[14] However, as time went by, it became clear that this would not be the end of the League's involvement in this controversial agreement.

COLBAN'S SECRET DIPLOMACY

In the last two decades, much has been written about the Greco-Turkish population exchange, as the taboos surrounding the events have gradually lifted. Greek and Turkish historians have tried to understand why the two governments agreed to a forced population exchange which involved at least 1.4 million people, and how this unparalleled transfer of people affected the economy, politics and culture of the two states.[15] Many have also been puzzled by how Nansen – the great humanitarian – could have been one of the architects of an agreement that forced people to migrate based solely upon their religious affiliation. However, the involvement of the League has received less attention.

The League Archives, held in Geneva, reveal that its involvement in the Greco-Turkish population exchange extended way beyond the appointment of members to the Mixed Commission. First of all, several conflicts that had occurred between the two countries during the execution of the agreement had been brought before the Council and some even to the Permanent Court of International Justice. Admittedly, these official involvements of the League have been described several times in the literature and are well documented in the *Official Journal* of the League of Nations. However, based on the quantity of correspondence and internal documents related to the agreement, it is clear that the Secretariat, and particularly the Minority Section, followed the process closely from day one. Colban and his colleagues were all in close dialogue with the Mixed Commission, providing them with advice and support on how best to carry out their job.

As early as seven days after the appointment of the neutral members of the Mixed Commission, Colban invited them to his office in Geneva. Firstly, he wanted to provide them with some guidance on their obligations towards the League. This was broached early on in the meeting, when he emphasised that "[t]he Commissioners were not to receive any instructions from the League of Nations or from the Secretariat, and that the relations between the Commission and the Secretariat would not be in any sense of [an] obligatory character".[16] Secondly, he advised them to "present a united front" towards the Greek and Turkish mem-

Swiss stamp picturing Fridtjof Nansen, the League of Nations High Commissioner for refugees. Nansen became known for his humanitarian efforts in Armenia, Russia and Greece, all made possible by his ability to manoeuvre within the new international arena that the League represented.

Muslim refugees crossing the Aegean Sea on their way to Turkey. More than 400,000 Muslim residents of Greece were forced to leave the country as a result of the population exchange agreement. Muslims and Christians had been living side by side in relatively peaceful coexistence for centuries and the idea of Muslims having to move to a foreign country with a foreign language was difficult to accept not only for the Muslims of Greece, but also for their Christian neighbours.

bers, especially at the first meetings of the Mixed Commission, where important operational decisions would be settled. He also stated that "[i]n relations with the Greek and Turkish Delegations, it would be necessary to remember that the Turks were somewhat different from Europeans and looked with suspicion upon everything that came from Western Europe at the present time, [and] that it might be best first to present provisional proposals rather than give decided opinions and let the two Delegations take the initiative".[17] This contradictory message about the independence of the Commission, in tandem with precise recommendations about what to do and how to act, would be the hallmark of his involvement in the population exchange in the years to come. Acting through the Mixed Commission, the Minority Section would become heavily involved in the execution of the agreement itself, as well as play a pivotal role in its relatively successful and peaceful outcome.[18]

With his expertise on minority questions, Colban had several valuable insights to offer the neutral members of the Mixed Commission. From their correspondence, it is also apparent that the Commission and the Minority Section developed a close relationship. This is not surprising, as they shared not only similar tasks, but also language and background. In fact, four of the Presidents of the Mixed Commission between 1923 and 1934 were Scandinavian, and a lot of the correspondence between the Commission and the Section was in Danish, Swedish or Norwegian. Since secret and informal discussions formed an important part of the Minority Section's *modus operandi*, it is perhaps not that strange that its involvement in the population exchange has received little attention in the literature. The interesting question, however, is why the Secretariat chose to involve itself in the execution of an agreement they had no responsibility for, and did not even necessarily believe in. Further to this, why did the Turkish Government hold the League responsible for the agreement – and why did the League, at least on an unofficial level, accept this responsibility?

HUMANITARIANISM AND REALPOLITIK

It was only in the case of the Ottoman Empire that the transition from empire to nation state, as dictated by the Peacemakers in Paris, led to an immediate war: Mustafa Kemal had not accepted the marginalisation of the former Ottoman Empire that the Treaty of Sèvres undoubtedly entailed, and went to war to establish the new Turkish republic. France, Italy, the UK and the US were all war-weary and unwilling to defend the Sèvres Treaty militarily. The Greek Government, however, refused to give up their control over the west coast of Asia Minor, given to them as part of the treaty with the Sultan; with forces already in the region to protect the Greek Orthodox minority, a short but brutal war erupted. Led by Mustafa Kemal, an experienced officer who by then had successfully fought both the Italians in Libya and the British in Gallipoli, the Turkish army soon defeated the Greeks. This caused a massive exodus of refugees across the Aegean Sea, in numbers not seen in the region until the 2015-2016 refugee crisis. It also effectively demonstrated

Arrival of refugees in Chios, Greece. Christian minorities in Turkey could trace their presence back more than a thousand years. Most of them lived in the coastal areas in the west and in the north-west corner of Asia Minor. During the Greco-Turkish war and the execution of the population exchange agreement, more than 1.4 million people were forced to leave their homes. Only the Greek minority of Constantinople was exempted from the exchange.

the military capacity of the new republic, and when the Allied powers met in Lausanne to re-negotiate the peace treaty with Turkey in 1922/23, a lot was at stake.

There are no simple answers as to why Colban and Drummond decided to involve themselves in the Greco-Turkish population exchange, but two circumstances appear to be of particular importance. First, the growing legitimacy of the League, due to their expertise in international matters, brought about an expectation from both parties involved, and from within the organisation itself, that it would act. Second, the involvement of the League must be seen in the context of the contemporary geopolitical situation. Colban knew that the population exchange agreement was about more than the fate of the Greek and Turkish minorities: At stake was the peace and stability of a strategically essential region. From the correspondence regarding the population exchange, it seems as if Colban and his Department simply regarded it as their mandate and responsibility to help out, and keep the process from collapsing – not because they necessarily supported the agreement, but because no good alternative to a successful exchange existed.

As to the Turkish Minister's comment about the success of the population exchange having a bearing on the world's confidence in the League, this can probably be attributed to the fact that the Lausanne Treaty was a revision of the peace established in Paris, which the League was established to uphold. Thus, the question was tied to the League's very *raison d'être*. This must have been clear for Drummond, and also for the League Council, which several times involved itself in the execution of the agreement. The survival of the League and the new international system depended on the endorsement of the world, which in turn hinged upon finalising the peaceful establishment of new nation states on the remains of the former European and Middle Eastern empires. In the case of the Greek and Turkish minorities, strategic and humanitarian interests aligned – as they would several times in the history of the League of Nations in the 1920s.

CONCLUSION

The legacy of the League of Nations has traditionally been tied to its failure to withstand emerging totalitarian forces in the 1930s, often explained by the built-in political shortcomings of the organisation. However, over the last two decades, scholars have expressed an increased interest in the bureaucratic branch of the League, which achieved significant results spanning from public health issues to protective labour legislation – many of which survived the interwar period and the League itself. The Minority Section is one example of this rather advanced bureaucratic body, which in the case of the Greco-Turkish population exchange, managed to balance loyalty to the political branch of the organisation with pragmatic, swift diplomacy, securing both the rights of the minorities involved and stability in the region, neither of which were given outcomes. The population exchange itself remains controversial to this day, yet the understudied involvement of the Minority Section highlights a Secretariat ready to take on unthankful responsibilities.

NOTES

1 Letter from Ishmet Pasha to Eric Drummond on 8 November 1923, regarding Greek violations of the Lausanne Treaty. Files of the Administrative Commissions and Minority Section (hereafter ACM) at the League of Nations Archive, Geneva (hereafter LoNA). Box R82, 1923, File 2, Document 32150, Dossier 31152.

2 Protest from Adnan Bay to the League of Nations Council on Greek violations of the Lausanne Treaty, 1923, ACM, LoNA, Box R82, 1923, File 2, Document 32150, Dossier 31152.

3 Lauren: *The Evolution of International Human Rights*, 118.

4 Pedersen: 'Petitions', 232.

5 Rosting: 'Protection of Minorities by the League of Nations', 648-649.

6 Raitz von Frentz: *A Lesson Forgotten*, 38.

7 Guterman: *Das Minderheitenschutzverfharen des Volkerforbundes*, 345-375; Fink: 'Minority Rights as an International Question', 385-400.

8 Colban: 'The Minorities Problem', 313.

9 For the minorities system and the work of the minority section, see Fink: *Defending the rights of others*; Raitz von Frentz: *A Lesson Forgotten*; Guterman: *Das Minderheitenschutzverfharen des Volkerforbundes*; and Ranshofen-Wertheimer: *The International Secretariat*.

10 'Convention Concerning the Exchange of Greek and Turkish Population', Lausanne, 30 January 1923. Article 1.

11 Yildirimn: *Diplomacy and Displacement*, 4-5.

12 Tolleshaug: *Fridtjof Nansen*, 127.

13 There was a lot of opposition towards the idea of a forced population exchange, both because it violated important principles of freedom and justice, and because many saw it as a dangerous precedent for future conflicts. One of the critics was Lord Curzon, who was concerned that the world would "pay a heavy price for [it] in the future". Tolleshaug: *Fridtjof Nansen*, 122.

14 League of Nations. *Official Journal*, November 1923, 1468.

15 For an overview, see Hirschon (ed.): *Crossing the Aegean*; Yldirim: *Diplomacy and Displacement*.

16 Greco-Turk Exchange of Population Commission. Notes taken at meeting in Mr. Colban's room on 24 September 1923, ACM, LoNA. Box R82, 1923, File 2, Document 31412, Dossier 31152, page 1.

17 Greco-Turk Exchange of Population Commission. Notes taken at meeting in Mr. Colban's room on 24 September 1923, ACM, LoNA. Box R82, 1923, File 2, Document 31412, Dossier 31152, page 1.

18 The League involvement in the Greco-Turkish Population Exchange is the topic of my MA thesis: *Supervisor, Facilitator and Arbitrator: A Study of the Involvement of the Minority Section of the League of Nations in the Forced Population Exchange between Greece and Turkey in 1923*. Here, I have studied, amongst other sources, the internal communications within the Minority Section of the League of Nations regarding the population exchange agreement. These largely unutilised sources provide a new insight into the execution of the agreement, but also into how the Minority Section operated in general.

BIBLIOGRAPHY

Unpublished material

League of Nations Archive, Geneva (LoNA), Administrative Commissions and Minority Section (ACM), Letter from Ishmet Pasha to Eric Drummond on 8 November, regarding Greek Violations of the Lausanne Treaty. Box R82, File 2, Document 32150, Dossier 31152, 1923.

League of Nations Archive, Geneva (LoNA), Administrative Commissions and Minority Section (ACM), Protest from Adnan Bay to the League of Nations Council on Greek violations of the Lausanne Treaty. Box R82, File 2, Document 32150, Dossier 31152, 1923.

League of Nations Archive, Geneva (LoNA), Administrative Commissions and Minority Section (ACM), Greco-Turk Exchange of Population Commission. Notes taken at meeting in Mr. Colban's room on 24 September 1923. Box R82, File 2, Document 31412, Dossier 31152, page 1, 1923.

League of Nations. *Official Journal*, November 1923, 1468.

Published material

Colban, Eric: 'The Minorities Problem', *The Norseman* 5, 1944, 309-317.

Drange, Mads: *Supervisor, Facilitator and Arbitrator: A Study of the Involvement of the Minority Section of the League of Nations in the Forced Population Exchange between Greece and Turkey in 1923*, MA Thesis, University of Oslo, 2017.

Fink, Carol: 'Minority Rights as an International Question', *Contemporary European History* 9 (3), 2000, 385-400.

Guterman, Christoph: *Das Minderheitenschutzverfharen des Volkerforbundes*, Berlin: Duncker & Humbolt, 1979.

Hirschon, Renée (ed.): *Crossing the Aegean. An appraisal of the 1923 compulsory population exchange between Greece and Turkey*, New York: Berghahn Books, 2003.

Lauren, Paul Gordon: *The Evolution of International Human rights. Visions seen*, Philadelphia: University of Pennsylvania Press, 2011.

Pedersen, Susan: 'Samoa on the World Stage: Petitions and Peoples before the Mandates Commission of the League of Nations', *The Journal of Imperial and Commonwealth History* 40 (2), 2012, 231-261.

Raitz von Frentz: *A Lesson Forgotten. Minority Protection under the League of Nations. The Case of the German Minority in Poland, 1920-1934*, Münster: Lit Verlag, 1999.

Rosting, Hjalmar: 'Protection of Minorities by the League of Nations', *The American Journal of International Law* 17, 1923, 641-660.

Tolleshaug, Berit: *Fridtjof Nansen. En norsk helt i en Gresk tragedie?*, Oslo: Pax Forlag, 2001.

Yildirimn, Onur: *Diplomacy and Displacement: Reconsidering the Turco-Greek Exchange of Populations, 1922-1934*, New York: Routledge, 2016.

Haakon A. Ikonomou

'HE USED TO GIVE ME TURKISH LESSONS IN CONSTANTINOPLE'

How to Get a Job in the League Secretariat

Strangely, the early staffing of the very first permanent international bureaucracy of a world organisation was conducted in a distinctly unbureaucratic manner. This does not mean that the Secretariat of the League did not consider staffing of pivotal importance. This was, after all, how the Secretariat was filled with the people and personalities that came to shape the institution, and international politics more broadly, throughout its existence. Retaining the right to hire, fire and promote people as they saw fit was, moreover, among the most important sources of autonomy for the League Secretariat. If it could not choose its own human composition, how could it act independently of – or rather, manoeuvre relatively unconstrained between – narrow state interests?

But *how* did people get into the League Secretariat? This chapter will look at one specific road into international bureaucracy, in order to draw up some more general insights about the recruitment practices of the League: the overall argument being that while the recruitment practices of the Secretariat became increasingly institutionalised, professionalised and routinised – setting the standard for following generations of international organisations – early recruitments were often the product of haphazard encounters and nebulous networks. As this first generation of League officials arguably had a disproportionately large impact on the organisation, this seems a relevant point to explore.

There is a burgeoning interest in internationalists' biographies,[1] but few investigate the role of the international civil servant as such.[2] Indeed, research on the history of international public administrations is in its infancy.[3] The personal histories of civil servants – particularly if their practice, evidenced in the archives of the League in Geneva, can be interpreted through personal papers, diaries or interviews – can open up the 'black box' of international organisations, allowing researchers to probe into their social world and bureaucratic practices. One of the strengths of the biography is its ability to link the individual to the structural – the protagonist can act as a sensor for general trends and changes within a specific institution.[4] Thus, to shed light on the early recruitments of the Secretariat, we will follow the curious trajectory of Thanassis Aghnides.

The Music Club of Anatolia College (1910). Music held a central place in the curricula of the religious and missionary schools Aghnides attended. At t[he] Grand Patriarchal School, music shaped the turn-of-the-century Hellenism of the Ottoman Empire's orthodox community. At St. Joseph and Anatolia College, music formed part of a broad Christian civilizing doctrin[e]. Aghnides would continue to express his internationalism in musical terms throughout his lif[e].

MOMENT OF FLUX

From the looks of the early existence of the League Secretariat, setting up an international secretariat is a bit like dressing while running a race – you do not want to be left behind from the start, but you most definitely do not want to cross the finish line a half-dressed buffoon.

In other words, the first Secretary-General Sir Eric Drummond – himself not the first-choice candidate for the job – had to make the Secretariat functional and operational from the very beginning, to handle all kinds of political, social and economic matters following the Great War: matters that would not wait politely for the organisation to find its shape. On the other hand, Drummond also had to make strategic choices, both in terms of personnel and with regard to the structure of the Secretariat, which would have a long-term impact on its workings and ultimately determine whether it could 'go the distance'.

In the beginning, therefore, Drummond struck a balance between pragmatic *ad hoc* solutions and principled decisions, developing what his right-hand man and confidant Frank P. Walters called "a small but elastic organism".[5] His more principled decisions were mostly based

on two ideals. The first was that the Secretariat should be composed of a truly international staff, organised along functional, rather than national, lines. Thus, there would be no 'French Section', composed of French experts, bureaucrats and diplomats representing French interests, but rather a 'Health Section' and an 'Information Section', composed of people from different nationalities working together on a specific, functionally limited subject.

The other major ideal was to retain absolute autonomy in terms of staffing. This did not mean that the Secretariat was beyond pressure from Member States to take on certain candidates for specific posts – far from it. But the final decision in terms of staffing ultimately lay with Drummond himself, and this principle, whether real or cosmetic in practice, had to be upheld for the Secretariat to survive as a distinct "organism".[6]

Indeed, the clearest indicator of the growing crisis within the League Secretariat in the late 1920s and early 1930s was the erosion of these two principles. The new member state Germany, together with Fascist Italy and Imperialist Japan (both long-standing members), started to nominate staff to the Secretariat who were specifically instructed to be loyal and work for the home nation alone.[7] And, in tandem with this, these member states began blatantly to pressure the Secretary-General to take on specific "candidates".[8]

The principles under pressure in the 1930s had been formalised through bureaucratic procedures and formal institutions built around the Secretariat's staffing practices during the 1920s. But what about in the very beginning? Many of the League's first employees found their way into the Secretariat via the Paris Peace Conference. Thinking that Paris in the late spring and summer of 1919 held an unprecedented pool of talented men and women, Drummond strategically waited until the Peace Conference drew to a close and seized upon this great moment of flux to recruit a small team of employees that would shape the institution profoundly.[9] One of these people Drummond hired was a young Greek diplomat.

Macedonia Hall of Anatolia College's Thessaloniki campus. While working at the League Secretariat, Aghnides helped the President of Anatolia College get in touch with the Greek liberal statesman Eleftherios Venizelos, thus securing his old Alma Mater's move to Thessaloniki, Greece, in the midst of the catastrophic Greco-Turkish population exchange.

THANASSIS AGHNIDES GETS A JOB

Several of the men and women that landed jobs within the Secretariat in the spring and summer months of 1919 were people Drummond personally knew and trusted, or came recommended by people he knew and trusted. Furthermore, he had to consider the national composition of the early team: top positions were reserved for Britain, France, Italy and the United States (before their withdrawal), without whose support and involvement the League would have lacked legitimacy and force. Still, these early recruitments followed no structured pattern, had no formalised rules and was not assessed by any permanent competent body. It was this situation that gave the young Ottoman Greek, Thanassis Aghnides, an opportunity that would change the course of his life.

Born and raised in the Anatolian heartland and Constantinople, and part of the Greek Orthodox upper middle class of the Ottoman Empire, Aghnides attended three different religious schools during the course of his education. After graduating from the Grand Patriarchal School in Phanar, the most prestigious Greek Orthodox School in Constantinople, he received his *baccalaureat* from the French Catholic College of St. Joseph before taking a further degree at the American Protestant Anatolian College.[10]

This strange mixture of religious and linguistic experiences, and his excellent grades in calligraphy, arithmetic, geography and other disciplines, qualified him for legal studies in Constantinople.[11] Moreover, due to the close ties between the French and American missionary institutions and the expat community of the capital, Aghnides secured a traineeship "in the study of Sir Edwin Pears", President of the European Bar of the Consular Courts at the Porte.[12] Pears being one of the leading personas of the British community in Constantinople,[13] this acquaintance opened many doors for Aghnides. Among other things, and due to his proficiency in French, English, Turkish and Greek, Aghnides acted as the personal Turkish teacher of the ascending British diplomatic star Harold Nicolson.[14]

As Turkish nationalism grew more fervent, and Greek and Armenian minorities – themselves in the grasp of nationalist fever – faced an increasingly perilous existence in the crumbling Ottoman Empire, Aghnides moved to Paris in 1911, to retake his law degree in French at the Sorbonne. When war came, Aghnides, possessing many of the skills needed for the diplomatic trade, was recruited by the Greek Ministry of Foreign Affairs, and soon after appointed director of the Press Bureau at the Greek Embassy in London.[15] Though the circumstances are unclear, he did not get along with his superiors and quit the foreign service at the close of the war.[16]

Thus, in 1919, Aghnides found himself unemployed and looking for a new career. A strange encounter would decide his path. His former Turkish pupil from Constantinople and acquaintance from his London days, Harold Nicolson, was now a part of the British Delegation at the

Peace Conference. Not only that, Nicolson was working specifically with Greek territorial claims and British proposals for what to do with the territories of the defeated Ottoman Empire. He was in close contact with Eleftherios Venizelos – the Greek liberal statesman who would present the Greek claims before the Peace Conference – and was in fact deeply infatuated with him, as well as with Greek antiquity (as most of the educated classes in Britain were).[17] The same Venizelos had personally recruited Aghnides to the Greek Foreign Service a few years earlier, at a time when he was fighting vigorously to bring Greece into the war on the side of the British and the Allies.[18]

A blend of British imperial, Christian missionary and Greek diplomatic networks; the Peace Conference as a site where statesmen from around the world came to defend their claims of territory and self-determination; the education and skill of Aghnides; and pure chance, brought Nicolson and Aghnides together in the streets of Paris. After Aghnides had confided to Nicolson that he was searching for some kind of professional direction, Nicolson wrote to Drummond:

> I wish to recommend to you a young Greek who would, I think, be extremely valuable on the International Secretariat [...] I have known him for the last six years as he used to give me Turkish lessons in Constantinople. [...] I can guarantee that he is exactly the sort of person you would want, and I think it would be a great pity if we failed to secure his services.[19]

Nicolson was so keen on conveying the virtues of this young Greek, it seems, that he forgot to mention his name. "You do not mention his name: could you kindly let me have it?", Drummond wrote back.[20]

Thus began Thanassis Aghnides' remarkable career in the League Secretariat. After spending most of his first years in the Minority, Disarmament, and Political Sections, he rose to the post of Director of the Disarmament Section in 1930, heading it in the crucial years of the failed World Disarmament Conference (1932-1934). From 1939 to 1942, he was Under-Secretary-General of the League of Nations in charge of Department I of the Secretariat, playing an important role, together with Secretary-General Seán Lester, in keeping the machinery going and rendering the technical and humanitarian elements of the League operational. Aghnides would stay with the Secretariat for 23 years; after a few years as Greek Ambassador to London during the Second World War, he continued to work for the United Nations until the 1960s.

In 1924, Thanassis Aghnides visited Greece as an envoy of the League Secretariat, to report on the population exchange between Greece and Turkey, after the Greek military defeat in Asia Minor forced the first revision of the order established at the Paris Peace Conference. Aghnides wrote to Secretary-General Drummond about the hardships of the refugees who had fled their homes in what was once the Ottoman Empire to start a new life in Athens. He did not write that his mother was one of the refugees.

THE LASTING SIGNIFICANCE OF THE FIRST EMPLOYEES

The circumstances of Aghnides' recruitment to the League Secretariat are significant for several reasons. First, they very clearly show the relative randomness of the early staffing of the Secretariat, which was the product of the acute need for able men and women in order to become operational as soon as possible, as well as Drummond's remarkable autonomy in recruiting staff in the first months of the Secretariat's existence and the unprecedented pool of talent gathered in, or connected to, the Paris Peace Conference. People like Alexander Loveday, Jean Monnet and Pierre Comert all joined the provisional Secretariat (located in London) in this moment of flux. Second, as is displayed in the

Average length of first employment interval

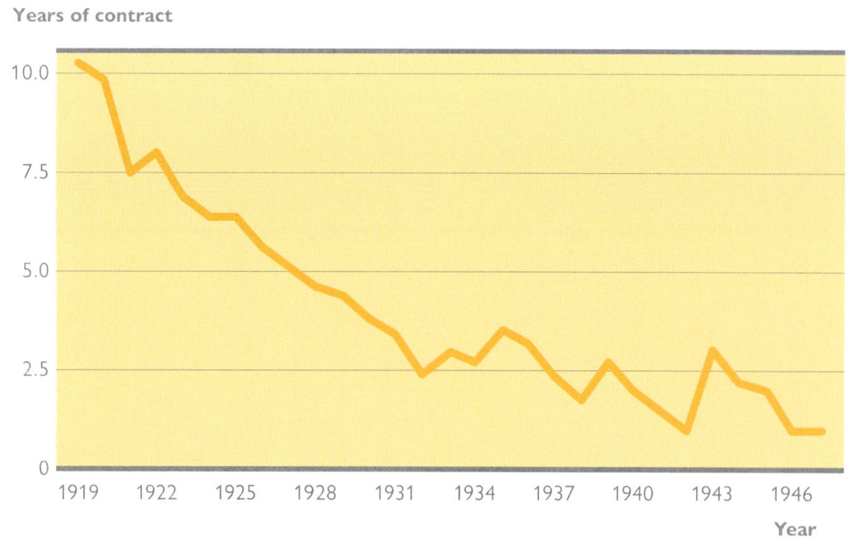

graph, those employed in 1919 and the subsequent three or four years stayed on the staff significantly longer than the international bureaucrats recruited in the following years.

Third, the fact that these employees stayed for longer, combined with the many early strategic and institutional decisions they had to make, which would shape the League of Nations' organisational make-up for the remainder of its existence, meant that the first cohorts of international bureaucrats wielded a disproportionate amount of administrative power.[21] Some, like Erik Colban (Director of the Administrative and Minorities) or Alexander Loveday (Member, then Chief of the Economic and Financial Section, and Director of the Financial Section and Economic Intelligence Service), would develop entire sub-fields of international governance.[22] To understand how this came to be, this chapter has demonstrated that we need to consider historical contingencies and biographical trajectories just as carefully as we analyse institutional structures, political procedures and administrative norms.

As for Aghnides, he would go on to shape the very procedures of staffing in international organisations that were about to be formulated when he joined the League Secretariat in 1919. Heading the United Nation's International Civil Service Advisory Board, set up in 1949, Aghnides was instrumental in producing the 'Report on Standards of Conduct in the International Civil Service (1st Ed. 1954)' which came to serve as a handbook for international civil servants in the UN, the ILO, the WHO, GATT and many other international organisations for the remainder of the twentieth century. Central to this document were Drummond's two principles of an *international* staff appointed by an *independent* administration.[23]

Drawing on the raw material of the LONSEA database, developed as part of the research cluster "Asia and Europe in a Global Context" at the University of Heidelberg, we can place Aghnides' career within a broader statistical context. As part of the first generation of League civil servants, Aghnides climbed the first steps of the career ladder in a formative phase of the Secretariat's lifespan and enjoyed an unusually long career within the organisation.

NOTES

1 Knudsen and Gram-Skjoldager (eds): *Living Political Biography*.

2 Ludlow: *Roy Jenkins*; Winter and Prost: *René Cassin & Human Rights*; de Haan and Everard (eds): *Rosa Manus*.

3 Gram-Skjoldager and Ikonomou: 'The Construction of the League of Nations Secretariat'.

4 Panter, Paulmann and Szöllösi-Janze: 'Methodological Challenges & Perspectives'.

5 League of Nations Archives (hereafter, LoNA), Geneva, R182, 17.07.1919, Walters to Secretary-General Drummond.

6 Gram-Skjoldager and Ikonomou: 'The Construction of the League of Nations Secretariat'.

7 See for example, Tollardo: *Fascist Italy and the League of Nations*.

8 One of the clearest violations came in 1930, when the German Foreign Minister Julius Curtius simply blocked a British candidate for the job of Director of the Disarmament Section, put forth by Eric Drummond himself, paving the way for Thanassis Aghnides. Gram-Skjoldager, Ikonomou and Kahlert: 'Scandinavians and the League of Nations Secretariat, 1919-1946'.

9 LoNA, R1455, 30.04.1919, Response to Wiseman's scheme by Drummond.

10 Aghnides: 'About the author' in *Status of the Oecumenical Patriarchate*.

11 Institut des Frères des Écoles Chrétiennes. Collège Saint-Joseph A Kadi-Keuï. Distribution Solennelle des Prix présidée par Son Excellence Monsieur Constans, Ambassadeur de France, prés la sublime porte, Le 8 Juillet 1903, Contantinople; McGrew: *Educating Across Cultures*, 126.

12 Pears: *Forty Years*, 28-29, 340. Edwin Pears was close to both the prestigious Robert College and Anatolia College, both run by American missionaries, and saw their presence in the Ottoman Empire as part of the civilisation mission of the Christian West: "no one who has a higher appreciation than I of the work done by American missionaries in Turkey. Whenever such mission exists, it is a centre of light and civilisation".

13 Pears: *Forty Years*, 2.

14 'Obituary, Thanassis Aghnides', *The Times*, date not found.

15 Aghnides: 'About the author' in *Status of the Oecumenical Patriarchate*.

16 LoNA, P273, 'Interview with Thanassis Aghnides', Geneva: Centre de Reserches sur les institutions internationales, 1966, 3-4.

17 'Diary entry, 28.01.1919', Nicolson (ed.): *The Harold Nicolson Diaries*, 20; Prott: *The Politics of Self-Determination*.

18 Smith: 'Venizelos' Diplomacy, 1910-1923', 134-192; LoNA, P273 'Interview with Thanassis Aghnides', 3-6.

19 LoNA, S699-700, 04.07.1919, British Delegation, Paris, My dear Drummond, by H. Nicolson.

20 LoNA, S699-700, 23.07.1919, Sunderland House, London, My dear Nicolson, by E. Drummond.

21 For the formative administrative practices, see Gram-Skjoldager and Ikonomou: 'The Construction of the League of Nations Secretariat'.

22 Smejkal: 'Protection in Practice'; Clavin: *Securing the World Economy*.

23 International Civil Service Advisory Board (ICSAB), 'Report on Standards of Conduct in the International Civil Service', *United Nations*, 1954, 2; Auberer, 'Digesting the League', 424.

BIBLIOGRAPHY

Aghnides, Thanassis: *Status of the Oecumenical Patriarchate based on the Provisions of the Treaty of Lausanne – International Standing of the Oecumenical Throne*, New York, 1964.

Clavin, Patricia: *Securing the World Economy: The Reinvention of the League of Nations, 1920-1946*, Oxford: Oxford University Press, 2013.

de Haan, Francisca and Myriam Everard (eds): *Rosa Manus. The Internationalist Life & Legacy of a Jewish Dutch Feminist*, Leiden and Boston: Brill, 2016.

Gram-Skjoldager, Karen and Haakon A. Ikonomou: 'The Construction of the League of Nations Secretariat. Formative Practices of Autonomy and Legitimacy in International Organizations', *International History Review*, 2017.

Gram-Skjoldager, Karen, Haakon A. Ikonomou and Torsten Kahlert: 'Scandinavians and the League of Nations Secretariat, 1919-1946', *Scandinavian Journal of History*, 2019.

Knudsen, Ann-Christina L. and Karen Gram-Skjoldager (eds): *Living Political Biography – Narrating 20th Century European Lives*, Aarhus: Aarhus University Press, 2012.

Ludlow, N. Piers: *Roy Jenkins and the European Commission Presidency, 1976-80: At the Heart of Europe*, London: Palgrave Macmillan, 2016.

McGrew, William: *Educating Across Cultures. Anatolia College in Turkey and Greece*, Lanham: Rowman & Littlefield, 2015.

Nicolson, Nigel (ed.): *The Harold Nicolson Diaries, 1907-1964*, London: Phoenix, 2005.

Panter, Sarah, Johannes Paulmann and Margit Szöllösi-Janze: 'Mobility and Biography: Methodological Challenges and Perspectives', *Mobility and Biography*, 1-14.

Pears, Sir Edwin: *Forty Years in Contantinople. The Recollections of Sir Edwin Pears, 1873-1915*, 3rd ed., London: Herbert Jenkins Limited, 1916.

Prott, Volker: *The Politics of Self-Determination. Remaking Territories and National Identities in Europe, 1917-1923*, Oxford: Oxford University Press, 2016.

Smejkal, Thomas: *Protection in Practice: The Minorities Section of the League of Nations Secretariat, 1919-1934*, New York: Columbia University Academic Commons, 2010.

Smith, Michael Llewellyn: 'Venizelos' Diplomacy, 1910-1923: From Balkan Alliance to Greek-Turkish Settlement'. In Paschalis M. Kitromilides (ed.): *Eleftherios Venizelos. The Trials of Statesmanship*, Edinburgh: Edinburgh University Press, 2008.

Tollardo, Elisabetta: *Fascist Italy and the League of Nations, 1922-1935*, London: Palgrave Macmillan, 2016.

Winter, Jay and Antoine Prost: *René Cassin & Human Rights. From the Great War to the Universal Declaration*, Cambridge: Cambridge University Press, 2013.

Søren Friis

THE SCANDINAVIAN CENTRE

Denmark and the Early Years of International Studies under the League of Nations

In December 1926, a small group of scholars met at the Copenhagen home of P. Munch, a prominent politician and historian. The outcome of their meeting was the founding of a new research institute, *the Institute of Economics and History*.[1] With Munch as its head, the institute was to serve as an independent, interdisciplinary platform for cooperation among Danish economists and historians, particularly senior scholars of the University of Copenhagen.

Yet this new institute was not founded on purely national or scholarly motives. For one thing, Munch – a former Minister of Defence (1913-1920) and future minister of foreign affairs (1929-1940) – was already a highly active internationalist, who had been a delegate to the League of Nations since its inception. To understand the creation and evolution of the institute in Copenhagen one needs to look to institutional developments within international cooperation during this period; the Institute of Economics and History was a small but vital component in an interwar history now being rediscovered, that of formalised networking and collaboration among scholars and experts under the umbrella of the League of Nations.

A key forum for cooperation within the social sciences was the yearly *International Studies Conference* (ISC), organised by the League's International Institute for Intellectual Cooperation from 1928 onward.

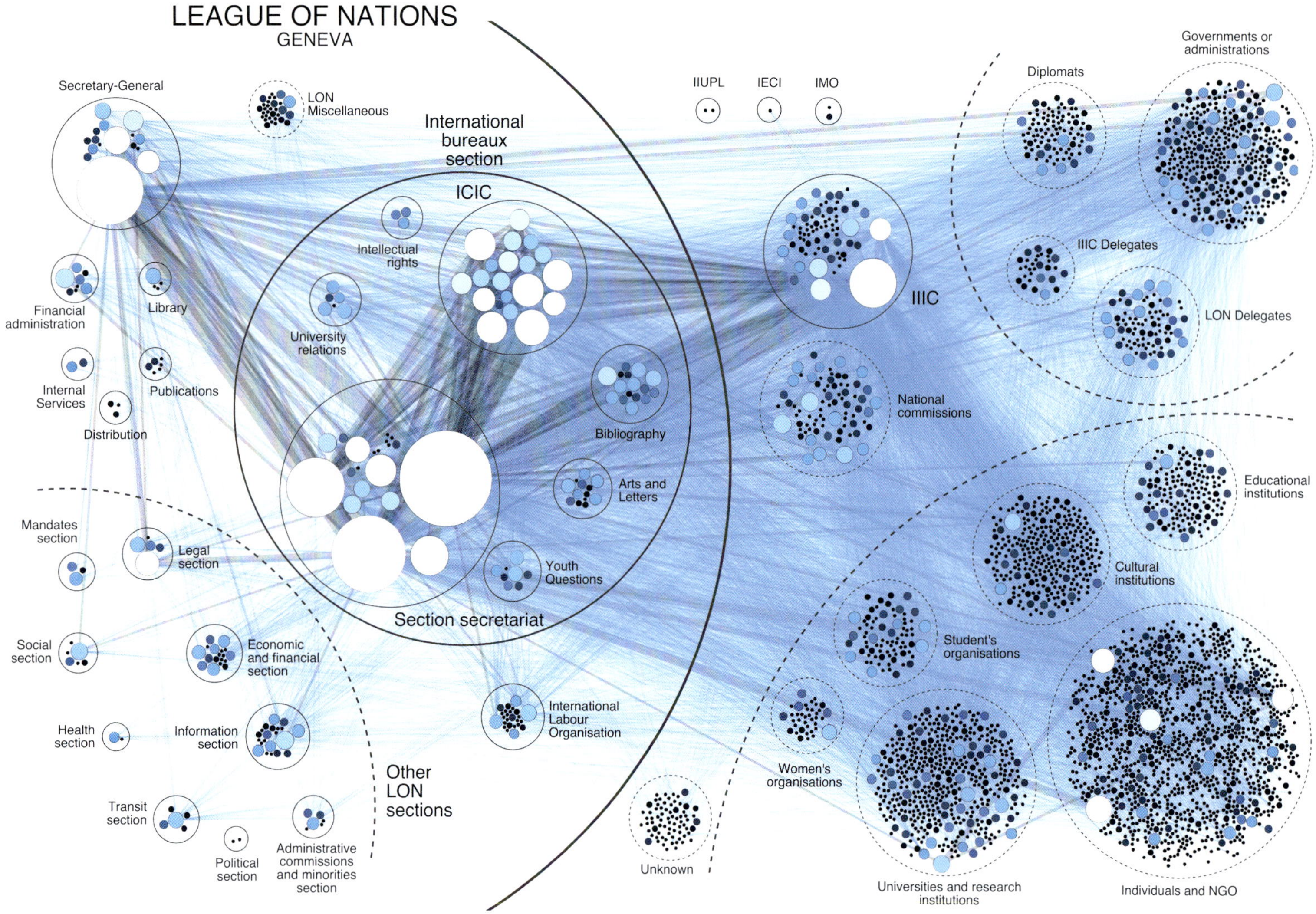

The ISC came to encompass a sprawling network of research institutes in the emerging field of International Studies, as well as the diverse range of social scientists who inhabited these institutes. The conference represented a novel and multi-layered kind of internationalisation: it gathered together a transnational group of scholars not to discuss a pre-defined field of research but rather to *define* what it meant to undertake "international studies" (its aims and methods) in a time of international crises. This endeavour was also based on a clear desire to *influence* the very object of this would-be discipline, that is, the real-world practice of "international relations", specifically in a liberal internationalist direction stressing the importance of formalised cooperation among nations.

In its earliest years, there was nothing very "international" about the research carried out at the Danish institute. Early research projects consisted mainly of historical studies of social and economic developments in Denmark (the institute's quarterly journal *Økonomi og Politik*, however, did take an interest in international politics and the world economy). Despite the keen international interests and early pronouncements of Munch and other colleagues, no written studies with an international or foreign focus were undertaken.

In 1929, the Institute of Economics and History was first represented at the International Studies Conference. Soon thereafter, the relatively small Institute in Copenhagen came to be considered – by its funders, at least – one of the centres in the network of institutes connected through the ISC. This puzzling state of affairs would seem to challenge the focus on American, British and a few other powerful institutional actors that still persists.[2] The question here, then, is: how and what did institutions outside the centres of London, New York, Paris and Geneva contribute to the flourishing social science diplomacy of the interwar years? And to what effect? While a focus on larger institutes within powerful states seems warranted, to understand the dynamics and impact of transnational networks, such as those centred within the League, I argue that we should also look to the peripheries (in this case, Northern) as key sites where grand ideas and schemes met with local practices and concerns. This chapter will focus on a few key developments in the changing relations between the Danish institute and its international network, several of which may be explained through such a tension between internal and external motivations for international networking during the interwar period.

This graph by Martin Grandjean visualises the League of Nations' early work on intellectual cooperation as a network of nearly 1700 archival "actors", i.e. every sender and recipient of ICIC documents at the UN Archives in Geneva, 1919-1927. Social network analysis helps us understand the League as an "organic" organisation in this sphere and others, as it highlights close relationships which bypass the formal hierarchy, as well as links built with the diplomatic and scientific world outside.

Peter Munch (1870-1948), Danish social liberal politician and historian, was the founder and president of the *Institute of Economics and History* (1927-59), the first Scandinavian institute welcomed by the League's *International Studies Conference*. Munch, whose legacy is still hotly debated, pushed for a liberal internationalist orientation in Danish policy, research and education for four decades, holding numerous positions of power in government and public life.

THE INTERNATIONAL STUDIES CONFERENCE AND ITS COMPONENTS

With the peace agreement at Versailles weeks away, on the evening of 30 May 1919, experts from the British delegation to the Paris Peace Conference met with American colleagues at the Hotel Majestic in Paris. Each group saw a need for a form of scholarly collaboration that would be international in both its object of study and its method. For a peaceful world order to last, they agreed, it was necessary to establish a regular forum of liberal international thinkers. These plans first resulted in the creation from 1920 of two sister institutes for research in international affairs in Britain and the United States – Chatham House and the Council on Foreign Relations, respectively.

The long-envisioned founding of an International Institute of Intellectual Cooperation (IIIC) under the League of Nations in 1926 created a structure which allowed for international expansion. Thus, from 1928, the annual International Studies Conference was organised under the IIIC, binding together the emerging network of 'think tanks', many set up following the Treaty of Versailles in Europe and North America, including the still very young Copenhagen institute. For the purposes of the ISC, these member institutes were labelled "institutions for the scientific study of international relations",[3] yet they were more diverse than this simple categorisation would suggest, encompassing institutes that conducted social, economic, political, historical and legal research with varying emphasis. Indeed, the annual conferences drew not only a varied crowd of scholars but also League of Nations officials and agents of key philanthropic foundations – such as the Rockefeller Foundation and the Carnegie Endowment for International Peace.

The first conference was hosted by Berlin's Deutsche Hochschule für Politik in 1928. This was followed by plenary sessions in London (1929, 1933, 1935), Paris (1930, 1934, 1937), Copenhagen (1931), Milan (1932), Madrid (1936), Prague (1938) and finally Bergen, Norway (1939), an abbreviated session held just before the outbreak of war. From 1931, when the Copenhagen institute played host, the ISC took on a more permanent character and it was decided to pursue biennial "study cycles" devoted to specific topics of general interest.[4] The 1932-1933 cycle was devoted to the theme of "The State and Economic Life"; 1934-1935 to "Collective Security"; 1936-1937 to "Peaceful Change"; and finally, 1938-1939 to "Economic Policies in Relation to World Peace".

THE INSTITUTE OF ECONOMICS AND HISTORY – COPENHAGEN AND BEYOND

The Institute of Economics and History opened its doors in January 1927 in offices afforded it by the University of Copenhagen. It was headed by a board comprising the University's instructors in history and economics, and individual representatives of Denmark's four main political parties (Munch himself represented the centrist Social Liberal Party), as well as various elected scholars and state officials. Munch chaired the board and served as President of the Institute until his death in 1948 at age 77. The Institute comprised a small regular staff and affiliated students, while its day-to-day management was carried out by the Secretary of the Institute and the heads of its different sections (economic, historical and journal), under the board's supervision.

Among the most prominent scholars in residence during its first decade was the young Swedish economist Bertil Ohlin. Ohlin had been appointed a professor of economics at the University of Copenhagen at the age of only 25. This granted him a seat at the board at the Institute's founding, where he participated actively in shaping its agenda. As evidenced by the initial name of its economic section, *Konjunkturafdelingen*, the Institute adopted an early interest in business cycle research, as well as a general one in the relationship between economic research and social issues. Ohlin had pragmatically suggested such a focus at a founding meeting; business cycle research, he stressed, was "important, current, central, and of interest to the Americans",[5] by which he was referring to the Rockefeller Foundation as potential funders.

At first glance, the initial aims of the Institute of Economics and History seemed to be based on more grounded concerns of strengthening social scientific research within Denmark, rather than participating in the kind of ambitious transnational networking epitomised

Bertil Ohlin (1899-1979), Swedish economist and liberal politician, played a little-acknowledged role in creating the first institutes for international studies in Denmark and Sweden. Ohlin was a prominent member of the "Stockholm school" of economics and authored the League's report *The Course and Phases of the World Economic Depression* (1931). He later led Sweden's People's Party (1944-67) and received the Nobel Memorial Prize in Economic Sciences (1977) for his work on international trade.

by the ISC. Yet early declarations from its founders did reveal the highly international context for its creation. Introducing the institute, its key figures stressed the need for cooperation and collaboration modelled on the natural sciences, seeing interdisciplinary and transnational social science research as an emerging necessity. With the enormous wealth of materials becoming available, the founders argued, scholars within the humanities could no longer hope to succeed without collaborative efforts and the use of scientific methodologies. As such, Munch and his colleagues argued for combining the historical craft with the methods of the social sciences, particularly economics and statistics. They lavished praise on existing research institutes, both economic and political – soon connected through the ISC – from Britain's Chatham House and Sweden's Socialvetenskapliga institutet to Weimar Germany's Hochschule für Politik. They also heaped praise on the New York-based Rockefeller Foundation and its newly founded programme to support the social sciences in Europe.[6] This praise seemed very much in anticipation of a future relationship: the American foundation would become the institute's primary source of financing with a multi-year grant awarded in 1928.

AN INTERNATIONAL AFFAIR – WHO, WHEN AND WHERE?

The Institute of Economics and History was first represented at the second annual International Studies Conference in London in March 1929 by the economists Bertil Ohlin and Jørgen Pedersen, Secretary of the Institute for its first decade. Extending from this meeting, it crossed the Atlantic and entered into cooperation with the U.S. Social Science Research Council (as the Scandinavian contributor to its world-wide bibliography on the social sciences), and the Council on Foreign Relations (contributing to its quarterly bibliography on international relations in the journal *Foreign Affairs*).

The opportunity to engage regularly with the ISC network from 1929-1930 onward seemed to herald a first turning point for the Institute. In 1930, on Munch's request, the IHS set up a new study group in international postwar history with the Paris Peace Conference as its starting point, whereas all its previous study groups had dealt with domestic historical issues. This led to an increasing number of study groups and published studies on such diverse issues as colonial problems, issues of international trade, contemporary German foreign policy and Franco-Italian relations.

By the dawn of the 1930s, then, what began as a *national* research institute seemed in the process of becoming an "Institute of International Affairs" more in line with the model of its Anglo-American forerunners.[7] There were at least two connected factors contributing to this partial transformation. The first was financing from the Rockefeller Foundation, which also funded several other think tanks in Europe,[8] and became the largest contributor to the Copenhagen institute by its second year. In fact, the promise of such funding seems to have a been a vital driver behind the institute's creation, as evidenced by discussions at its founding meetings. Secondly, there was the opportunity to undertake more substantial international(ised) research and networking activities, which participation in the ISC allowed – and which, in a circular fashion, would also strengthen the prestige of the Institute in the eyes of collaborators and funders.

Initially supportive of the Institute's basic mission of strengthening the state of interdisciplinary social science work, reports by the Rockefeller Foundation by the mid-1930s began to tout the Copenhagen institute as a particularly successful node in its network of international affairs institutes in Europe – a Nordic bastion of sorts. "[T]he Danish Institute", argued the Rockefeller Foundation in 1938, "led the Scandinavian countries in creating a center of interest in international relations, and served as the model for the centers set up by Norway and Sweden".[9]

For its American funders, then, the value of the institute in Copenhagen was strongly tied to its role – largely imagined, one must note – as the centre of a Scandinavian group of foreign affairs think tanks.[10] The archives of IHS in Copenhagen, not utilised until now, make it clear that the first small steps toward Nordic cooperation in the field of international studies were only undertaken in the mid- to late 1930s, and were explicitly geared toward obtaining continued Rockefeller funding. Nordic cooperation in international studies, in other words, was not driven mainly by organic ideological commonalities, as the proponents of a Scandinavian "peace tradition" might have it, but just as much by external attempts to *imagine* such a coherent Nordic tradition and the role it might play in furthering liberal internationalist aims from the perspective of New York, London and Paris.

These differences in motivations would sometimes lead to some curious discrepancies in perception. For instance, Rockefeller Foundation reports claimed that it was funding an "International Relations Section" at IHS,[11] but the institute itself did not make any mention of such a section in any of its annual reports or elsewhere. This suggests that the institute in Copenhagen did not have much input or stake in its expected role as "the chief Scandinavian center for scientific interest in international relations",[12] as the Foundation claimed it was. Yet the Copenhagen institute was certainly motivated to meet such ambitious expectations to the extent it was able – and able to gauge these expectations correctly. By the late 1930s, after a decade in existence, IHS could credibly report on a host of activities encompassing both the study of a range of international problems and formalised cooperation with other institutes in Scandinavia, Europe and beyond.

POSTSCRIPT: INTERNATIONAL STUDIES AND THE NEW ERA

Under the League of Nations, the social sciences and humanities had jointly experienced a flowering of cross-border cooperation, as significant new venues for scholarly cooperation emerged. As the United Nations and a host of new international organisations arose, a more streamlined brand of social science expertise took over. Many of the surviving institutes of international affairs, not least their original flagships in New York and London, were well-situated to meet these demands, with their assemblages of expertise covering newly prominent Cold War concerns such as international relations, area studies and development economics. Others fell by the wayside.

In a sense, the International Studies Conference itself fell victim to the postwar creation of UNESCO, under which the International Political Science Association (IPSA) superseded it as the official forum for cooperation in the field of international studies.[13] By the early 1950s, the field of International Relations (IR) had formally become the domain of political scientists rather than of the diverse group of historians, economists, sociologists, classicists, philosophers and others who shaped its discussions during the interwar years. Similarly, the Copenhagen institute – financially weakened after the loss of Rockefeller funding – became something of an anachronism at the University of Copenhagen, where its own leadership engineered its division into separate departments for history, economics and political science during the late 1950s.

During the course of its existence from 1927 to 1959, and even in its dissolution, the Institute of Economics and History reflected the importance and impact of transatlantic philanthropy on the streamlining of the European social sciences – including their separation into clearly defined disciplines, with the arguable exclusion of history as one unforeseen outcome. The agents of this project in Copenhagen and many other cities on each side of the Atlantic – academics and organisers alike – worked as something akin to social science diplomats. By and through transnational networks, this plethora of actors dispersed and legitimised the idea of social science as a result of its international standardisation (of which the networks were ipso facto evidence); through its concern with common international problems; and by power of its claims to offer social scientific solutions to these problems.

Indeed, decades after the Institute of Economics and History had shut its doors, one could argue that the model of the international affairs institute born at the Paris Peace Conference in 1919 was still being re-adapted worldwide. With its own Danish forerunner long forgotten, but still consciously modelled on the sister institutes in Stockholm and Oslo that had long outlived it, a publicly funded Danish Institute for International Studies (DIIS) would finally see the light of day in 2003, its "independence" this time mandated by government decree. By then, the Norwegian Institute of International Affairs (NUPI) and the Finnish Institute of International Affairs (FIIA) had both celebrated four decades in existence, while the Swedish Institute for International Affairs was nearing 65.

Yet there are clear limits to the perspective that "international studies" or IR simply spread unquestioned from centre to periphery, beginning in the interwar years and continuing until today. The early local agents of this diffusion had their own array of pragmatic as well as scholarly motivations – funding, recognition, even basic survival in the fraught political landscape of the interwar years – for bothering to engage in this exercise in the first place. The large academic and ideological diversity of the European institutes and academics engaged in the International Studies Conference and its offshoots, with Copenhagen only being one example, forces us again to question notions of structural Anglo-American hegemony. Without the participation of the peripheries, the (re)creation and promotion of the idea of International Studies would be unthinkable, then and now.

NOTES

1 The Institute of Economics and History will be referred to here by its common abbreviation 'IHS', short for *Institutet for Historie og Samfundsøkonomi*, as 'the Copenhagen institute', or simply 'the Institute'. This chapter is based on working papers previously presented at the APH 4th International PhD Conference, Aarhus, June 2016, and the European Social Science History Conference, Belfast, April 2018. I am indebted to commentators at these events. I also want to acknowledge the Velux Foundation, which supported the inception of this research through its grant to the project *'Towards Good Society': Conceptualizing the Social through the Economic, 1930s-Today* (2013-2016), and give my many thanks to fellow participants in this project.

2 Recent general contributions on the ISC and IIIC include Laqua: 'Transnational intellectual cooperation'; Laqua: 'Internationalism and Nationalism'; Pemberton: 'Changing Shape'; and Riemens: 'International academic cooperation'. Classic contributions include Goodman: *League and Cultural Cooperation*; Renoliet: *L'UNESCO Oubliée*; and Wright: *International Studies Conference*. On individual institutes outside the US/UK, see Giona: *Ispi*; Steine: *Fred, forskning og formidling*; and Stöckmann: 'Studying the International'.

3 Royal Institute of International Affairs: 'The Conference of Institutions'.

4 A. Zimmern, Fourth Conference of Institutions for the Scientific Study of International Relations (Held at Copenhagen, June 8th-10th, 1931). Report submitted by Professor A. Zimmern to the International Committee on Intellectual Co-Operation. Annex 4, C.471.M.201.1931.XII, 15 August 1931. CICI, UNESCO Archives, Paris.

5 Remarks by Bertil Ohlin. Minutes of meeting at Dr. Munch's home, 13 December 1926. Box 1-2, IHS/10009, Danish National Archives, Copenhagen.

6 Munch: 'Aartiers Historie'; Arup: 'Det nye historiske institut'; and Pedersen: 'Om Instituttet'.

7 See, e.g., Parmar: 'Anglo-American Elites'.

8 Rietzler: 'Experts for Peace', 45-65.

9 Rockefeller Foundation: *Annual Report 1938*, 264.

10 It has also been convincingly suggested that institutes such as that in Copenhagen afforded U.S. agents a lookout post into the politically murky European landscape. For a Danish account, see Buus: *Indflydelse og efterretning*.

11 Rockefeller Foundation: *Annual Report 1936*, 248-249, *Annual Report 1938*, 263-264.

12 Rockefeller Foundation: *Annual Report 1936*, 249. Annual financial statements and activity reports by IHS in University of Copenhagen: *Årbog for Københavns Universitet* 1927-47 and *Økonomi og Politik* 1-34, respectively, were also consulted.

13 Long: 'Who killed the ISC?'.

BIBLIOGRAPHY

Unpublished material

Danish National Archives, Institut for Historie og Samfundsøkonomi (IHS/10009), Box 1-2, Minutes of meeting at Dr. Munch's home, 13 December 1926.

UNESCO Archives, International Committee on Intellectual Cooperation (CICI), C.471.M.201.1931.XII, 15 August 1931, Annex 4, Fourth Conference of Institutions for the Scientific Study of International Relations (Held at Copenhagen, June 8th-10th, 1931). Report submitted by Professor A. Zimmern to the International Committee on Intellectual Co-Operation.

Published material

Arup, Erik: 'Det nye historiske institut', *Dagbladet Politiken*, 1 December 1927.

Buus, Henriette: *Indflydelse og efterretning - Rockefeller Foundations indflydelse på den danske velfærdsstat 1920-1970*, Copenhagen: Museum Tusculanums Forlag, 2008.

Giona, Federico: *Think tanks and international affairs during the interwar period: Ispi (Institute for Studies in International Politics) between foreign policy and public opinion (1919-1943)*, PhD Dissertation, IMT Lucca, 2016.

Goodman, Abraham Henry: *The League and Cultural Cooperation: A Survey of the History, Aims, Methods and Achievements of the League of Nations Intellectual Cooperation Organisation*, MA Thesis, University of British Columbia, 1946 (01.01.2019).

Laqua, Daniel: 'Transnational intellectual cooperation, the League of Nations, and the problem of order', *Journal of Global History* 6 (2), 2011, 223-247.

Laqua, Daniel: 'Internationalism and Nationalism in the League of Nations' Work for Intellectual Cooperation'. In Miguel Bandeira Jerónimo and José Pedro Monteiro (eds): *Internationalism, Imperialism and the Formation of the Modern World*, Basingstoke: Palgrave Macmillan, 2017, 59-85.

Long, David: 'Who killed the International Studies Conference?', *Review of International Studies* 32 (4), 2006, 603-622.

Munch, P.: 'Studiet af de sidste Aartiers Historie'. In Poul Nørlund (ed.): *Festskrift til Kristian Erslev den 28. Decbr. 1927 fra danske Historikere*, Copenhagen: Den danske Historiske Forening, 1927, 655-675.

Parmar, Inderjeet: 'Anglo-American Elites in the Inter-War Years: Idealism and Power in the Intellectual Roots of Chatham House and the Council on Foreign Relations', *International Relations* 16 (1), 2002, 53-75.

Pedersen, Jørgen: 'Om Institutet for Historie og Samfundsøkonomi. Foredrag ved Dansk historisk Fællesforenings Aarsmøde i Rønne, 29. Maj 1930', *Fortid og Nutid* 17, 1930, 249-261.

Pemberton, Jo-Anne: 'The Changing Shape of International Cooperation: From the League of Nations to UNESCO', *Australian Journal of Politics & History* 58 (1), 2012, 34-50.

Renoliet, Jean-Jacques: *L'UNESCO oubliée. La Société des Nations et la coopération intellectuelle (1919-1946)*, Paris: Publications de la Sorbonne, 1999.

Riemens, Michael: 'International academic cooperation on international relations in the interwar period: the International Studies Conference', *Review of International Studies* 37 (2), 2011, 911-928.

Rietzler, Katharina: 'Experts for Peace: Structures and Motivations of Philanthropic Internationalism in the Interwar Years'. In Laqua (ed.): *Internationalism Reconfigured: Transnational Ideas and Movements between the World Wars*, London: I.B. Tauris, 2011, 45-65.

Rockefeller Foundation, The: *The Rockefeller Foundation Annual Report 1936*, New York: The Rockefeller Foundation, 1936.

Rockefeller Foundation, The: *The Rockefeller Foundation Annual Report 1938*, New York: The Rockefeller Foundation, 1938.

Royal Institute of International Affairs: 'The Conference of Institutions for the Scientific Study of International Relations', *Journal of the Royal Institute of International Affairs* 8 (3), 1929, 185-202.

Steine, Bjørn Arne: *Fred, forskning og formidling. Internasjonale studier i Norge og Sverige 1897-1940*, PhD Dissertation, University of Oslo, 2016.

Stöckmann, Jan: 'Studying the International, Serving the Nation: The Origins of International Relations (IR) Scholarship in Germany, 1912-33', *The International History Review* 38 (5), 2016, 1055-1080.

University of Copenhagen: *Årbog for Københavns Universitet*, Copenhagen: University of Copenhagen, 1927-1947.

Wright, F. Chalmers: *The International Studies Conference: Origins – Functions – Organisation*, Paris: International Institute of Intellectual Cooperation, 1937.

Økonomi og Politik (journal), Copenhagen: Institutet for Historie og Samfundsøkonomi, Vols. 1-34, 1927-1960.

Hagen Schulz-Forberg

NEOLIBERALS AND THE LEAGUE OF NATIONS

On the Incidental Birth of Neoliberalism within the League's Dot-Connecting System

Children love it: connecting the numbered dots on an otherwise blank page. Doing so, an image emerges that in most cases is more complex than previously thought. In transnational history, the League of Nations is quite similar to such a dot-connecting drawing game, as its study yields increasingly complex images of the transnational past. The global claims of the mandate system in a world shifting from an imperial to a nation-state order constitute one of those complex images, the increasingly more nuanced history of international law another.[1] And increasingly, historiography also uncovers the origins of neoliberalism, one of today's major critical paradigms and catchphrases, in relation to the League.[2] This chapter contributes to the ongoing rewriting of neoliberalism's history by looking at the decade during which the concept took shape, the 1930s, from a broader historical perspective than most. While historical research increasingly recognises the 1930s as the period when neoliberalism was born, a deeper analysis of the institutional setup within which it emerged is still mostly missing.[3] The fact that the League's universe of global governance can be identified as its birthplace recasts the history of neoliberalism as transnational, necessitating rereadings, since much of this history has so far focused on a handful of intellectuals or schools of thought. These intellectuals and schools were in fact all related to the League's networks, which

incentivised their research. Here intellectual history is linked with international and institutional history, as well as a prosopography-inspired reading of what might best be captured as normative agency carried out by the actors involved. Conscious of their norm-making, economists and internationalists more generally engaged in the shaping of states and their economies in order to help build a certain image of society. Neoliberalism emerged transnationally in deliberations by these normative actors.[4] It was thus a self-proclaimed concept designed for a global order. The argument developed here arose from a transnational approach that combined three points of access to its topic – *actors*, *institutions* and *concepts* – assuming that each has a bearing on the other.[5] The material on which the argument rests has been found in the archives of the International Institute of Intellectual Co-operation

The ICIC in session. Gilbert Murray, classicist, liberal activist and humanist – and the ICIC's president from 1928 to 1939 – chairs the meeting from the head of the central table. Murray had a planet, the '941 Murray', named after him in honour of his post-war support for Austria. José Castillejo, Spanish expert in Roman law, long-standing ICIC board member and participant at the Walter Lippmann Colloquium where the term 'neoliberalism' was coined, is the third person along on the left-hand side of the table.

(IIIC), the Rockefeller Foundation and the League of Nations, as well as the personal papers of key actors. Additionally, publications by actors involved in shaping transnational expertise and by relevant institutions, such as the International Studies Conference (ISC), help to strengthen the points made.

In the following, the role of experts and the functioning and impact of the League's widely spun networks of expertise and knowledge-making are highlighted; John Bell Condliffe (1891-1981), a tireless transnational economist often involved in shaping expertise for policy-making, serves as an illustrative case to reveal the depth and breadth of the League's dot-connecting web. All institutions, actors and concepts mentioned here emerged from the vast material retrieved in order to reconstruct the transnational economic expertise of the 1930s in particular. The role of Condliffe is investigated here to shed light on the productivity and impact of the League's web, while the fuller argument and story are currently being developed for a forthcoming monograph.

For economic thought and the beginnings of neoliberalism, the League not only appears as the maker and self-proclaimed saviour of civilisation and the kind of world economy needed to sustain it; indeed, the various schools of thought in economics, such as the early Chicago School,[6] the Lausanne School[7] or the Geneva School,[8] can be connected via the League's institutional tentacles, and its overall mission and normative drive towards thinking in terms of peaceful global orders. Neoliberalism emerged within this new world of academic expertise and transnational policy-making.[9]

The League created a complex global landscape of research and policy-making in which connected institutions carried out research with a mission. In some countries, existing institutions for the study of international affairs or social and economic policies served as the source of expertise, particularly the London School of Economics (LSE); countries that lacked such an institution founded one. The Instituto de Estudios Internacionales y Económicos in Madrid, for example, began its work in early 1931.[10] A kind of early version of private–public partnership was practised. The League contributed financially, together with the member state's government and the Rockefeller Foundation.

Within the web established by an increasing number of institutional dots, neoliberalism took shape as an unintended consequence of larger efforts at conceptualising world peace and its economic design. What is the relation between markets and peace? What is the role of economics for peaceful change? How and on what economic basis can collective security be organised nationally and internationally? And vice versa – what economic conditions lead to insecurity? In a man-made world, what basic norms and values should inform economic and social organisation?[11]

A GLOBAL WEB

Throughout the 1920s and 1930s the League addressed these and more questions by creating a landscape of research institutions with a global spread. The organisation was complex and mainly facilitated by the League's various associated organisations, the International Committee for Intellectual Co-operation (ICIC) and its operationalising arm in Paris, the International Institute for Intellectual Co-operation (IIIC) and the International Studies Conference (ISC), which emerged within the IIIC and its own more official institutionalisation in 1929.[12] Each member state joined with its major dots, that is, its leading research institutions. National institutions were gathered under the umbrella of National Committees for Intellectual Co-operation (NCICs), to which specialised committees were attached, for example for International Studies.

The reach and complexity of these webs became apparent in the tenth ISC conference, of 1937. It needed ten preliminary meetings on specific sub-topics, held in Geneva, London, Paris and Vienna. The conference then had to digest more than one hundred memoranda from Australia, Canada, the United States and thirteen European countries. Overall, 142 participants came to Paris for a week, representing twenty national research institutes and national coordinating committees. They came mostly from Europe, but also from Australia, Brazil, Canada and the US (which, despite not being a member of the League, nevertheless ran its own national committees closely connected to the IIIC and ISC throughout). Five countries sent invited experts or observers: China, Germany, Italy, Japan and Mexico. Germany and Italy had participated prominently at meetings and conferences until they left the League. Furthermore, organisations grouped under the headline "international" also participated or sent experts: the Carnegie Endowment, the Rockefeller Foundation, the Pacific Institute of International Affairs, the Graduate Institute of International Studies in Geneva, the Academy of International Law, the New Commonwealth Institute (which published Hayek's essay on the effect inter-state federation might have on the economy – seen by many as an original script for contemporary neoliberalism)[13] and the International Labour Organisation (ILO) all came to the ISCs.[14]

FROM HAMBURG TO HONOLULU – TO CHRISTCHURCH

The task of this new network was to produce sustainable policies for global order and the necessary elite personnel to staff the dots. Each of the larger questions mentioned above was broken down into smaller research questions and divided among the participating institutions. In many cases, the actors shaping this world of research were able to build their careers within the institutional web that spun its threads from, for example, Hamburg's Institut für Auswärtige Politik, founded in 1923, to Honolulu's Institute of Pacific Relations from 1925, to the city of Christchurch in New Zealand, where Condliffe received his MA in economics in 1915 and began lecturing on economics, constitutional history and economic thought in 1916. Condliffe does not rank among the intellectually more prominent early neoliberals. Yet his biography illuminates the effects of the League's institutional and intellectual landscape, particularly during the 1930s when neoliberalism found its discursive shape and was given its name at the Walter Lippmann Colloquium in August 1938, in the presence of Condliffe and twenty-five other participants.[15]

Originally from Footscray, Victoria, in Australia, Condliffe attended Canterbury College in Christchurch after his family relocated to

New Zealand in 1904. Following his prize-winning MA thesis (the first ever economic history of New Zealand based on the systematic use of trade statistics) and his first experience as a lecturer, Condliffe was engulfed in the First World War. Wounded on the battlefields near Ypres in February 1918, he then gained a scholarship at the University of Cambridge. There, John Maynard Keynes made a lasting impression on him, not only intellectually, but also on the level of agency, driving home the insight that economics needed to propose policy solutions for the urgent problems of the time. In 1920, he returned to Christchurch, this time as professor of economics. Remaining close to policy-making, Condliffe was affiliated with the Canterbury Chamber of Commerce and published analyses of economic news on a monthly basis. He wrote reports, memoranda, protocols or reviews of events and proceedings throughout his career. Though a prolific academic writer, his administrative-academic and policy-related output had a more lasting effect. It peaked during his time at the League's Economic Intelligence Service, from 1931 to 1939. Before joining Geneva, Condliffe had changed address from Christchurch to Honolulu, where he began work as a research director in 1926. While based on Hawaii, his responsibilities saw him touring the globe, organising conferences and research projects in China, Japan and America, as well as Europe.[16]

FROM GENEVA TO LONDON – TO CHRISTCHURCH

A major dot within his own co-creation: David Rockefeller, in the 1930s a student of Schumpeter at Harvard and of Hayek at the LSE, in a wheelchair with UN Secretary-General Ban Ki-Moon in front of the tapestry copy of Picasso's *Guernica* at the UN headquarters, November 2016. Rockefeller, who lived to the age of 101, not only co-financed substantial parts of the dot-connecting system via the Rockefeller Foundation, but also acted in it as an economist, policy-making expert and leading global banker.

The following eight years saw Condliffe managing an impressive workload. He authored the final report of the World Economic Conference from 1933 and put together the first *World Economic Survey* (and the following five) based on data from the intelligence service and the ILO.[17] The surveys were the first and most authoritative documents about the Great Depression, providing data, explanations and visualisations for an unprecedented crisis. As Quinn Slobodian remarks, the graphic depiction of the global economy's contraction in the 1930s could rightly be called the Condliffe graph.[18]

As if this were not sufficiently demanding, Condliffe became the research manager for the collaboration between the Rockefeller Foundation and the IIIC, and fundamentally changed the way in which the ISC went about organising its conferences. The ISC's two-year study cycles (ongoing since 1932) were introduced, with the Rockefeller Foundation increasingly influencing its overall design. Condliffe became the official rapporteur of the ISC, a go-between for private foundations and international organisations and research institutions. Highly trusted by the foundation, he also wrote a stream of letters of reference for colleagues who applied for Rockefeller fellowships. In 1938, he joined the LSE as a lecturer and, needless to say, continued to write reports, for example for the International Chamber of Commerce Congress in Copenhagen in June 1939,[19] and was a member of the Committee on International Economic Policy at the Carnegie Endowment for International Peace.

While in London, Condliffe must have encountered Hayek and possibly also the talented and wealthy young economics student David Rockefeller (who studied with Hayek from late 1937 onwards). He did not meet another crucial figure of postwar neoliberalism associated with the LSE, however, even though he shared many of his views: Karl Popper was on the other side of the globe at the time.

Popper rose to fame during his time at the LSE. Yet *The Open Society and Its Enemies* was written in Christchurch in New Zealand, at Canterbury College, Condliffe's alma mater. Before moving to New Zealand, Popper visited London for some months and made the acquaintance of Hayek. Sometime in 1936, he came across a job announcement for a position to be filled – in New Zealand. It is not fully clear how Popper learned about the position. Yet the simple fact that job announcements for rather remote places apparently fluttered through the transnational system illustrates just how wide the web was spun by the mid-1930s.[20]

The impressive complexity of the League's dot-connecting system. Neoliberalism's coincidental birth took place within only a small fraction of a mind-bogglingly complex web. The International Committee of Intellectual Cooperation reported to the International Bureaux Section, here depicted next to the Health Section, the second and largest field of the Rockefellers' philanthropic activity since the 1930s – when it co-financed the Danish health system, among others.

THE INCIDENTAL BIRTH OF NEOLIBERALISM

The events preceding the Walter Lippmann Colloquium that are of importance for the birth of neoliberalism include the ISC conferences since 1932, the Danubian Studies group and a string of conferences organized by the IIIC in collaboration with the Rockefeller Foundation, in particular the Economists' Conference held in Annecy in 1936 and the meetings of the Permanent Committee of Business Cycle Institutes that was created as a follow-up of Annecy.[21] The League commissioned and broadly supported emergent forms of economic research: statistics, econometrics, macro-economics, business cycle research and economic as well as scientific theory in more general terms.[22] The leading economists of the time worked within the League's system of institutional affiliations. Neoliberalism developed within this world of transnational deliberation and it continued to nest within the fabric of international organisations alongside and in contestation with other perspectives.

Condliffe was not among the handful of economists whose ideas changed the rules of the game, but he was a leading figure among those

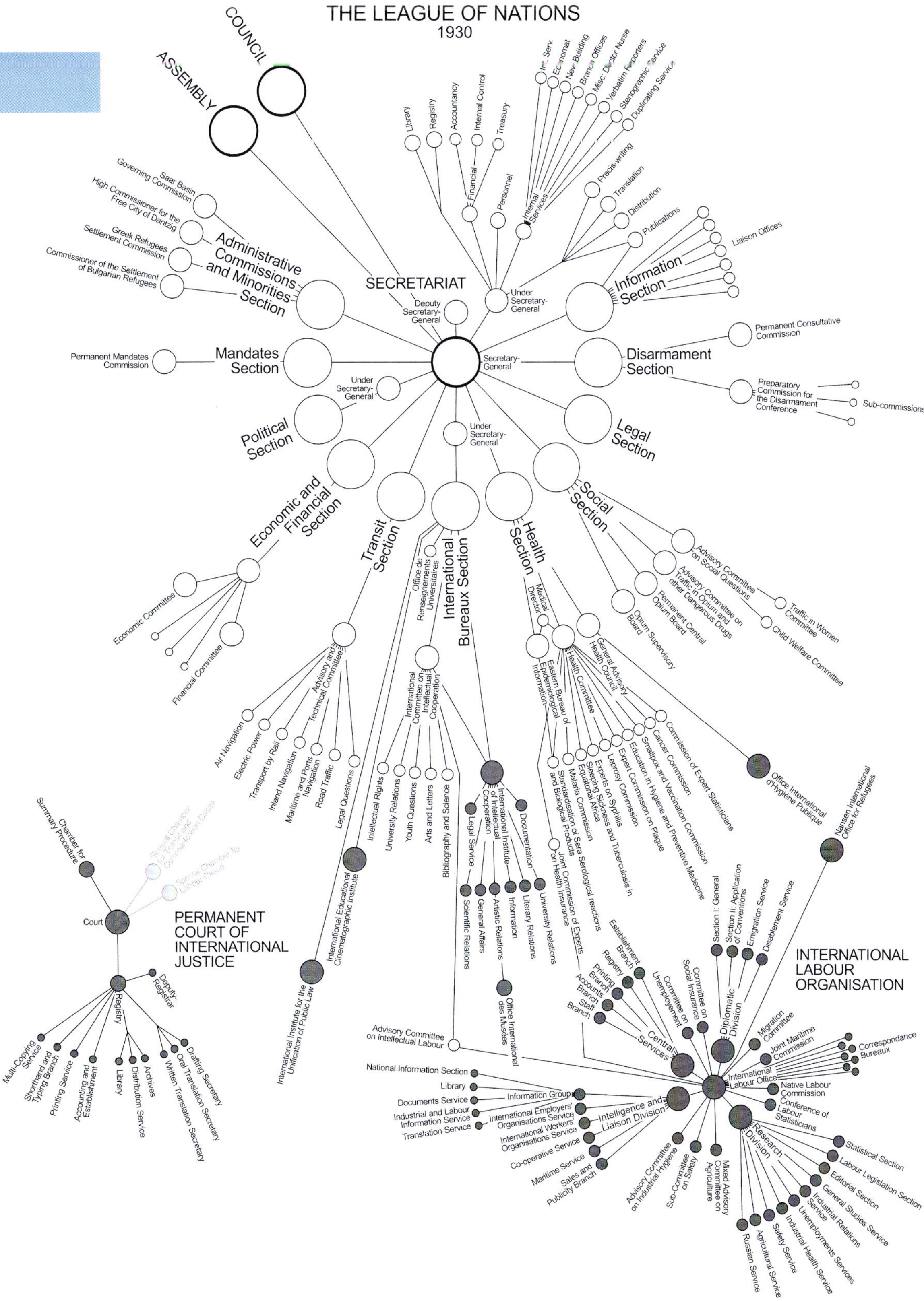
THE LEAGUE OF NATIONS
1930
COUNCIL
ASSEMBLY
SECRETARIAT
Secretary-General
Deputy Secretary-General
Under Secretary-General
Under Secretary-General
Under Secretary-General
Library
Registry
Accountancy
Internal Control
Treasury
Financial
Personnel
Internal Services
Int. Serv.
Economat
New Building
Branch Offices
Misc. Doctor Nurse
Verbatim Reporters
Stenographic Service
Duplicating Service
Precis-writing
Translation
Distribution
Publications
Information Section
Liaison Offices
Administrative Commissions and Minorities Section
Saar Basin Governing Commission
High Commissioner for the Free City of Danzig
Greek Refugees Settlement Commission
Commissioner of the Settlement of Bulgarian Refugees
Mandates Section
Permanent Mandates Commission
Disarmament Section
Permanent Consultative Commission
Preparatory Commission for the Disarmament Conference
Sub-commissions
Political Section
Legal Section
Economic and Financial Section
Economic Committee
Financial Committee
Transit Section
Advisory and Technical Committee
Air Navigation
Electric Power
Transport by Rail
Inland Navigation
Maritime and Ports Navigation
Road Traffic
Legal Questions
International Bureaux Section
Office de Renseignements Universitaires
International Committee on Intellectual Cooperation
Intellectual Rights
University Relations
Youth Questions
Arts and Letters
Bibliography and Science
International Institute of Intellectual Cooperation
Legal Service
Documentation
Scientific Relations
General Affairs
Artistic Relations
Information
Literary Relations
University Relations
Office International des Musées
International Educational Cinematographic Institute
International Institute for the Unification of Public Law
Advisory Committee on Intellectual Labour
Health Section
Medical Director
Eastern Bureau of Epidemiological Information
Health Committee
General Advisory Health Council
Joint Commission of Experts on Health Insurance
Standardisation of Sera Serological reactions and Biological Products
Malaria Commission
Sleeping Sickness and Tuberculosis in Equatorial Africa
Experts on Syphilis
Leprosy Commission
Expert Commission on Plague
Education in Hygiene and Preventive Medicine
Smallpox and Vaccination Commission
Cancer Commission
Commission of Expert Statisticians
Office International d'Hygiène Publique
Social Section
Advisory Committee on Social Questions
Advisory Committee on Traffic in Opium and other Dangerous Drugs
Permanent Central Opium Board
Opium Supervisory Board
Traffic in Women Committee
Child Welfare Committee
Nansen International Office for Refugees
PERMANENT COURT OF INTERNATIONAL JUSTICE
Court
Chamber for Summary Procedure
Special Chamber for Transit and Communication Cases
Special Chamber for Labour Cases
Registry
Deputy-Registrar
Multi-Copying Service
Shorthand and Typing Branch
Printing Service
Accounting and Establishment
Library
Distribution Service
Archives
Written Translation Secretary
Oral Translation Secretary
Drafting Secretary
INTERNATIONAL LABOUR ORGANISATION
International Labour Office
Diplomatic Division
Section I: General
Section II: Application of Conventions
Emigration Service
Disablement Service
Committee on Social Insurance
Committee on Unemployment
Central Services
Establishment Branch
Registry
Printing Branch
Accounts Branch
Staff Branch
Migration Committee
Joint Maritime Commission
Correspondance Bureaux
Native Labour Commission
Conference of Labour Statisticians
Intelligence and Liaison Division
Information Group
National Information Section
Library
Documents Service
Industrial and Labour Information Service
Translation Service
International Employers' Organisations Service
International Workers' Organisations Service
Co-operative Service
Maritime Service
Sales and Publicity Branch
Advisory Committee on Industrial Hygiene
Sub-Committee on Safety
Mixed Advisory Committee on Agriculture
Research Division
Statistical Section
Labour Legislation Section
Editorial Section
General Studies Service
Industrial Relations Service
Unemployments Services
Industrial Health Service
Safety Service
Agricultural Service
Russian Service

who played the game itself. He pronounced his arguments with the urgency of a politically conscious intellectual. Neoliberalism had been defined as a certain way of organising the state in 1938. It needed to guard the price mechanism and establish the rule of law; it was allowed to raise taxes for national defense, social security, education, social insurance and scientific research. This much was agreed upon in the 'agenda of liberalism' identified as neoliberalism at the time.[23] Condliffe's dedication to the project (despite his Keynesian leanings) of rebuilding global order transpires from his remarks at the colloquium:

> Those who are here are convinced that the liberal philosophy is the best one: but they cannot be in agreement with restricting themselves to an apologia for a bygone economic system. [...] It will be necessary to reduce monopolies, re-establish the equality of classes, notably in education. [...] It is necessary to make clear and understandable to the mass the social role of the system, that is to say how work must contribute to the enrichment of all.[24]

There were surely more eloquent and elaborate contributions to the discussion, but Condliffe's convictions sum up what neoliberalism needed to achieve in the eyes of the normative actors that shaped it discursively in the 1930s. His influence and references supported highly relevant and influential research. In his function as a go-between he facilitated the groundbreaking work of others. Without the transnational landscape of the League's research and policy-making institutions, this would simply not have been possible. For instance, Condliffe would probably not have been asked to write a recommendation in the early 1940s for a Hungarian émigré who applied for a Rockefeller grant in support of his book project. His enthusiastic recommendation for Karl Polanyi resulted in a two-year fellowship; the ensuing publication, *The Great Transformation*, inspires scholars to this day.[25] Meanwhile, reaching out from Christchurch with a finished manuscript, Popper remembered that Condliffe was a Canterbury College alumnus and a friend of his own old acquaintance from the mid-1920s onwards, the same Karl Polanyi. Condliffe handed the script to Alfred Braunthal and through the latter, *The Open Society and Its Enemies* arrived at Routledge.[26]

THE LANDSCAPE OF THE LEAGUE

Condliffe's career is exemplary in illustrating the League's transnational research and its policy-making landscape's breadth and depth. Its cosmos brought forth a wide variety of perspectives on how to run the state and the economy. Condliffe was part of the process, holding leading and decisive positions, facilitating projects, events and publications, and, almost as a side effect, participating in the making and publication of two of the most long-standing achievements in twentieth-century social theory. Taking Condliffe as the starting dot, the image that emerges is one of a large, transnational web of research that gave birth to an immense number of innovations in the social and political sciences. One was neoliberalism.

NOTES

1 Pedersen: *The Guardians*; Anghie: *Making of International Law*; Koskenniemi: *Gentle Civilizer of Nations*.

2 Schulz-Forberg: 'Laying the Groundwork', 13-39. Slobodian: *Globalists*.

3 Mirowski and Plehwe: *Road from Mont Pèlerin*; Burgin: *Great Persuasion*; Peck: *Neoliberal Reason*; Audier: *Néo-libéralisme(s)*.

4 See Schulz-Forberg and Olsen: *Re-inventing Western Civilisation* for an introduction of the concept of 'normative agency'.

5 This approach served as the basis for a larger research project entitled *Towards Good Society: Constructing the Social through the Economic since the 1930s* and funded by the VELUX Foundation. For more information, see: http://goodsociety.au.dk.

6 Jacob Viner, who shaped the first so-called Chicago School of Economics together with Frank Knight and Henry Simons, participated regularly at annual ISC deliberations. Viner was also advisor to the New Deal government of Franklin D. Roosevelt.

7 Making reference to Léon Walras, the Lausanne School's predilection for mathematics and general equilibrium theory deeply influenced a number of French economists, among the early neoliberals Jacques Rueff in particular.

8 Coined by Slobodian: *Globalists*.

9 Schulz-Forberg: 'Embedded Early Neoliberalism'.

10 Castillejo: Letter to Ortega y Gasset, 673-677.

11 These questions, here paraphrased, were put to the network of experts at the ISC and IIIC with exactly this vocabulary. The concept of collective security was not purely a global concept, imagining a global order, but encompassed what was necessary to create social security within nation states. Insecurity, in return, mostly referred to societies unable to provide enough perspective for its workforce in relation to job and life security. Social peace was clearly foregrounded as a major policy goal. Economic models were thus always scrutinised on their possible effects for social fabric.

12 See Søren Friis' chapter in this volume.

13 See Streeck: *Gekaufte Zeit*. Magnusson and Stråth: *A Brief History of Political Economy*, 119-121.

14 Moresco: *Peaceful Change*.

15 Schulz-Forberg: 'Embedded Early Neoliberalism'. See also Reinhoudt and Audier: *The Walter Lippmann Colloquium*.

16 New Zealand Biography: *Condliffe, John Bell*.

17 Economic Intelligence Service: *World Economic Survey*, 7.

18 Slobodian: *Globalists*, 59.

19 https://teara.govt.nz/en/biographies/4c28/condliffe-john-bell.

20 Hacohen: *Karl Popper*, 118-120.

21 See Audier: *Néo-libéralisme(s)*. Slobodian: *Globalists*, 73-78.

22 Clavin: *Securing the World Economy*.

23 Schulz-Forberg: 'Laying the Groundwork'.

24 Reinhoudt and Audier: *The Walter Lippmann Colloquium*, 170-171.

25 Rockefeller Archives, Folder 3694.

26 Popper to Condliffe, 19 May 1943.

BIBLIOGRAPHY

Anghie, Antony: *Imperialism, Sovereignty and the Making of International Law*, Cambridge: Cambridge University Press, 2005.

Audier, Serge: *Néo-libéralisme(s). Une archéologie intellectuelle*, Paris: Grasset, 2012.

Burgin, Angus: *The Great Persuasion. Reinventing Free Markets since the Depression*, Boston, MA: Harvard University Press, 2015.

Castillejo, José: Letter to Ortega y Gasset, 31 January 1931. In *Epistolario de José Castillejo, Vol. III, Fatalidad y Porvenir, 1913-1937*, Madrid: Editorial Castalia, 1999, 673-677.

Clavin, Patricia: *Securing the World Economy: The Reinvention of the League of Nations, 1920-1946*, Oxford: Oxford University Press, 2013.

Dictionary of New Zealand Biography: *Condliffe, John Bell*, https://teara.govt.nz/en/biographies/4c28/condliffe-john-bell (12.05.2018).

Economic Intelligence Service: *World Economic Survey*, Geneva: League of Nations, 1933.

Hacohen, Malachi Haim: *Karl Popper: The Formative Years – 1902-1945. Politics and Philosophy in Interwar Vienna*, Cambridge: Cambridge University Press, 2000.

Koskenniemi, Martti: *The Gentle Civilizer of Nations: The Rise and Fall of International Law, 1870-1960*, Cambridge: Cambridge University Press, 2001.

Magnusson, Lars and Bo Stråth: *A Brief History of Political Economy. Tales of Marx, Keynes and Hayek*, Cheltenham Glos: Edward Elgar, 2016.

Mirowski, Philip and Dieter Plehwe (eds): *Road from Mont Pèlerin. The Making of the Neoliberal Thought Collective*, Boston, MA: Harvard University Press, 2009.

Moresco, Emanuel: *Peaceful Change International Studies Conference, Vol. III, Colonial Questions and Peace*, Paris: International Institute for Intellectual Co-operation, 1939.

Peck, Jamie: *Constructions of Neoliberal Reason*, Oxford: Oxford University Press, 2013.

Pedersen, Susan: *The Guardians: The League of Nations and the Crisis of Empire*, Oxford: Oxford University Press, 2015.

Popper, Karl: Letter to John Bell Condliffe, 19 May 1943. In Papers of Karl Popper, Hoover Institute, Folder 28, 4.

Reinhoudt, Jurgen and Serge Audier: *The Walter Lippmann Colloquium. The Birth of Neoliberalism*, London: Palgrave, 2018.

Rockefeller Foundation Records, RG 1.1. (FA368), Benington College – Polanyi, Karl – (Refugee Scholar), Folder 3694.

Schulz-Forberg, Hagen: 'Laying the Groundwork: The Semantics of Neoliberalism in the 1930s'. In H. Schulz-Forberg and N. Olsen (eds): *Re-inventing Western Civilisation: Transnational Reconstructions of Liberalism in Europe in the Twentieth Century*, Nottingham Upon Trent: Cambridge Scholars Publishing, 2014, 13-39.

Schulz-Forberg, Hagen: 'Embedded Early Neoliberalism: Transnational Origins of the Agenda of Liberalism Reconsidered'. In Q. Slobodian, D. Plehwe and P. Mirowski (eds): *Nine Lives of Neoliberalism*, London: Verso, 2019, forthcoming.

Slobodian, Quinn: *Globalists: The End of Empire and the Birth of Neoliberalism*, Boston, MA: Harvard University Press, 2018.

Streeck, Wolfgang: *Gekaufte Zeit: Die vertagte Krise des demokratischen Kapitalismus*, Berlin: Suhrkamp, 2013.

Quincy Cloet

'A FULLER KNOWLEDGE OF THE FACTS'

The League of Nations' Endeavours to Produce International Expertise

The League of Nations was dedicated to the organisation of peace after the First World War. But how can we explain its preoccupation with knowledge, evident from the myriad reports and statistics generated by the Secretariat and the various Committees during the League's lifetime? The League's organisation favoured the involvement of experts from multiple countries in its decision-making and pushed towards the use of fact-finding and information in the conduct of international politics. Taken together, this constituted a comprehensive approach towards knowledge and expressed a veritable desire to produce international expertise.

As this chapter will demonstrate, such knowledge production was a framework that tied together the fact-based work patterns and routines of League staff members and representatives with the institution's decision-making process. It identifies an institution's capacity to enact change in international affairs through knowledge-gathering and expertise, making it a promising approach for the study of international organisation more generally.

UNFINISHED DREAM, UNDEREXPLORED SUBJECT

Knowledge was essential to the League's functioning: its *Monthly Bulletin of Statistics* and *Statistical Yearbook*, as well as custom reports written by experts, were meant to inform Council and Assembly discussions. As a French statistician observed in 1921, "a precise knowledge of the economic and social condition of peoples, their strength and productive power, would be the best guarantee for universal peace, as it would prevent the practice of underhand economical struggles which often are a prelude to political conflicts".[1]

The history of the League and its myriad forms of knowledge production, however, is one that has not been the subject of academic scrutiny. Although interest has grown in the League's technical work and the role of experts in certain fields of activity, such as health and social affairs, an overall consideration of knowledge as part of the organisation's fabric is not yet available.[2] In contrast, the United Nations' management of knowledge in the twenty-first century has been studied from a holistic perspective, albeit one that appraises rather than questions the objectives of knowledge accumulation and utilisation.[3] The League, as its predecessor, so far lacks any exposition of its knowledge system.

To understand the (political) objectives of knowledge production within international organisations, International Relations scholars have made some promising steps in the development of a framework. Although their scholarship presents neither a unified theory nor a methodological toolset, we can learn from the approaches and questions used by the discipline. Broadly speaking, International Relations scholars seek to find out how international organisations employ knowledge to attain prescribed aims, such as conflict-resolution or development goals. To this end, they look at organisations' discourses and the practices developed by their workforces.[4]

How to approach the League of Nations from the perspective of knowledge production? For reasons of brevity, this chapter will focus on one aspect of the League's quest for reliable information: inquiry commissions. Several examples are used to explain the characteristics of these League commissions, as well as the challenges and complexities they had to overcome. Although these knowledge-producing bodies submitted themselves to compromise in their search for answers, inquiries created a set of institutional practices which are still in vogue at the international level today.

KNOWLEDGE PRODUCTION AND INQUIRY COMMISSIONS

The League relied on inquiries to gather 'the facts' about issues with repercussions for the international community. Inquiries were used in a domestic context to investigate issues of public concern and from the early twentieth century by the Hague Court to facilitate solutions in minor bilateral disputes. Inquiries were primarily fact-finding bodies but could take the formal shape of a court or engage with other means of dispute settlement, such as conciliation and arbitration. The League was the first of its kind to rely extensively on this semi-judicial tool for the resolution of a broad range of international issues. It sent out inquiries to disputes in Manchuria (China) and the Chaco (Bolivia-Paraguay) to assemble reliable accounts of what had occurred there. In other instances, it investigated issues that had provoked public outrage and required international action, such as the trafficking of women and children.

Inquiry commissions occupy a slightly odd position within the League's international bureaucracy, because they were created on an *ad hoc* basis and composed solely of commissioners with no permanent ties to the League.[5] In other words, for each inquiry a mandate was set, and a new team of people was assembled to investigate and report the issue of concern. Thus, they were distinct from the Secretariat and other permanent League bodies. Despite their *ad hoc* structure, inquiries are a useful case study because they appear across the board in the League's institutional history.

Inquiries are an exhaustive subject; therefore, this chapter will focus on three areas deemed relevant for understanding the League's approach to knowledge production.[6] First is the conception of expert knowledge conceived by the relevant actors, for instance, in the hiring practices for experts in preparation for the inquiry. Second is the types of knowledge that were gathered, produced and disseminated by the inquiry commissions. Third and last is the purposes that were assigned to the production of knowledge as part of the inquiries. These three areas should help to obtain an overall image of the inquiries, their potential

Victor Bulwer-Lytton (first row, left) upon arrival in Japan. The Lytton Commission was instructed by the League of Nations to investigate a dispute between China and Japan regarding the region of Manchuria. In 1932, the Commission concluded that Japan had staged an explosion near the town of Mukden a year earlier which resulted in the Japanese occupation of Manchuria and the creation of a puppet state named Manchukuo.

success as 'truth-seeking' tools and how they laid the grounds for international investigations today.

PUTTING TOGETHER AN INQUIRY COMMISSION

The hiring practices reveals that there was no one-size-fits-all approach to finding experts to serve on inquiry commissions. The composition of inquiries into political disputes primarily revolved around the nationalities of the individual commissioners – rather than their professional backgrounds – with large member states eager to have a representative on the team. Other inquiries allowed for more leeway, by mediation of the Secretariat, to approach individuals for their subject-related expertise or exposure to the situation on the ground. However, in no cases were women seriously considered to serve on a commission, regardless of their expertise.

In the case of an investigation into opium production in Persia, the Assembly gave specific instructions about the sought profile of the three-member Commission: a person suitable to act as chairman, an expert on transport and commerce and someone knowledgeable about agriculture. Nationality had no discernible influence on the appointment process, but the instructions meant that the Secretariat struggled to find individuals who fitted the criteria. An expert "acquainted with agricultural conditions in that country and with the Persian language" proved to be a particular challenge.[7] The Secretariat settled for a botanist who had researched opium extraction for medical purposes, with work experience in Libya. Overall, the Commission knew little about Persia. In fact, one staff member admitted: "Persia was quite different from what I had expected but not from what I should have been prepared for if I had looked more carefully into its geography."[8]

THE ULTIMATUM.

JAPAN. "IF YOU GO ON SAYING I'M NAUGHTY, I SHALL LEAVE THE CLASS."

The Persian case exemplifies how 'expert knowledge' was the subject of compromise, depending on the availability of people and their knowledge of the region in question, or general professional background. Work experience in the colonies was often perceived as a strength when dealing with the non-Western world. Although the League was built around ideas of 'New Diplomacy' and a changed political landscape after the First World War, much of the experiences and practices undertaken by its members were steeped in the idioms, networks and institutions of empires.[9] The inquiry into forced labour in Liberia in 1930 had a British doctor as chairman, who had worked extensively on sleeping sickness in colonial central Africa. Although the chairman had never previously set foot in Liberia and possessed no relevant expertise, his familiarity with the environmental conditions was seen as more important than his grasp of the complexities of the issue.

After the publication of the Lytton Report, in 1933, a special gathering of the League of Nations' Assembly concluded that Japan had violated Chinese territorial sovereignty by the unlawful occupation of Manchuria and the creation of Manchukuo. Soon after the Assembly's resolution (depicted as 'The Ultimatum' in the adjacent image), the Japanese representation gave notice of withdrawal from the League of Nations.

HOW TO FIND THE FACTS

In preparation for the actual inquiry, commissioners needed knowledge about the subject matter and the places they intended to visit as part of the investigation. The League's Secretariat gathered memoranda, maps and pamphlets from individuals they considered experts, as well as academic societies and national ministries. Although ostensibly providing general knowledge for the inquiries, these sources could also frame the subject matter and introduce bias. For example, in the League's dealings with the non-Western world, it often relied on imperial and colonial administrations to fetch reliable statistics and surveys. In the example of the Persian opium inquiry, the information gathered via representatives of the British Empire was considered to be more reliable than local sources, but difficult to separate from Britain's economic interests in the country.

Most investigations followed the pattern of a three- to four-month stay on the ground, including meetings with officials as well as the collection of data and witness testimonials. The collected information provided the foundation for a final report, which was a composite document reflecting the views of several commissioners. Consensus had to be found amongst commissioners, although often it was only reached after a series of disagreements. For instance, the members of the Persian inquiry debated whether the report should be concerned solely with the substitution of opium by other agricultural crops, or whether it should offer recommendations of a general nature on the domestic economy.[10]

Debates about the nature of the assignment were a consequence of the League's tendency to give each investigation a broad and distinctive mandate, rather than rely on a codified protocol. A wide range of issues were investigated, from border disputes to women trafficking, and commissioners were given a large degree of discretion in their assignment.

For instance, the League Council could be tempted to put the objective of peaceful resolution before an investigation of the facts. With the Chaco War, a territorial dispute between Bolivia and Paraguay in the 1930s, the Council insisted upon a broad mandate: to study all aspects of the conflict and do "whatever it takes" to end the conflict.[11] The Chaco Commission fairly quickly saw the limits of this approach, since the facts of the conflict, particularly the question of who had provoked the hostilities, precluded a sustainable reconciliation. In its final report, it abandoned its inquiry into the causes of the Chaco War, favouring the description of a possible peace agreement.[12]

Overall, commissioners used a multitude of investigatory methods, and tried to leave their personal mark on their final reports.

INQUIRY: WHAT IS IT GOOD FOR?

Inquiries were talked about in terms of high ideals, i.e. impartial investigations seeking the truth. As the Spanish politician Salvador de Madariaga expressed it at a Council session in 1931, inquiries were "the surest guarantee we have today that difficulties will be settled in the fairest manner and in the interest of peace. A Commission provides guarantees of knowledge and impartiality".[13] Although the League could rely on local observers or press reports for information, the possession of its proper fact-checking tool was deemed as a vital help to decision-making in the Council and Assembly. In 1932, Council President and French Foreign Minister Aristide Briand stressed "the importance to the League of obtaining information by its own methods, by methods for whose accuracy it can vouch", especially in cases where facts were disputed by opposing parties.[14]

In practice, the ideal of the inquiry was fraught with tension and impossible expectations. The lack of a clear protocol for the conduct of inquiries meant that their mandates could be too broadly defined, and unclear with regard to their ultimate aims. Diplomacy counteracted fact-finding: for example, a Japanese representative's referral

Under the reign of Emperor Hirohito, depicted in the adjacent image as Crown Prince in 1919, Japan sought territorial expansion abroad during the inter-war period. Although the events at Mukden in 1931 that led to a confrontation between China and Japan were committed without the Emperor's explicit approval, he acquiesced to the military-led expansion of the Japanese Empire on the Chinese mainland.

to truth as "a condition for the League's life and growth" did not stop him defending his country's actions in Manchuria based on security reasons.[15] Truth-seeking was hampered by power politics: quests for leadership within the commission, but also countries competing over economic interests in the international arena. Notwithstanding these practical setbacks, knowledge could act as a catalyst and set about political change. For example, the League's inquiry into forced labour led to a series of political resignations in Liberia.[16] In the case of Manchuria, the commission concluded that there were no legitimate grounds for Japanese troops to occupy Chinese territory.[17] Overall, inquiries stimulated talk at the international level about atrocities and violations of international law.

INTERNATIONAL LEGACY

Questions of the success and legacy of the League's inquiry commissions are difficult to gauge; *ad hoc* decisions and compromise underlie many of the examples cited above. The value of inquiry was contested because fact-finding did not produce a clear-cut outcome that satisfied all stakeholders. In other cases, the conclusions of reports were not acted upon by decision-makers; the absence of action contributed to an impression that inquiries were ineffective. However, the League's experimentation with inquiry commissions testifies to a belief in rational and technocratic means that was to underscore international politics. In the end, the League built a set of institutional practices for international investigation that, at least in theory, allowed for dispassionate fact-finding and the disentangling of issues from their politicised contexts. Moreover, the League created an important precedent for future international organisations, by placing knowledge-gathering at the centre of its conduct in international affairs.

For this reason, it is valuable to look beyond the individual examples to the framework of international inquiry that was set in place and still underpins the United Nations' fact-finding missions today.[18] The commissions on Syria and Burundi established by the United Nations are only the latest examples of a tried and tested method that continues to be employed to investigate human rights violations and issues of public concern. Following the flexible technique adopted by the League, the United Nations' inquiries are *ad hoc* and autonomous, though this has produced similar flaws regarding structure, transparency and effective outcomes.[19] Despite these practical shortcomings, knowledge production at the international level has pushed diplomacy's covert channels towards greater public scrutiny and made discussion over matters of war and peace accessible to all.

NOTES

1 March: 'International Statistics', 629-635.

2 Akami: 'Imperial Polities', 4-25; Rodogno, Kozma and Garcia (eds): *The League of Nations' Work on Social Issues*.

3 Svenson: *The United Nations as a Knowledge System*.

4 For an overview of International Relations scholarship about knowledge production, see Bliesemann de Guevara and Kostić: 'Knowledge Production', 1-20.

5 The general exceptions to this rule were the opium and women trafficking inquiries which were supported by the Secretariat's Social Section, and as a result could rely on a semi-permanent structure and logistical support for their investigations.

6 The source material for this chapter comprises the official inquiry reports and correspondence relevant to the commissions (which are at the League archives at the UN offices in Geneva), as well as the diaries and written correspondence of a number of commissioners. This material sheds light on the establishment of inquiries but also on the protagonists' perceptions of what constituted impartial knowledge in international politics.

7 International Institute for Agriculture to League of Nations Secretariat 3. December 1925. Services of an agricultural expert, appointment of Professor Cavara, R801. League of Nations Archives (LoNA).

8 Knight to Purves, 19 May 1927. Services of Mr. Jewell B. Knight, R801. LoNA.

9 Jerónimo: 'A League of Empires', 87-126.

10 MacLeish to Delano, n.d. Draft report to Council, Delano Papers, Series 3-20, Folder I. Frederic Delano Roosevelt Presidential Archives (FDRA).

11 'Council Meeting held on January 20th, 1934 – Dispute between Bolivia and Paraguay – Report of the Committee of Three'.

12 *Dispute between Bolivia and Paraguay – Report of the Chaco Commission*.

13 'Discussion at the 65th Session of the League of Nations Council September-December 1931'. R1865. LoNA.

14 'Discussion at the 66th Session of the League of Nations Council January-February 1932'. R1870. LoNA.

15 'Discussion at the 66th Session of the League of Nations Council January-February 1932'. R1870. LoNA.

16 'Foreign Relations of the United States: Diplomatic Papers', 1930, volume 3, 378-379. United States Department of State (USSD).

17 *Report of the International Commission of Enquiry into the Existence of Slavery and Forced Labour in the Republic of Liberia*.

18 Recently this has been the subject of a doctoral thesis, with a focus on the legal implications of the use of inquiry to examine mass atrocities; Harwood: *Navigating between principle and pragmatism: the roles and functions of atrocity-related United Nations Commissions of Inquiry in the international legal order*.

19 Méndez: 'Commissions of Inquiry', 49.

BIBLIOGRAPHY

Unpublished material

'Discussion at the 65th Session of the League of Nations Council September-December 1931'. R1865. League of Nations Archives (LoNA).

'Discussion at the 66th Session of the League of Nations Council January-February 1932'. R1870. League of Nations Archives (LoNA).

Harwood, Catherine: *Navigating between principle and pragmatism : the roles and functions of atrocity-related United Nations Commissions of Inquiry in the international legal order*, Doctoral Thesis, Leiden: Leiden University, 2018.

International Institute for Agriculture to League of Nations Secretariat 3. December 1925. Services of an agricultural expert, appointment of Professor Cavara, R801. League of Nations Archives (LoNA).

Knight to Purves, 19 May 1927. Services of Mr. Jewell B. Knight, R801. League of Nations Archives (LoNA).

MacLeish to Delano, n.d. Draft report to Council, Delano Papers, Series 3-20, Folder I. Franklin Delano Roosevelt Presidential Archives (FDRA).

Published material

Akami, Tomoko: 'Imperial Polities, Intercolonialism, and the Shaping of Global Governing Norms: Public Health Expert Networks in Asia and the League of Nations Health Organization, 1908–37', *Journal of Global History* 12 (1), 2017, 4-25.

Bliesemann de Guevara, Berit and Roland Kostić: 'Knowledge Production In/about Conflict and Intervention: Finding "facts", Telling "truth"', *Journal of Intervention and Statebuilding* 11 (1), 2017, 1-20.

'Council Meeting held on January 20th, 1934 – Dispute between Bolivia and Paraguay – Report of the Committee of Three', *League of Nations Official Journal*, February 1934, 242-249.

'Dispute between Bolivia and Paraguay – Report of the Chaco Commission', Geneva: League of Nations, 1934.

March, Lucien: 'International Statistics and the League of Nations', *Quarterly Publications of the American Statistical Association* 14 (133), 1921, 629-635.

Méndez, Juan: 'Commissions of Inquiry: Lessons Learned and Good Practices', *Politorbis* 54 (2), 2012, 47-54.

Report of the International Commission of Enquiry into the Existence of Slavery and Forced Labour in the Republic of Liberia, Geneva: League of Nations, 1930.

Rodogno, Davide, Liat Kozma and Magaly Rodriguez Garcia (eds): *The League of Nations' Work on Social Issues*, Geneva: United Nations, 2016.

Svenson, Nanette: *The United Nations as a Knowledge System*, London: Routledge, 2015.

United States Department of State: *Foreign Relations of the United States: Diplomatic Papers*, Vol. 3, Washington, DC: GPO, 1930, 378-379.

Tomoko Akami

BEYOND THE FORMULA OF THE AGE OF REASON

Experts, Social Sciences, and the Phonic Public in International Politics

In recent years, the League of Nations has been examined as a "harbinger of global norms" for its successor, the UN,[1] rather than as a failed attempt at the world's first collective security organisation. Accordingly, scholars' attention has shifted from diplomats, politicians and military officers to the experts who were in charge of the various norm-making projects of the League. One could even claim that the League was the first intergovernmental organisation to consolidate the work of experts in the task of governing the world. It mobilised experts, their 'non-governmental' expert organisations, and their networks across the globe.[2]

In order to understand the role of the League in shaping global governing norms, we need to examine the experts who carried out this core activity, many of whom continued their work in the UN and its agencies. This chapter will discuss two problematic assumptions held by both the historical protagonists and the historians, in the hope that this will prompt further debate: (1) that the experts belonged to the 'liberal professions' and represented civil society; and (2) that the 'public' was believed by the League, the experts and the foreign policy elites to be the reading middle-class public, while technology and politics brought a 'new' kind of the public, namely the phonic public, to the fore (by the 'phonic public', I mean the public whose political actions were based mainly on information gained from sound bites of radio and speeches, as opposed to the reading public, who relied on newspapers, books and journals).

I suggest that the League inherited these assumptions about experts and the public from the social sciences that emerged in the Enlightenment era, and that it failed to adjust to the new era of mass-based politics and electronic media. I further suggest that since then historians have also been constrained by these assumptions.

The League of Nations mobilised experts in diverse fields for its technical work. The Health Committee, the advisory body of the League's Health Section, consisted of medical and other scientific experts from leading research institutions and ministries of health from across the world. The committee established the Malaria Commission in 1924, which became one of the longest-living and most active bodies in the Health Section, with operations going beyond Europe and North America, to Asia and Africa.

PROBLEM 1: Assuming that the experts belonged to the 'liberal professions', independent from the state, and were actors of and for 'civil society'

The League's global norm-setting took various forms, which required experts in diverse fields. For setting trans-border norms, the expertise of international law was crucial. Its experts, including many career diplomats, who were trained in university faculties of law and/or professional legal institutions, became central in the codification of these international norms at the League.[3] Global norm-setting also required the standardisation of terminologies, codes and practices.

The League set up various 'technical committees', which initiated such standardisation in their respective fields. The standardisation also provided the common ground for experts who came from different countries to conduct cooperative operations. These operations were wide-ranging, and the League mobilised experts in medicine, natural sciences, engineering and other technologies and infrastructures. Many, however, came from the social sciences. While they were initially largely focused on domestic issues,[4] their expertise in national and colonial affairs proved to be the basis of their international work for the League.

In the era of the League, the social sciences, with origins going back to the Enlightenment,[5] developed into more specialised, 'scientific' disciplines, such as political science, economics, sociology, statistics, demography, anthropology and psychology. The speed and scope of this "scientific compartmentalization" differed, however, from country to

country. It was well advanced in the US, for instance, but much less so in other countries, even after the Second World War.[6]

The League got experts of these yet-to-be clearly compartmentalised social sciences, as well as experts in other diverse fields, working together for its programmes, and produced useful approaches and results. Social medicine, for example, saw social and economic conditions, such as poverty, as having a significant impact on people's health; it became a core tenet of the League's Health Committee in the 1930s. Its programmes sought collaboration among experts of medicine, sociology, economics, psychology and public administration.[7]

Pressures to create more 'scientific', streamlined, and specialised 'disciplines' of social sciences were strong in the interwar period, which affected the experts who worked for the programmes of the League. This was evident, for example, in the case of the League's International Studies Conference (ISC, 1928-1954), which aimed to establish the

"scientific study of international relations".[8] The experts themselves had their own reasons for establishing their separate disciplines; they wanted to gain greater legitimacy, influence over policy-makers and prestige for their particular profession. They also wanted strong and separate chairs and departments at universities. Furthermore, the major philanthropic organisations, such as the Rockefeller Foundation and the Carnegie Endowment for International Peace, which funded the ISC as well as other programmes of the League, expected 'scientific' methods and knowledge out of their investments. As a result, the League's committees, as well as relevant non-governmental organisations, tried to eliminate 'non-scientific' (namely 'religious' or 'activist') elements, and stressed 'scientific' aspects of their programmes when they applied for funding from these foundations.[9]

The Standardisation Commission was an active body in the League's Health Section. It was led by Thorvald Madsen, also Director of the State Serum Institute, Copenhagen, and the President of the Health Committee. Tirelessly promoting the Commission's work, he facilitated international collaboration among top researchers and organised conferences to compare findings. By 1935, the Commission had "established international standards for 11 therapeutic sera, one bacterial extract, four vitamins, [and] three sex hormones", among other agents.

This development of the social sciences made the relationship between their expertise and the state increasingly symbiotic, rather than oppositional. In this context, the analytical framework of the state versus civil society, in which the experts and their 'non-governmental' organisations tend to be associated with the latter, becomes artificial or even misleading. Some social scientists were certainly committed to social activism, and maintained a critical stance with regards to the state and state policies. Yet the prototype of social sciences, sociology, began as a response to the need of the modern state to expand its functions into social policies in order to deal with the complex issues resulting from industrialisation, democratsation, and class conflicts.[10]

While further specialisation of social sciences occurred in the interwar period, these newly established disciplines also remained largely policy-relevant studies, and the states needed their experts to formulate and execute these specialised policies. As a result, although some experts of social sciences pursued their careers in academia or in private practices, others worked in public administrations at a municipal, national, imperial or colonial level. While some experts remained 'independent from the state' throughout their careers, many did not; they became 'advisors', 'consultants' or 'think tank' members for state policy-makers, or switched between public offices, universities and the private sector.

This symbiotic relationship between the experts and the state affected the relationship between the experts and the League. To start with, many policy-relevant experts who worked at the League's technical committees had worked at the state level before their prominence in the field was recognised. The League mobilised these eminent experts for its committees and projects, whom their governments would sanction to send to the League as expert members and/or official representatives. At the League, then, while the experts had to work with various states, they also balanced their professional ethics with the interests of the states they (unofficially) represented.

In these complex power dynamics, what defined their actions (their reformist agenda, professional sense of mission, sense of service to their own state or the League or their more technical concerns) is hard to discern. Some patterns are clear, however: experts of the League committees and its agencies advanced certain social causes, such as control of trafficking of women and children and dangerous drugs, abolition of slavery, repatriation of refugees, protection of minorities, improvement of labour conditions and equal legal status for women. The documents of the various committees of the League also indicate a general trend that they supported democratic changes, opposed fascism and militarism and wanted to avoid war and conflict.

Yet the League was not a pacifist organisation. Although many who supported it have been conventionally categorised as 'utopians'/'liberals' as opposed to 'realists' who understood world affairs based on power politics,[11] recent works have questioned this dichotomy, and revealed the complexity of the thinking of each camp.[12] The League certainly did not reject the prevailing colonialism of the victorious empires, and was ultimately counter-revolutionary. Its primary concerns were to maintain order, prevent or manage major crises and conflicts and govern the existing system. Its reform projects, therefore, served as a means to this end. Accordingly, more radical supporters of the League became increasingly frustrated in the mid- to late 1930s and advocated an alternative League with a stronger commitment to pacifism.[13] Any analysis of the expertise at the League needs to be located in this complex political and ideological terrain, not in a simple framework of civil society versus the state, 'liberals' versus 'realists' or national versus international.

PROBLEM 2: Experts in the era of electronic media, mass-based politics and the phonic public

The League inherited its views on the role of experts and the public from the founders of the social sciences in the era of the Enlightenment. While these views were outmoded in the interwar period, the League and its experts did not adjust to the new forces at play.

Put simply, the League held that rational, impartial and science-based accurate information and knowledge would lead the people in the right direction (peace). Conversely, irrational, biased and inaccurate information and knowledge would cause conflicts and wars. The best strategy of moral disarmament, to avoid conflicts and wars, was therefore to prevent such false information and knowledge from entering the public arena.[14] The League accordingly stressed the significance of public opinion in international politics, and took its publicity work very seriously. It set up an Information Section at the Secretariat and overseas publicity offices in London, Paris, Rome, Tokyo, Berlin, New Delhi (initially in Mumbai [Bombay]) and Beijing. It created a pressroom within the building of the League's Secretariat in Geneva and fed its 'news' to journalists and news media organisations across the globe.

Moreover, the League, like the founders of the social sciences, equated the public with the well-educated, rational and reading middle class. Experts were to digest the issues and communicate them to this public. The League did not change this assumption about the public, or the role of experts, despite the fact that politics were becoming more mass-based. Accordingly, its publicity efforts remained directed towards the experts who would enlighten and educate the reading 'public'.[15] All these assumptions inevitably defined the nature of the publicity activities of the League, conducted by its Information Section, and various projects, such as Intellectual Cooperation, International Media Conferences and International Studies Conferences.

The danger of 'fake news', then, was clearly recognised by the League, and while the accuracy and impartiality of information was seen as the very basis for democracy and peace,[16] there were serious shortcomings in its assumptions. First, it overestimated the public's powers of rationality, while largely dismissing the significance of its emotions. The League's experts produced accurate and scientific material for the public so that it could make rational decisions. Meanwhile, especially (but not exclusively) fascist and socialist regimes deployed experts to create materials, such as posters, slogans, leaflets or broadcast speeches, that appealed directly to the emotions of the political masses. Combined with coercion, their tactics proved effective in achieving their own objectives.

Such tactics were not foreign to capitalist democracies. Flourishing advertising companies (particularly in the US) were developing tactics to lure consumers in, appealing to their psychologies and emotions. Indeed, Woodrow Wilson's wartime propaganda machine was led and staffed by these advertising gurus. The League, however, chose not to use this commercial and emotion-oriented advertising formula. Rather, they preferred to educate the public indirectly through experts.[17]

Second, the League did not make fundamental changes to their publicity strategies and tactics, despite the fact that they were outmoded by the emergence of electronic media (especially radio broadcasting), mass-based politics (though largely male) and the phonic public. Political leaders in many countries quickly recognised the significance of domestic radio broadcasting. It was the first 'direct' means for political leaders to appeal to the masses across the nation. By the mid- to late 1930s, overseas radio broadcasting services became possible, which states quickly utilised for external policy purposes.[18]

Tosaka Jun (1900-1945) was a Marxist. Studying physics and philosophy at Kyoto Imperial University, he became the founder of a study group on materialism in 1932, led the grou and edited its journal, *Study on Materialism*. Although he becam a professor at Hōsei University, he was arrested several times fo his writings on materialism, and died in prison, only days before the end of the Second World War. He nonetheless published extensively on philosophy, ideology, science, technology, materialism, ethics and politics in his short life. Known for his clear writing, his insights remain relevant to the politics and society of our own time.

How were these political masses and the phonic public theorised by contemporary social sciences? Walter Lippmann's *Public Opinion* (1922) and *Phantom Public* (1925) recognised the emergence of mass-based politics as a new political development and warned about its detrimental effects on democracy.[19] Here, he reinforced the importance of experts in enlightening the masses, and in this sense, it was a call for a return to the 'age of reason', rather than adjustment to the new era. A Marxist public intellectual in Japan, Tosaka Jun, was critical of the neglect of the political masses, and concluded in 1932 that contemporary theorists were incapable of recognising public opinion beyond that of the bourgeois class. They remained in the Enlightenment era, he argued, and dismissed proletariat public opinion as "mob utterance".[20]

While the proletariat public was not identical with the phonic public (as Tosaka also recognised), both were new formations of 'the public'. The League failed to appreciate the emergence of the proletariat public and the phonic public as significant new political phenomena, and to adjust their formula. Although the League's Information Section created promotional photos, slides and films, and used radio broadcasting, even creating its own 'Radio Nations' (1929-1939), there is little evidence of discussions about the need to change their basic assumption regarding the public, nor how to adjust to the era of mass-based politics and the phonic public.

Last, the League's heavy reliance on experts also had an indirect detrimental long-term effect on the transparency and public appeal of subsequent international organisations, and for our understanding of international affairs. As Nicholas Guilhot's recent work demonstrates, in the US of the 1950s, the lessons of fascism did not make postwar experts of international affairs adjust to the era of electronic media and mass-based politics. Instead, they "distrusted the masses"; they wanted to "insulate politics from democracy" and to reserve their field for statesmen and an elite circle of foreign policy experts.[21]

AND BEYOND THE FORMULA OF THE AGE OF THE REASON

There is a serious danger in the exclusive and compartmentalised nature of current experts at international organisations, as the knowledge they produce is understood only among the experts who can decode the jargon of their narrow disciplinary borders and remains unattainable for most of the public. Though the current public may be better educated than any preceding generation, it is predominantly a phonic public, getting its information through digital sound bites. Have experts at international organisations and theorists of international affairs today gone beyond the formula of the age of reason, which was already outmoded in the era of the League, but nonetheless restored in the immediate postwar period? Our analyses of experts at the League must grapple with this long overdue question.

NOTES

1 Pedersen: 'Back', 1092.

2 Giddens: *Nation-state*, 163-164. See also Herren: *Internationale Organisationen*; Akami: *Internationalizing*.

3 Koskenniemi: 'History', 2. See also their role in shaping the mandate system in Anghie: *Imperialism*.

4 Conrad: *What is*, 3.

5 Porter: 'Genres', 16-22.

6 Ross: 'Changing', 213-214.

7 This was evident in the League's programmes, such as the reform of the Chinese public health system, rural hygiene, nutrition, housing and malaria treatment. Borowy: *Coming*, 325-342; Amrith: *Decolonizing*, 28-40.

8 On the ISC, see Long: 'Who'; Riemens: 'International'; Cotton: 'Early'.

9 Rietzler: 'From', 185-187; Akami: *Internationalizing*, 50-53.

10 Bannister: 'Sociology', 331-332.

11 Carr: *Twenty*.

12 Long and Wilson (eds): *Thinkers*.

13 Accinelli: 'Militant', 30-33.

14 Tworek: 'Peace'.

15 Akami: 'The limits', 76-77.

16 See for instance: http://projects.au.dk/inventingbureaucracy/blog/show/artikel/the-league-and-the-combating-of-false-information/.

17 Akami: 'The limits', 71.

18 Akami: *Soft Power*, 108, 125, 168, 210.

19 Luskin: *Lippmann*, Chapter 2.

20 Tosaka: 'Yoron', 60-61.

21 Nicolas Guilhot: 'Introduction'.

BIBLIOGRAPHY

Accinelli, Robert D.: 'Militant internationalists: The League of Nations Association, the Peace Movement, and US foreign policy, 1934-38', *Diplomatic History* 4 (1), 1980, 19-38.

Akami, Tomoko: *Internationalizing the Pacific: the US, Japan and the Institute of Pacific Relations in War and Peace, 1919-1945*, London: Routledge, 2002.

Akami, Tomoko: *Soft Power of Japan's Total War State: The Board of Information and Dōmei News Agency in Foreign Policy, 1934-45*, Dordrecht: Republic of Letters, 2014.

Akami, Tomoko: 'The limits of peace propaganda: the Information Section of the League of Nations and its Tokyo office'. In Jonas Brendebach, Martin Herzer and Heidi Tworek (eds): *International Organizations and the Media in the Nineteenth and Twentieth Centuries: Exorbitant Expectations*, London: Routledge, 2018, 70-90.

Amrith, Sunil S.: *Decolonizing International Health: India and Southeast Asia, 1930-65*, New York: Palgrave, 2006.

Anghie, Antony: *Imperialism, Sovereignty and the Making of International Law*, Cambridge: Cambridge University Press, 2007.

Bannister, Robert: 'Sociology'. In Theodore M. Porter and Dorothy Ross (eds): *The Modern Social Sciences*, Cambridge: Cambridge University Press, 2003, 329-353.

Borowy, Iris: *Coming to Terms with World Health: the League of Nations Health Organization, 1921-1946*, Frankfurt: Peter Lang, 2009.

Carr, E.H.: *The Twenty Years' Crisis: 1919-1939: An Introduction to the Study of International Relations*, New York: Perennial, 2001 (first published 1939).

Conrad, Sebastian: *What is Global History?*, Princeton: Princeton University Press, 2016.

Cotton, James: 'Early international relations teaching and teachers in Australia: Institutional and disciplinary origins', *Australian Journal of International Affairs* 67 (1), 2013, 71-97.

Giddens, Anthony: *Nation-state and Violence*, Berkeley: University of California Press, 1985.

Guilhot, Nicolas: 'Introduction: One discipline, many histories'. In N. Guilhot (ed.): *The Invention of International Relations Theory: Realism, the Rockefeller Foundation, and the 1954 Conference on Theory*, New York: Columbia University Press, 2010, 1-32.

Herren, Madeleine: *Internationale Organisationen und globale Ordnung*, Darmstadt: Wiss Book Company, 2009.

Koskenniemi, Martti: 'History of international law, World War I to World War II'. In *Max Plank Encyclopedia of Public International Law*, Oxford: Oxford University Press.

Long, David: 'Who killed the International Studies Conference?', *Review of International Studies*, 32 (4), 2006, 603-622.

Long, David and Peter Wilson (eds): *Thinkers of Twenty Years' Crisis: Inter-war Idealism Reassessed*, Oxford: Clarendon Press, 1995.

Luskin, John: *Lippmann, Liberty, and the Press*, University of Alabama Press, 1972.

Pedersen, Susan: 'Back to the League of Nations', *American Historical Review* 112, 2007, 1091-1117.

Porter, Theodore M.: 'Genres and objects of social inquiry, from the Enlightenment to 1890'. In Theodore M. Porter and Dorothy Ross (eds): *The Modern Social Sciences*, Cambridge: Cambridge University Press, 2003, 13-39.

Riemens, Michael: 'International academic cooperation on International Relations in the interwar period: the International Studies Conference', *Review of International Studies* 37 (2), 2011, 911-928.

Rietzler, Katharina: 'From peace advocacy to international relations research: the transformation of transatlantic philanthropic networks, 1900-1930'. In Davide Rodogno, Jakob Vogel and Bernhard Struck (eds): *Shaping the Transnational Sphere: Experts, Networks and Issues from the 1840s to the 1930s*, New York: Berghahn Books, 2014, 173-193.

Ross, Dorothy: 'Changing contours of the social science disciplines'. In Theodore M. Porter and Dorothy Ross (eds): *The Modern Social Sciences*, Cambridge: Cambridge University Press, 2003, 205-237.

Tosaka, Jun: 'Yoron no kōsatsu [On the public opinion]', *Yuibutsuron kenkyū [Study on Materialism]*, Vol. 2, 1932, 60-65.

Tworek, Heidi: 'Peace through truth: the press and moral disarmament through the League of Nations', *Medien und Zeit* 4, 2010, 16-28.

Online source

http://projects.au.dk/inventingbureaucracy/blog/show/artikel/the-league-and-the-combating-of-false-information/ (12.02.2019).

Niels Brimnes

BANDUNG REVISITED

From Rural Hygiene to Primary Health Care

'Rural Hygiene' – a field connecting health, nutrition and agriculture – is often seen as an area in which the League of Nations' engagement was successful, and it was certainly an area that left a profound legacy in the postwar world.[1] The interest in rural hygiene arguably culminated in a major conference organised by the League's Far Eastern Bureau in Bandung, Indonesia in August 1937. Representatives from across South and South East Asia gathered and debated the best way to improve the health and lives of millions of Asians living in rural settings. Rural hygiene was closely associated with the doctrine of 'social medicine', which had gained ground during the interwar years, not least through the activities of the League of Nations Health Organization (LNHO). Social medicine was sceptical of expensive medical solutions based on advanced technology, which often targeted single diseases for the benefit of elite segments in society. Instead, it promoted simpler, broader and more affordable solutions to problems of health. General sanitation, better housing and improved nutrition were among the preferred strategies of social medicine and rural hygiene.[2]

While these ideas reached a zenith in Bandung in 1937, they also lived on after World War II. Most conspicuously they resurfaced in 1978 at another major conference, this time in Alma-Ata in the Soviet Republic of Kazakhstan, where WHO – LNHO's most direct successor – adopted the 'Primary Health Care' strategy. While the similarities between the two conferences are relatively obvious and have been noted by other scholars, this article offers a systematic comparison between the notion of 'Rural Hygiene' as it appeared in Bandung in 1937, and 'Primary Health Care' as it manifested itself forty years later in Alma-Ata.[3] It further discusses how one of the conveners of the Alma-Ata conference, the WHO Director-General Halfdan T. Mahler, engaged with idea of Rural Hygiene in his promotion of Primary Health Care.

THE LEAGUE OF NATIONS' CONFERENCE ON RURAL HYGIENE

The Bandung conference on rural hygiene is a much discussed and often celebrated moment in the history of international health. Theodore Brown and Elisabeth Fee described it as a "milestone event" in health and development.[4] According to Iris Borowy, the conference in Bandung

> might have been one of the first, if indeed not the first, major international event in public health in which Asian voices were heard and representatives of non-Western regions were allowed to speak for themselves and challenge the idea of one universal Western model for world health.

Borowy further found the Conference to be "both the high point and the end" of the League of Nations Health Organization's work in Asia.[5] More modestly, Sunil Amrith described Bandung as perhaps the first "formal dialogue on questions of health and welfare which was at once imperial, and international".[6] Randall Packard saw it as the "culmination" of the interest in rural reconstruction and hygiene outside Europe, but noted in a more critical vein that it also reflected the continued entanglement of international health organisations with colonial medicine.[7]

The discussions at the Conference were organised around five general themes: 1) health and medical services, 2) nutrition, 3) sanitation and sanitary engineering, 4) rural reconstruction and collaboration with the population, and 5) measures for combating certain diseases in rural areas.[8] This agenda illustrates the influence of social medicine. The favoured topics of nutrition and sanitation were conference themes

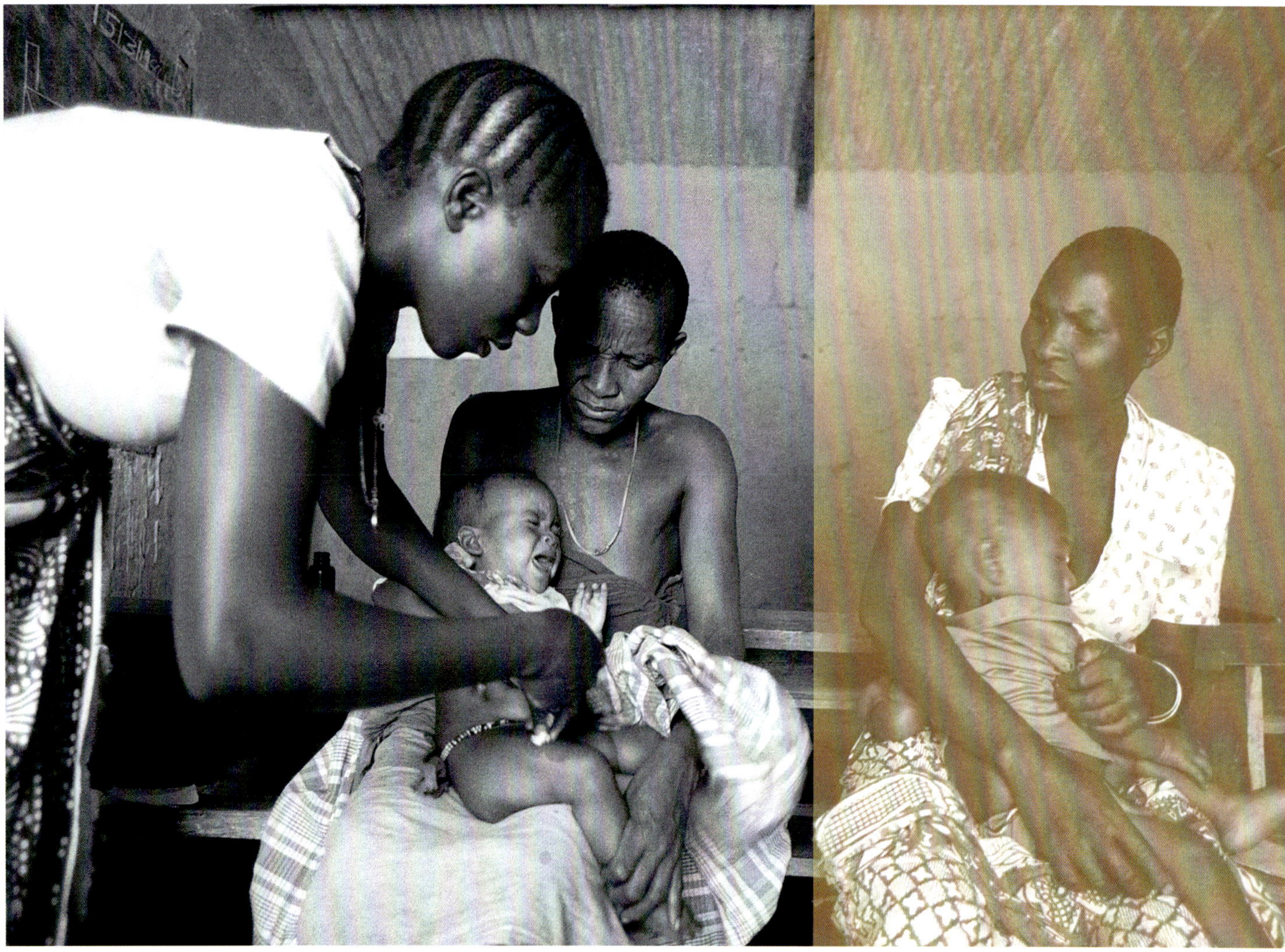

in their own right, while the attempts to combat a range of specific diseases were lumped together under one heading.

In order to explore how the legacy of the Bandung conference lived on, let me jump forty years forward to identify the core principles of Primary Health Care as they were established in Alma-Ata. I will then return to Bandung to discuss the extent to which these principles can be traced back to this meeting. Methodologically, I am therefore working my way backwards: my reading of the Bandung report is informed by a brief analytical distillation of the core principles of Alma-Ata.[9]

THE ALMA-ATA CONFERENCE AND THE PRINCIPLES BEHIND PRIMARY HEALTH CARE

The Alma-Ata conference was the product of a specific juncture in ways of thinking about both health and international politics. First, it offered a new direction to WHO, after the organisation had abandoned its Malaria Eradication Programme in 1969, thereby ending two decades dominated by technology-driven health interventions against single diseases. Second, it aligned itself with an emerging criticism of both established development strategies and sophisticated biomedicine.[10] The policies endorsed by the conference therefore appeared radical to many observers.

The official declaration adopted at the conference referred explicitly to the notion of a 'New International Economic Order' (NIEO), as carried by the UN General Assembly in 1974, and thus openly sided with the demand for a global redistribution of wealth promoted by many developing countries in the political climate of the early 1970s.[11] An official report published in the run-up to Alma-Ata called for "the transfer of a greater share of health resources to the underserved majority of the population", and requested affluent countries to commit themselves "to a more equitable distribution of international health resources".[12] An internal document used more dramatic language. Primary Health Care was here presented as "a code word describing a health related response to the international and national cry for social equality and justice with equal emphasis upon the developing world and the underserved groups of many countries".[13]

A community health worker immunises a child in Tanzania in 1984. Immunisation did not feature significantly at the Bandung Conference in 1937. Mass vaccination against plague was recommended, but the conference failed to endorse the controversial BCG vaccine against tuberculosis. In 1978, by contrast, "immunization against the major infectious diseases" was listed among the basic components of Primary Health Care in the Alma-Ata Declaration. Immunisation was a technological solution that qualified as "appropriate technology".

The particular approach to health care sanctioned at Alma-Ata challenged policies providing sophisticated medical technology to "the privileged few" and suggested an alternative that sought to make essential health care universally accessible.[14] This alternative was embedded in three principles: *intersectoriality*, *community participation* and *appropriate technology*.

For want of a better word, I use 'intersectoriality' to refer to the insistence that health issues be seen in the context of general social and economic development. As stated in the post-conference report,

"Primary Health Care is an integral part of the socioeconomic development process".[15] 'Community participation' was defined in the pre-conference report as "the process by which individuals and families assume responsibility for their own health and welfare", a principle that enabled them "to become agents of their own development instead of passive beneficiaries of development aid".[16] 'Appropriate technology' meant that apart from being scientifically sound, the technology applied through the health services should be simple, affordable and "in keeping with the local culture". It therefore challenged a pharmaceutical industry that preferred to develop expensive, sophisticated drugs for elites across the world.[17] The notion of appropriate health technology was closely interwoven with an emphasis on community health workers, who had not received extensive or clinical training. References were made not only to the importance of nurses, "feldshers" and the famous Chinese "barefoot doctors", but also to the value of "indigenous" practitioners of other medical traditions and to the possibility of including women in health-related work.[18]

FROM BANDUNG TO ALMA-ATA

Let me now return to 1937, in order to determine more precisely the extent to which the vision of Primary Health Care discussed at Alma-Ata was a continuation of – or a return to – the ideas on Rural Hygiene discussed in Bandung.

First, as noted by Packard above, the event at Bandung was situated firmly within a colonial world order, and the majority of the participants were colonies under European authority. While Alma-Ata emerged as a cry from a decolonised world for a more just distribution of resources invested in health, Bandung did not call for changes in the colonial, international order. It did touch upon the need for a redistribution of resources within nations and colonial possessions, but the voice was kept low and only surfaced in scattered suggestions for "land reform".[19] In Packard's analysis, the discussions at Bandung did highlight the social and economic problems behind poor health, yet "at almost every turn, the conference participants backed away from recommendations that would have radically changed the status quo in order to improve rural hygiene in their countries".[20] Interestingly, the Alma-Ata participants were as cautious in demanding internal reforms. Presumably, this was in adherence to the principle of "non-interference in the internal affairs of other states", as stated in the NIEO declaration.[21] If colonialism was not up for discussion at Bandung, the privileges of national elites in the global south was not a target at Alma-Ata.

'Intersectoriality' was openly embraced at Bandung. The letters of convocation had stated that "delegations should represent all the activities having an influence on rural hygiene: health, civil administration, rural reconstruction, agriculture, co-operatives, social questions".[22] This was indeed a broad agenda, and the conference report gladly noted that governments had understood the message and sent delegations consisting of representatives from several sectors other than health:

> This may be taken as a positive indication that those responsible for the medical services and health protection of the rural populations in the East realise that their work is made difficult, if not impossible, unless activities in the fields of economics, sociology, agriculture and education are carried on at the same time.[23]

This concern had a clear parallel in the preparations for Alma-Ata, where invitations were deliberately sent both to the ministries of health and to the ministries of foreign affairs in order to reach stakeholders beyond a narrowly-defined circle of health officers.[24]

'Community participation' formed a significant part of the discussions at Bandung, and 'Rural Reconstruction and the Collaboration of the Population' was one of the five overarching themes on the conference agenda. The relevant discussions concluded that it was necessary "to work through the people, and avoid, as far as possible, imposing systems from above", and produced resolutions that advocated village committees.[25] Another panel impressed that "the people should be led, not driven". This phrase indicates, however, that even though the active collaboration of communities was solicited, it was in a more patronising way than was recommended forty years later at Alma-Ata. Village

Halfdan Mahler (1922-2016) was the idealistic and charismatic Director-General of WHO from 1973 to 1988. His scepticism towards advanced and expensive technological solutions to health problems and his insistence on social equity in health makes him a successor to the doctrine of social medicine of the inter-war years and aligns him with people such as the Belgian doctor and philanthropist René Sand (1877-1953) and LNHO Director Ludwik Rajchman (1881-1965).

communities had to be supervised or "led" by a "committee of management" consisting of government experts, and several speakers emphasised that "improperly trained personnel cannot secure the confidence of the rural people".[26]

The emphasis on 'appropriate technology' is another of the obvious similarities between Bandung and Alma-Ata. One example is the 'naturalistic' method of controlling malaria, which was endorsed by the delegates at Bandung in a way that could have been copied directly into the reports from Alma-Ata. Naturalistic methods of controlling malaria were seen as "relatively inexpensive" and they could "suitably be carried out by the peasants themselves".[27]

When it comes to the corollary of appropriate technology, the promotion of semi-skilled auxiliary personnel or community health workers, the similarities between Bandung and Alma-Ata are less obvious. Borowy has shown how the authors in charge of compiling the important preparatory report for Bandung were not only strongly in favour of semi-skilled personnel, but also saw indigenous medical traditions as a valuable resource.[28] In the introductory section to the report from the conference, this issue was first framed in an open and inconclusive way. It was noted that there were two options: to insist on academic training up to the standard found in central universities, or to accept that diplomas be issued to less educated health workers. The introduction ended ambiguously by insisting that "there should be no compromise" in the training of qualified medical staff, while also noting that the training of auxiliary personnel was "no less important".[29] The resolution adopted by the conference was equally ambiguous. On the one hand, it insisted that "every country should, in the sphere of medical education, attain the highest level of theoretical and practical training". On the other, it referred to the importance of "adequately training a large body of auxiliary personnel".[30]

Halfdan Mahler addresses the United Nations General Assembly in 1980 to launch the Water Supply and Sanitation Decade. An adequate supply of safe drinking water was emphasised as crucial to rural hygiene at the Bandung Conference and became one of the essential elements of Primary Health Care. In both the 1930s and the 1970s, safe water and basic sanitation exemplified the broad fields of intervention that were promoted as alternatives to technological, disease-specific solutions to health problems.

While the delegates in Alma-Ata embraced the semi-skilled community health worker, it was more difficult to challenge, even denounce, the highest level of medical education and theoretical training in 1937. Interestingly, the idealistic WHO Director-General and convener of the Alma-Ata conference, Halfdan T. Mahler, deployed this contrast in his promotion of Primary Health Care.

REMEMBERING BANDUNG 1937

A few months before the Alma-Ata conference, Mahler published an article in an international journal in which he explicitly discussed the legacy of the 1937 conference and its obvious links with the conference he was preparing. Mahler noted that the delegates at Bandung had understood how health was inextricably connected to broader economic, social and educational developments, had realised the importance of community participation and had been sceptical about schemes superimposed by the government.[31] He then reviewed the principles of Primary Health Care, in the form in which he had presented them to the World Health Assembly in 1975, and noted: "The similarity between these principles and the conclusions reached in 1937 cannot be denied. Clearly, PHC is not 'new'". He then rhetorically asked: "Why has it been necessary to resurrect ideas that were put forward decades ago? What happened between 1937 and 1975?"[32]

Mahler's answer was that the delegates in Bandung had made one crucial mistake. In his words: "Even in the 1937 report, the seeds of failure had been sown". The culprit was the abovementioned recommendation that every country should strive to attain the "highest scientific level of theoretical and practical training" in medical education. According to Mahler, this inevitably led to a preference for advanced medical technology and a health service biased towards catering for the few and wealthy: "[r]efinement of knowledge for the sake of knowledge and of the techniques for the sheer cleverness of them".[33]

Primary Health Care was now being developed as an alternative "that has more than once been recognized as the best road to take", and while in many ways it reiterated the principles stated in Bandung, it differed by finding more space for various kinds of community health workers, including "traditional healers and local midwives".[34] This was not a fair reading of the recommendations from Bandung, because it ignored the ambiguity of its statements about the use of semi-skilled health workers – but it was a reading well suited to Mahler's purposes.

THE LEGACY OF THE LEAGUE

It is not surprising that Mahler sought to identify an important difference between the health strategy advocated in Bandung before World War II and the new concept of Primary Health Care he was promoting in the run-up to the Alma-Ata conference. Mahler obviously needed to brand Primary Health Care as a genuinely new strategy that had learned from mistakes in the past. It is equally unsurprising that it is possible to demonstrate profound similarities between Bandung and Alma-Ata, even where Mahler claimed there were differences. Ideas branded as 'new' are rarely without solid connections to the past, and when it comes to international cooperation in the late twentieth century, the League of Nations is an obvious place to look. The case of the Primary Health Care strategy and its core principles of intersectoriality, community participation and appropriate technology is no exception.

NOTES

1 Staples: *The Birth of Development*, 73-74.

2 Weindling: 'Social medicine'; Amrith: *Decolonizing International Health*, 29-36.

3 For references to the similarities between Bandung and Alma-Ata, see Packard: *A History of Global Health*, 228; Brown and Fee: 'The Bandoeng Conference of 1937'.

4 Brown and Fee: 'The Bandoeng Conference of 1937'.

5 Borowy: *Coming to Terms*, 355-356.

6 Amrith: *Decolonizing International Health*, 38.

7 Packard: *A History of Global Health*, 84.

8 *Report of the Intergovernmental Conference*, 6-7.

9 The analysis is based on a comparative reading of three official published reports – one from Bandung and two relating to Alma-Ata – and is therefore a comparison of endorsed and deliberately communicated health strategies.

10 Packard: *A History of Global Health*, 105-131, 231-248.

11 'Declaration of Alma-Ata', in *Primary Health Care. Report of the International Conference*, 2-6.

12 *Primary Health Care. A joint report*, 12-13, 16.

13 *The Third Ten Years*, 302.

14 *Primary Health Care. A joint report*, 7-8.

15 *Primary Health Care. Report of the International Conference*, 17.

16 *Primary Health Care. A joint report*, 20-21.

17 *Primary Health Care. Report of the International Conference*, 19.

18 *Primary Health Care. A joint report*, 31-34. See also Nunes and Medcalf: 'Visualizing primary health care'.

19 *Report of the Intergovernmental Conference*, 26, 56.

20 Packard: *History of Global Health*, 85.

21 'Declaration on the Establishment of a New International Economic Order'.

22 'Report of the Intergovernmental Conference', 6.

23 'Report of the Intergovernmental Conference', 23.

24 *The Third Ten Years*, 299.

25 'Report of the Intergovernmental Conference', 51, 54-55.

26 'Report of the Intergovernmental Conference', 38, 41, 54. See also Packard: *History of Global Health*, 86.

27 'Report of the Intergovernmental Conference', 92.

28 Borowy: *Coming to Terms*, 351.

29 'Report of the Intergovernmental Conference', 8, 35.

30 'Report of the Intergovernmental Conference', 44.

31 Mahler: 'Promotion', 107.

32 Mahler: 'Promotion', 108.

33 Mahler: 'Promotion', 108.

34 Mahler: 'Promotion', 109, 111.

BIBLIOGRAPHY

Unpublished material

'Declaration on the Establishment of a New International Economic Order', para 4 a., A/RES/S-6/3201, http://www.un-documents.net/s6r3201.htm (08.09.2018).

Published material

Amrith, Sunil S.: *Decolonizing International Health. India and Southeast Asia 1930-65*, Basingstoke: Palgrave, 2006.

Borowy, Iris: *Coming to Terms with World Health. The League of Nations Health Organisation 1921-46*, Frankfurt a.M.: Peter Lang, 2009.

Brown, Theodore M. and Elizabeth Fee: 'The Bandoeng Conference of 1937: A Milestone in Health and Development', *American Journal of Public Health* 98 (1), 2008, 42-43.

Mahler, Halfdan: 'Promotion of Primary Health Care in Member countries of WHO', *Public Health Reports* 93 (2), 1978, 107-113.

Nunes, João and Alexander Medcalf: 'Visualizing primary health care: World Health Organization Representations of community health workers, 1970-1989', *Medical History* 62 (4), 2018, 401-424.

Packard, Randall M.: *A History of Global Health. Interventions into the Lives of Other People*, Baltimore: Johns Hopkins University Press, 2016.

Primary Health Care. A joint report by the Director-General of the World Health Organization and the Executive Director of the United Nations Children's Fund, Geneva and New York: WHO and UNICEF, 1978.

Primary Health Care. Report of the International Conference on Primary Health Care, Alma-Ata, USSR, 6-12 September 1978, Geneva: WHO, 1978.

Report of the Intergovernmental Conference of Far-Eastern Countries on Rural Hygiene, Geneva: League of Nations, 1937.

Staples, Amy: *The Birth of Development. How the World Bank, Food and Agriculture Organization, and World Health Organization changed the world, 1945-65*, Kent: The Kent State University Press.

The Third Ten Years of the World Health organization, 1968-1977, Geneva: World Health Organization, 2008.

Weindling, Paul: 'Social medicine at the League of Nations Health Organization and the International Labour Office Compared'. In Paul Weindling (ed.): *International Health Organizations and Movements 1918-1939*, Cambridge: Cambridge University Press, 1995, 134-153.

PART 3

THE LEAGUE PROJECTIONS AND PRESENCE

IN his 2018 article "Narratives and Bodies: Culture beyond the Cultural Turn" (*The International History Review* 40 (3), 2018, 609-630), historian Patrick Finney usefully categorised the mushrooming catalogue of culturalist international history into works that dealt with narratives and those that dealt with bodies. By 'narratives' we mean, broadly speaking, stories communicated by people, institutions, objects, sites and cultures that shape both identities and behaviour. How state officials portray and narrate external threats, for instance, shapes what a given population perceives as dangerous (and external for that matter). Narrative approaches have become one of the enduring legacies of the 'cultural turn' not only in international history, but in IR too. A sub-field of IH and IR has been particularly interested in how states and IOs narrate themselves (often under the heading of 'public diplomacy'). The European Union (EU) has received ample attention – perhaps because it has so consciously and persistently sought to legitimise its existence through the production of coherent, strategic narratives. The League was the first IO to pursue such coherent legitimation strategies, and IOs in general – lacking the more traditional 'hard' tools of power – are remarkably conscious of how they are interpreted in their contemporary world, seeing good standing with (an imagined) global public and with states as sources of potency.

A recent edited volume on *International Organizations and the Media in the Nineteenth and Twentieth Centuries* (London: Routledge, 2018), edited by Jonas Brendebach,

Martin Herzer and Heidi Tworek, questions both the reach and impact of their communication strategies, but also recognises and illustrates how seriously the production of narratives was taken by the IOs themselves.

Unsurprisingly, then, the League of Nations Secretariat's largest section was the Information Section; battling 'false' information while trying to uphold its own story and legitimising its own existence was arguably one of its biggest challenges. The two first contributions of *Narrating the League* explores how these strategies unfolded in print and on film. But narratives about the League were also woven into the broader cultural imagination at the time, and even today. The third and fourth chapters, therefore, explore these visions of the League through the many generations of fictional literature on, and contemporary cartoon drawings of, the Geneva world, respectively.

The other category in Finney's taxonomy is 'bodies', which in recent years has meant flesh and bones, memories and emotions, but which in its essence denotes the return of the material after many years of text and discourse. The 'material turn', picking up speed from the 2000s onwards, sought to shift our attention to what the material *does* in the world, and how the material is *done* in concrete historical contexts. It explores the material as performative and as possessing agency. In less abstract terms, it means that the site chosen for diplomatic negotiations; the working conditions within an IO; or the mountains causing turbulence on a flight to an economic conference all matter, and potentially shape history. The three contributions to

Materialising the League do not pursue avant-gardist conceptions of the material (where the categories of subject and object are broken down), but explore how the material League was done, as well as the symbolic and more tangible repercussions of this; and, not least, what the material League did to the social world of those working there. This third part, then, on the League's projections and presence, is meant as a further step towards a broad, cultural history of the League of Nations, and IOs more generally.

Haakon A. Ikonomou

Emil Eiby Seidenfaden

FROM THE GALLERY TO THE FLOOR

The League of Nations and the Combating of 'False Information'

Since the US election in 2016, the use of false news stories for mass propaganda purposes and the potential harm done to the public's knowledge about current affairs and trust in governments and elites has reemerged as a matter for concern. In this context, international organisations are scrambling to tackle the threat, with initiatives like NATO's release of an online game that will equip teachers to identify false news and the EU's nascent fight with social media giants regarding the responsibilities of news outlets.[1]

While the use of false news is in fact old news – it has existed as long as print media – its reach and potential impact on international stability seems more unpredictable now, given increasingly globalised communication and the rise of social media. But while times have certainly changed, it is interesting that observers in the interwar period – who witnessed virulent nationalism, social conflict and geopolitical stirrings – worried about false news too. Indeed, false news or "misleading information" was investigated by the League of Nations in a series of international conferences in 1927, 1932 and 1933.

In this chapter, I ask how the League and its Information Section used increasing concerns over the use of false information to publicly legitimise themselves. I argue that the section sought to embed the Secretariat in a transnational network of journalists and news agencies as part of its ambitious efforts to legitimise the League through a vast network of individuals and groups who were in favour of the organisation, who would spread information about it and argue its cause. I draw on my research on the public legitimisation strategies of the League of Nations as performed by the Information Section, in which I use material from several archives, including the League of Nations Archives in Geneva and the Library of Congress in Washington D.C.[2]

The story of the international conferences for press experts is not new; it has been explored by Heidi Tworek, who presented the League's broader efforts in securing "peace through truth". But whereas Tworek recounted the first conference as originating in a resolution of the League's Assembly and merely organised by the Secretariat, I approach the story from among the Secretariat officials, arguing that the idea for the conference was first planted by them. Later, during the Second World War, when the experience of the League was evaluated in terms of publicity, the conferences were highlighted by a prominent official as part of the Secretariat's efforts to publicly legitimise the organisation.

The story of these League initiatives is striking for several reasons. First, it mirrors our own discussion of false news in a period when the media landscape was very different from today's, and reminds us that history cannot be understood backwards; in a world that was brought together by the telegraph, still recovering from a world war full of propaganda and the violent instrumentalisation of nationality, the combination of lies with mass media was frightening even if the masses on the receiving end were fewer in number than today. Second, the League's involvement in the discussion of this threat demonstrates a striking element of its public legitimisation strategies, which constituted an ambitious part of its work in Geneva.

THE INFORMATION SECTION

The League attributed much importance to publicity and public information, based on the Wilsonian vision of international relations in which diplomatic negotiations would be laid out for the public to scrutinise. Between the close of the 1920s and 1932, between 15 and 19 percent of salaries paid to personnel in the Secretariat went to its Information

Section, a department tasked with press relations and with propagating the League to the public.[3] The idea of public opinion as a democratic force with the potential to determine the rise and fall of regimes is what sustained this level of ambition. The Section was engaged in press services, the publication of books, pamphlets and audiovisual material and various kinds of liaison work with national and international collaborators. Its members travelled extensively and nurtured connections in governments, private organisations and philanthropic associations. In the interwar period, the written press was considered paramount when it came to public relations, so the Section was particularly keen on securing good relations with journalists, and its officials had worked as political journalists themselves before entering the young international civil service.

After 1933, as international tensions reverberated in the League's Assembly, the Information Section had its budget severely cut. However, one of the activities that persisted right up until the end of the League's existence was the invitation of influential guests to Geneva as "temporary collaborators" to observe the League at work and spread its message in their home countries. Many were journalists or experts. This picture shows an unspecified group of visitors at the Palais des Nations in 1938 or 1939.

THE INTERNATIONAL CONFERENCES OF PRESS EXPERTS

According to the League's own version of the story, its first independently organised conference was initiated as follows. At the Assembly in 1925 the Chilean delegate, Mr. Yanez, had proposed that the League should host an international conference of press experts to discuss matters of universal interest to journalists.[4] Such a conference, it was hoped, would ensure a better transmission of news "with a view to reducing the risk of international misunderstanding".[5] After careful preparation in the Secretariat, the conference convened in August 1927. The participants included directors of news agencies, journalists and directors of governmental press offices. The success of the first conference in 1927 led to two more being held under League auspices: in Copenhagen in 1932 and in Madrid in 1933. The idea for the conference, it will be seen, came from the Information Section.

All three conferences discussed the threat posed by false news, but the priority given to the question seems to have increased in the 1930s. The Copenhagen conference stated that "the campaign against the dissemination of inaccurate news is one of the necessities of international life". To prevent the press from using tendentious sources in the first place, "rectifying it" afterwards and coordination between national press bureaux were suggested as the best weapons against "inaccurate and sometimes tendentious" news.[6] The first conference in 1927 simply called the problem "tendentious news", recommending university courses for journalists as a countermove.[7] At the League Assembly in 1931, in a discussion of a "method of stopping the spread of false news", the Danish government offered to host the next conference to deal with such problems.[8] Prior to the third and final conference in Madrid, the League answered the call of the Copenhagen conference for increased coordination, and asked press organisations from 64 countries to suggest how to combat false news. The problem was interpreted differently among the delegations, and the exact consequences of the conferences, apart from resolutions, are hard to determine.[9]

Still, in this phase of the history of international organisation the conversation across borders, between both states and private agencies, was significant in itself and illuminates a stage in the rise of modern European news. For example, in 1927 it was not given that private agencies would be allowed as delegates at the conference. Objections were raised, but seemingly subsequently dropped, by the owner of the British News Proprietor Organization, Lord Burnham, who would eventually be elected President of the Conference. Burnham wanted governments to have the largest say at the conference, and wanted delegations to be "national, not sectional". He was eventually convinced otherwise by the Information Section – possibly calmed by assurances that press offices of all governments of members of the League were invited as observers.[10] Governmental oversight of transnational meetings was important in the interwar period.

The procedure leading to the setting of the agenda for the first conference involved officials of the Information Section corresponding intently with journalists, news editors and news agencies (381 "groups or individuals" to be precise),[11] which were divided into three committees to prepare for the conference. Section officials insisted in this correspondence with journalists, as well as in publications about the event, that the idea for the conference had been spawned by the Chilean delegation and had not come from the Secretariat. The refutation was crucial at the time because the Secretariat could not be seen to be initiating international action in matters this political.[12] But 25 years later Arthur Sweetser, a high-ranking member of the section, wrote a letter to his old chief – the French former director of the section Pierre Comert:

> Dear Pierre,
> Thoughts of you kept coming into my mind yesterday as I read the attached "International Code of Ethics for Information Personnel" and recalled our famous Conference of Press Experts in Geneva, not such an unconscionable time ago [...] Do you remember our starting out our tumultuous voyage by getting the Council to ask the Assembly ... to consider the advisability ... of asking some journalists ... to consider the advisability ... of asking the Council ... to consider the advisability of calling a Conference of Journalists to discuss such questions?[13]

Pierre Comert (1880-1964) directed the Information Section from 1919 to 1932 and illustrated how politics permeated most parts of the Secretariat. He was ousted by the Germans, who could not accept another powerful Frenchman in the Secretariat after Joseph Avenol's ascent to Secretary-General. Before that he was a staunch internationalist and at the same time Eric Drummond's preferred informal line to the French government after the early exit of Jean Monnet.

Aware of this near admission that the conference was the brainchild of the section, one may read through the correspondence between the section's officials and interested journalists from all over the world in the months leading up to the conference. Time and again in these letters, the officials refuted the suggestion that the section was the initiator, often using the phrase that the idea was a "baby left on our doorstep".[14] This suggests internal coordination of statements had taken place. It also resonates well with Tworek's uncovering of how from 1924 Pierre Comert corresponded with agents of the vast European alliance of news agencies Agences Alliées (led by French Agence Havas, British Reuters and German Wollf, together with several newer European agencies) about ways for the international press to cooperate better across borders – an obvious motivation for the network-oriented Comert and his section to propose an international conference. Indeed, one of the three preparatory committees for the conference consisted mainly of the Agence Alliées.[15] There is thus no doubt the initiative fitted well into the Information Section's understanding of liaison work, which would secure promotion of the League by maintaining a network of pro-League journalists and media, of private organisations favourable to the League and of semi-governmental connections that would help facilitate League action when necessary. The former official of the section Egon Ranshofen-Wertheimer, who was also the only chronicler of its history, curiously hinted at the initiative when in his 1945 discussion of the conferences he stated that: "*Officially* these activities originated in a resolution adopted by the 1925 Assembly".[16]

MORAL DISARMAMENT

The final conference in Madrid in 1933 ran parallel with a less-known part of the great Disarmament Conference (1932-1934) concerning "Moral disarmament", a concept that bridged the League's efforts within disarmament and the press, as well as international cooperation within science, education and cultural understanding. The fight against incorrect news resonated well with the League's desire to mobilise public opinion to the cause of peace and internationalism.

The organisation aimed to establish international ethics codes with regards to news and journalism, with the aim of countering nationalist interpretation and dissemination of news by opponents of the League. On top of visions of an "open diplomacy" and of using publicity actively in the fight for international peace, the League's efforts to standardise press conditions played into the idea of moral disarmament. The concept meant that disarmament ought to go further than simply reducing the build-up of arms among the Great Powers. It was particularly prevalent in the League's "Organization on Intellectual Co-operation" (the predecessor of today's Specialized Agency of the UN, UNESCO), in which it encompassed things like international coordination of public education in League matters, educative broadcasting, film production and academic cooperation, such as student exchange and international scholarships.[17] But moral disarmament also meant that the press had to play an active role as a promoter of peace and understanding among peoples – and thus that journalists had to be made to understand and fulfil that role. It is within this context that the conferences of press experts under League auspices must be understood.

Thus, the League's three conferences constitute an essential part of the story of its vision for furthering the cause of peace through the press – what Tworek has called "Peace through truth". It demonstrates one of the ways in which the role of the League was negotiated in international life – it tried to facilitate the

creation of a new and more 'responsible' press, and to establish transnational networks of journalists who spoke the internationalist language.[9] Equally important, it may be observed that the initiative of the Information Section, while well hidden, was a demonstration of how it perceived its role in the emerging international society. One publication by the section from the following year is suggestive of its ideal narrative about the League *vis à vis* the international press:

The relation between the League and the press is seen in this cartoon, drawn at the occasion of a dinner hosted by the Association of Journalists Accredited to the League during the failing Disarmament Conference in 1932. A reporter tries to make sense of the Great Power "sphinxes" who can only make vague speeches, while the arms race continues unabated. The cartoon endorsed an "open diplomacy" so central in League internationalism, while also criticising the impotency of the League system.

> The Press Conference brought journalists from the Press gallery to "the floor of the house" and, through the President of the Council, to the League Council table for the discussion of League of Nations problems.[18]

We see that the hosting of the press conference was connected to a vision of open diplomacy – in this case particularly for the press. Rather than being held back in the role of spectators, journalists were to be engaged directly in the international deliberations of the League. "Newspapermen" were to be operationalised in keeping at bay the forces that sought to bring the world back to the trenches, and thus they were important in the struggle for moral disarmament. In addition, the publication stated that the preamble to the final resolutions of the conference might be described as "the Magna Charta [*sic*] of the International Press".[19]

THE GREATER LEAGUE OF NATIONS

To a large extent, a division of labour in terms of public information took place among promoters of the League. While the Information Section itself dealt with strictly 'factual' information, like the publication of a *Monthly Summary* and of informative pamphlets on the various League organisations, more clear-cut pro-League propaganda was nurtured indirectly through maintaining a wider international network of private organisations (today called NGOs) and international private associations (today called INGOs). Liaison with media and journalist associations was just one branch of the League's public relations. Thomas R. Davies has shown that the League "sometimes asked INGOs to campaign for certain proposals" and that it relied on them to legitimate its policies.[20] A wide array of "private" channels was employed by the section to secure collaboration in spreading the League's message, including women's organisations, organisations for wounded war veterans, national League of Nations Unions and large American philanthropic foundations like Rockefeller and the Carnegie Endowment.[21] These efforts were noticed and debated in the interwar period. INGOs whose work and interests overlapped with the League were said to constitute "The Greater League of Nations" – a vast transnational network that worked as a forum for League debate.[22] In 1934, the Information Section declared that up until that point, its work had been "based on the assumption that public opinion is in a large degree informed through these organisations", leaving it somewhat unclear whether they were seen as mediators to the wider public or as constituting that public themselves.[23]

To the Information Section, press organisations belonged to this group of collaborators. Arthur Sweetser categorised them as such in a postwar conference evaluating the work of the Secretariat: the press was part of the "Greater League of Nations". Among important organisations present at the conferences of press experts were the International Federation of Journalists (IFJ), founded only one year before the first conference, and the International Association of Journalists Accredited to the League of Nations.[24]

CONCLUSION

In 1942, during a confidential conference on League experiences to be used in a future organisation (what would emerge as the United Nations), Arthur Sweetser was pressed on the value of collaborating with private groups and individuals to promote the League; he answered "Oh yes", and elaborated that publicity efforts should be divided into "the things that the [...] agency itself does by and for itself like in the sense of its own publications and broadcasts, and the secondary things and material it gets other people to do". He continued: "we had one or two large conferences in Geneva on common affairs of the press. You can develop this in very great detail if you want to."[25]

The League's fight against false information was part of its effort not only of providing an open diplomacy, but also of combating hostile public opinion through the "Greater League of Nations". A key instrument employed by the officials of the Information Section in reaching what they perceived as the international public was establishing liaisons with associations, organisations, foundations and individuals who were in favour of the League. Although the interactions of the Secretariat with private agents and with the press were formally two different things, its initiation of the International Conference for Press Experts in Geneva in 1927, which inspired two others in 1932 and 1933, was articulated as part of its work to promote the League and spread knowledge about it. Making the international press a collaborator in the cause for peace and international cooperation, or bringing it "from the gallery to the floor", was one of the public legitimisation strategies of the League of Nations.

NOTES

1 NATO Stratcom News release on 'The News Hero', 24 July 2018, (17.08.2018); Fioretti: 'Exclusive: EU to demand improvements on tackling fake news by the end of the year – draft', 12 April 2018 (17.08.2018).

2 In my research I have achieved an overview of the history of the section and its strategies by collecting a periodised sample of Secretariat registry correspondence originating in the Information Section, as well as material illuminating the agency of the three leading figures in the section: its first Director, Pierre Comert, its leading official and later second Director Adrianus Pelt and the influential second-in-command and short-term Director Arthur Sweetser.

3 *Official Journal of the League of Nations*, 1921-1922 and 1929-1933, October volume (02.11.2017). For 1923-1928 the budgets are public access UN documents at https://search.un.org/ (02.11.2017): C.713.M.425.1922.X; C.668.M.268.1923.X; C.618.M.217.1924.X; C.619.M.201.1925.X; C.581.M.220.1926.X; C.520.M.178.1927.X. All data is from 'Schedule B'.

4 Tworek: 'Peace Through Truth', 24.

5 Information Section: *The League of Nations and the Press*, 43.

6 'Conference of Directors of Press Bureaux and Press Representatives', January 1932, R3310, *Collaboration of the Press in the Organization of Peace*, League of Nations Archives (LoNA).

7 Information Section: *The League of Nations and the Press*, 47-48.

8 Information Section: *Monthly Summary of the League of Nations*, September 1931, 222.

9 Tworek: 'Peace Through Truth', 24.

10 Letter from Lord Burnham to Adrianus Pelt, 26 February 1926, *Press and Communication*, P192, Adrianus Pelt Papers, LoNA, 1; Information Section, *The League of Nations and the Press*, 45-46.

11 Information Section: *The League of Nations and the Press*, 44-45.

12 The conference had been authorised by the Assembly on the condition that the League "in no way seeks to create something resembling an official Press or to make propaganda". Société des Nations, Document Préparatoires - Conference d'Experts des Presse, C.231. M.93. 11 May 1927, https://search.un.org/ (30.04.2018), 6. My translation.

13 Letter from Arthur Sweetser to Pierre Comert, 23 October 1952, *Miscellaneous: General*, Box 28, Arthur Sweetser Papers, Manuscript Division, Library of Congress.

14 E.g. letter from Adrianus Pelt to Rey G. Howard, 24 December 1925, *Press and Communication*, P192, Adrianus Pelt Papers, LoNA.

15 Tworek: 'The Creation of European News', 734.

16 Ranshofen-Wertheimer: *The International Secretariat*, 212. Italics added.

17 League of Nations, Conference document 98, 'Moral Disarmament', *Documentary material forwarded by the International Organization on Intellectual Co-operation*, 24 March 1932 (28.04.2017).

18 Information Section: *The League of Nations and the Press*, 52.

19 Information Section: *The League of Nations and the Press*, 47.

20 Davies: 'A "Great Experiment" of the League of Nations Era', 411. 'INGO' is a term brought into use after the Second World War. In the interwar period, such

organisations were sometimes called 'private international unions', not to be confused with 'public international unions'.

21 E.g. a 1933 list of private associations with which the Information Section liaised: Pelt: 'Information Section – Liste des associations privée avec lesquelles la Section d'information est en rapport et analyse de chacune de ces liaisons', n.d., 1933, *Liaison Committee*, P191, Adrianus Pelt Papers, LoNA, 1-2.

22 E.g. Pickard: 'The Greater League of Nations', 465.

23 Committee to examine the organisation of the Information Section, Annex to 'Commission de Controle – Réorganisation de la Section d'Information. Note du Secrétaire general, 21 September 1933, *Section Reorganization*, P192, Adrianus Pelt Papers, LoNA, 3.

24 Tworek: 'Peace through truth', 24.

25 *Proceedings of the Exploratory Conference of the Experience of the League of Nations Secretariat*, Carnegie Endowment for International Peace, Box 244, Rare Books and Manuscript Library, Columbia University Libraries, 118.

BIBLIOGRAPHY

Unpublished material

Columbia University Libraries, Rare Books and Manuscript Library, *Carnegie Endowment for International Peace Records*, Box 244, 'Proceedings of the Exploratory Conference of the Experience of the League of Nations Secretariat', August 1942.

League of Nations Archives (LoNA), Adrianus Pelt Papers, *Liaison Committee*, P191, 'Information Section – Liste des associations privée avec lesquelles la Section d'information est en rapport et analyse de chacune de ces liaisons', n.d., 1933.

Library of Congress, Manuscript Division, Arthur Sweetser Papers, *Miscellaneous: General*, Box 28, Letter from Arthur Sweetser to Pierre Comert, 23 October 1952.

LoNA, Adrianus Pelt Papers, *Press and Communication*, P192, Letter from Adrianus Pelt to Rey G. Howard, 24 December 1925.

LoNA, Adrianus Pelt Papers, *Press and Communication*, P192, Letter from Lord Burnham to Adrianus Pelt, 26 February 1926.

LoNA, Adrianus Pelt Papers, *Section Reorganization*, P192, Committee to examine the organisation of the Information Section, Annex to 'Commission de Controle – Réorganisation de la Section d'Information. Note du Secrétaire general', 21 September 1933.

LoNA, R3310, *Collaboration of the Press in the Organization of Peace*, Conference of Directors of Press Bureaux and Press Representatives, January 1932.

Published material

Davies, Thomas R.: 'A "Great Experiment" of the League of Nations Era: International Nongovernmental Organizations, Global Governance, and Democracy Beyond the State', *Global Governance* 18, 2012, 405-423.

Information Section of the League of Nations Secretariat, *Monthly Summary of the League of Nations*, September 1931.

Information Section of the League of Nations Secretariat, *The League of Nations and the Press*, Geneva, 1928.

Pickard, Bertram: 'The Greater League of Nations – A Brief Survey of the Nature and Development of Unofficial International Organizations', *Contemporary Review* 850 (150), 1936, 460-465.

Ranshofen-Wertheimer, Egon: *The International Secretariat – A Great Experiment in International Administration*, Washington DC.: Carnegie Endowment for International Peace, 1945.

Tworek, Heidi J.S.: 'Peace Through Truth. The Press and Moral Disarmament through the League of Nations', *Medien & Zeit* 25 (4), 2010, 16-28.

Tworek, Heidi J.S.: 'The Creation of European News: News Agency Cooperation in Interwar Europe', *Journalism Studies* 14 (5), 2013, 730-742.

Online sources

Documentary material forwarded by the International Organization on Intellectual Co-operation, League of Nations, Conference document 98, 'Moral Disarmament', Geneva, 24 March 1932 (28.04.2017).

NATO Stratcom News release, 'The News Hero', 24 July 2018, (17.08.2018).

Official Journal of the League of Nations 1919-1940, Salaries, Wages and Allowances of the League of Nations Secretariat (Schedule B) 1921-1922 and-1929-1933, October volumes (02.11.2017).

UN document: *Société des Nations, Document Préparatoires - Conference d'Experts des Presse*, C.231. M.93. 11 May 1927 (30.04.2018).

UN documents: Salaries, Wages and Allowances of the League of Nations Secretariat (Schedule B) 1923-1928: C.713.M.425.1922-1927 (02.11.2017).

Reuters, Julie Fioretti: 'Exclusive: EU to demand improvements on tackling fake news by the end of the year – draft', 12 April 2018 (17.08.2018).

Helle Strandgaard Jensen,
Nikolai Schulz and Emil Eiby Seidenfaden

FILM-SPLAINING THE LEAGUE OF NATIONS

In 1937 the Warner brothers' *The Life of Emile Zola* won the Oscar for best picture and was praised by *The New York Times* as "the finest historical film ever made".[1] When cinemagoers went to see it, they might also have learned about the work of the League of Nations: not because the Warners or Zola were connected to the League, but because it was released in the same year as the League's infomercial *The League at Work*. In the 1930s, it was common to have so-called infomercials or newsreels playing before the feature films.[2]

The League's interaction with public opinion is only recently starting to attract attention from scholars. The information activities of the organisation were pursued primarily by the Information Section of its Secretariat, whose attempts to organise the international press in the cause of world peace in 1927, 1932 and 1933 were first discussed by Heidi Tworek,[3] but whose activities have only been evaluated in their totality by interwar observers.[4] The attempts made by the Information Section during the 1930s to use the emerging media of radio and film to promote the League have not been studied. While this part of the League's work was small, it communicates forcefully some of the challenges it faced and points to a future in which film would play a much more central role in propaganda and information.

This chapter reviews *The League at Work* as one of the most ambitious films produced for the section, and discusses how it presented the League to a 1930s audience.

Infomercials, like *The League at Work*, were short documentaries shown as opening acts for the popular feature films. One of the best-known British infomercials is *Night Mail*, directed by Basil Wright and Harry Watt.[5] This short documentary from 1936 about the Royal Mail train delivery service, together with Wright's *The Song of Ceylon* produced for the Ceylon Tea Propaganda Board in 1934, marks the height of the interwar British documentary film movement.[6] After making *Night Mail*, Wright left the Film Unit subdivision of the UK General Mail Service to found his own production company, The Realist Film Unit (RFU). In 1936-1937 the Information Section hired RFU to make an infomercial about the League.[7] *The League at Work* was the result.

Not until the last years of the existence of the League of Nations did it begin to work seriously with films, photographs and graphic promotion. Arguably, this hesitancy to use imagery to promote its cause was the result not only of budgetary constraints but equally of the fact that the League often targeted narrow European elites rather than a broad, global public. This changed in the United Nations, whose iconic posters were the result of international competitions.

LEAGUE FILMS AND THE PURPOSE OF THE LEAGUE AT WORK

Between the late 1920s and the outbreak of the Second World War the Information Section had a small number of films produced, ranging from short silent clips (showing delegates leaving the Assembly room, or the Secretary-General at his desk) to larger productions like *The League at Work*.

The League was not a frontrunner in film media. Its Assembly and its Supervisory Commission on the budget of the League made it clear to the Information Section in 1933 that "films and photographs should be strictly limited to those of exceptional interest".[8] These constraints were put on it as part of a general period of retrenchment in the organisation, and because activities that could be accused of constituting propaganda for the League were among the first targets when such cuts were made.[9] For this reason only a small handful of longer films were produced, and the *League at Work* was the most ambitious.[10]

In the well-preserved, two-part archived version of the infomercial the voiceover and all the participants speak English, but a French version (*La Société des Nations à l'oeuvre)* existed as well, the League being a bilingual organisation. A few films were published in other languages, including Spanish and German.

It is difficult to establish exactly where and how *The League at Work*

was distributed, as sources surrounding the production of the film are scarce. We know that films were distributed through a large network of League "collaborators" such as the League of Nations Unions, and new films were advertised in the League's other publications, like its *Monthly Summary*.[11] Finally, some films were showcased for delegates and journalists at League events, including the Assembly.[12]

The Information Section sometimes supplemented its official work with more discreet activities that circumvented the constraints put on it. In 1936 a confidential document shows Adrianus Pelt, the Director of the section, met a representative of the production company Gaumont British. The company agreed to financing and producing a series of small educational films on "international questions", while the Information Section would ask the Carnegie Endowment of International Peace to fund their distribution to schools all over Britain and the USA. Pelt requested that the films should contain "no direct propaganda", and that the involvement of the League should be unofficial.[13] While we do not know what came of the deal with Gaumont British, it was not uncommon for the Information Section to cooperate with the Carnegie Endowment as well as with the Rockefeller Foundation, which sponsored the League's library in 1927.[14] As discussed in Seidenfaden's chapter, the official rejection of propaganda methods characterised the work of the section throughout its existence.

Despite this insistence, the aim of information documentaries such as *Night Mail*, *The Song of Ceylon* and *The League at Work* was to promote the institutions that had paid for them. As such, the infomercial about the League fits well with the far-ranging publicity strategies already in place at this point in time. In the case of *The League at Work*, the institution's many activities are framed as relevant because they all support the League's overall goal – peacekeeping.

A broad range of NGOs and transnational movements pushed the League of Nations' member states to commit to lasting disarmament. An explicit part of the League's Covenant, the disarmament efforts collapsed spectacularly with the World Disarmament Conference (1932-1934) – a direct cause of Germany's withdrawal from the organisation. Unsurprisingly, therefore, *The League of Nations at Work* downplayed this theme, highlighting instead the organisation's administrative efficiency and broad range of technical expertise.

"JUDGE IT FOR YOURSELVES"

Turning to the film itself, the importance of the work done by the League of Nations was stated upfront. Immediately after the title information, viewers are shown pictures of crosses and war memorials from Flanders. A voiceover tells us about the League's aim to prevent war from happening again by making open and just relationships between nations possible. The voiceover's claims are supported in the next shot, where US president Woodrow Wilson is seen talking (it is implied at the League), while a voiceover explains how the organisation is designed to improve and strengthen the relationships between the world's nations.

The introduction ends with a request: "though this idea [of peacekeeping] may not be new, it has never been tried at such great a scale before. Here is the League of Nations at work, judge it for yourselves." This explicit invitation to the viewers to critically engage with the film and its content is somewhat surprising. Unlike *The Song of Ceylon* and *Night Mail*, the viewers of *The League at Work* were not positioned as an audience that should sit back and passively take in the information offered; rather, they had the right, in theory, to judge and assess the quality of the work done at the League.

Nevertheless, judging by the content of the rest of the film, we might attribute this openness to the self-confidence of the organisation. Although by 1937 the League carried little weight as an arena for solving problems of high politics, *The League at Work* conveys a strong belief and confidence in the organisation's bureaucratic capacity, and as a global technocratic body. This resonated well with a related tendency in the League's self-promotion during the 1930s: its focus on "technical" tasks, such as economic cooperation and international health, which would also be visible at the League's exhibition pavilion at the New York World's Fair in 1939.[15]

A SMOOTH-RUNNING, FAIR, EFFICIENT AND ABSTEMIOUS MACHINE

The League at Work shows the League of Nations as a smooth and efficient machine, where important men make important decisions assisted by neatly dressed women. As noted in Ikonomou's chapter on the translation and interpretation service, the Internal Services is the first section shown in the film. The prominent place of this section in the film helps to build a narrative about the League as central, and relevant, to the entire world community, as it contained the organisation's postal services, translations and print activities. The scenes from the Internal Services show us that the world was connected, organised and analysed from Geneva. A later sequence about the Information Section corroborates this narrative, as we get to see how the League hosts journalists from world-leading newspapers, broadcasts in English, French and Spanish and publishes a wide range of pamphlets, reports and books. The efficiency of the Geneva bureaucracy was visually fused with an idea of global technocracy and global communications.

Other parts of the film clearly expand and elaborate on this well-polished image of the League, as when we hear from the treasurer that "the League's finances are sounder than ever", assuring the viewers that the money their national governments pay to its upkeep is well managed. Equally, when we hear about the legal section, we are assured of the League's efficiency, as it is mentioned that it has published 4068 treaties to date. And when we hear about the mandate system, we are assured of its fairness by way of complicated calculations. Thus, when cinemagoers were invited to judge the League, they were provided with all the arguments for its efficiency, its fairness and its abstemiousness.

WHAT WE ARE NOT TOLD

The film's focus on bureaucratic efficiency, on *procedure*, serves to highlight some parts of its work, but also to downplay others. During the segment on the Political Section, the League's diplomatic service, which dealt with ongoing conflicts, we see nothing of the effects of this work outside the halls of Geneva. Sitting behind his desk, Frank Walters, the Section's Director, exhibits case files to the viewer. We are *not* shown the reality behind the case files: the Civil War in Spain, war in China or the Italian–Abyssinian war – although we get a glimpse in passing of titles on the League's characteristic yellow case folders, which are neatly stacked on a mahogany table in front of Walters. Bluntly put, the emphasis placed by the infomercial on *procedure* signals that in the 1930s procedure was all that was left of the League's original diplomatic machinery; there were few achievements to lay forth. Such an analysis may look like hindsight. But 1930s viewers will have sensed that at the end, the film communicates an atmosphere of crisis to try to defend the League's position. Its final scene features Anthony Eden, Foreign Secretary of Great Britain, sitting behind his desk in a calm, authoritative way, like Walters. Eden explains that the League is "not perfect" but that it represents a genuine step forward, if only the Great Powers will support it, as his own government will continue to do.

Using celebrities to attract attention to a good cause is not a recent phenomenon. Celebrities have endorsed products and brands, as well as helped heightening awareness of international organisations, for many years. Here popstar Beyoncé Knowles is shown onstage during the filming of the 'I Was Here' video at the General Assembly Hall of the United Nations for World Humanitarian Day 2012. In *The League at Work*, the American President, Woodrow Wilson, arguably filled the role of celebrity endorser.

AESTHETICS AND THE USE OF CUTAWAY SCENES TO LOOSEN UP THE LEAGUE

The invention of sound film was in some ways a throwback for the experimental and playful aesthetics that had marked filmmaking in the 1920s. The heavy equipment needed to record sound meant that the camera had to be still, otherwise the sound of moving it around would drown out everything else. Thus, the experimental style of the 1920s was replaced by films that seemed very still and dull in comparison in the 1930s. Many of the scenes from inside the buildings in Geneva in *The League at Work* are marked by this style, making its outlook seem quite uninspiring from today's perspective. Nevertheless, there are a great number of cutaway scenes (the interruption of a scene with the insertion of another scene) with voiceover in the film that help to loosen up this impression.

The cutaway scenes in *The League at Work* often help to further elaborate or explain the actions of the different sections or committees. In some of these scenes, we see pictures from exotic places with palm trees and deserts, as we are told that the League cares about people everywhere. We see moving pictures of horse carriages and artillery from the First World War replaced by a shot that pans over the dead bodies of a mother and a child, reminding us why disarmament is important. Later again, we see scenes from shady streets with even shadier hotels and junkies hooked on opioids, to make us aware that the League also combats social evils.

THE SCENE THAT WILL GIVE YOU GOOSEBUMPS

Audio-visual sources convey history in different ways from written documents: as we hear voices and see images from the past, they seem to draw us back in time, making distant events seem close and current. At the very end of the first of the two preserved reels, about nine minutes into the film, the voiceover tells us about the League's effort to protect the rights of minorities. From a present-day perspective, knowing how this failed then and is still failing now, hearing about these visions and dreams for a safe and just world is particularly poignant:

> Minorities have been guaranteed civic rights, they are protected against unfair discrimination, which national or religious feelings might cause. Any person or group has the right to apply for protection. Their petitions are submitted to special committees. If these fail to obtain redress, the council takes action. Thus, the League works for mutual understanding and tries to prevent outburst of national feelings, dangerous to the peace of the world.

CONCLUSION

The League's filmmaking activities came late and were experimental. Nevertheless, *The League at Work* can be considered an example of the organisation doing its utmost within the constraints put on it. The stifled aesthetics and rather didactic style that marks most of *The League at Work* can seem unappealing to a modern-day viewer. But while it is true that crisis obviously lurks behind its self-confidence, the infomercial represents an effort to remind the world why it needed an efficient international bureaucracy imbued with liberal and pacific visions. The League could not guarantee peace if its member states wanted war, but it could provide a transparent, smooth-running machine capable of securing orderly diplomatic relations that would stand ready for them whenever they chose to return to it. The film thus conveys the Leagues' idealism with a force that comes across clearly, even today.

NOTES

1 'The Life of Emile Zola', *The New York Times*, 12 August 1937.

2 McKernan: 'A History of the British Newsreel', http://bufvc.ac.uk/newsonscreen/learnmore/history (02.01.2018).

3 Tworek: *Peace through Truth*, 16-28. In addition, David Allen has discussed the League's Pavilion at the New York World's Fair in 1939: 'International Exhibitionism', 91-116. Tomoko Akami has studied the activities of the section as regards Japanese public opinion: 'The Limits of Peace Propaganda', 70-90. Timo Holste has discussed the tourism efforts made by the section at the League's headquarters in Geneva: 'Tourists at the League of Nations', 307-344.

4 E.g. Potter: 'League Publicity', 399-412.

5 Aitken: *Night Mail*, http://www.screenonline.org.uk/film/id/530415/ (02.01.2018).

6 Aitken: *The Documentary Film Movement: An Anthology*. Fosse and Fox: *The Guardian of a Small Flickering Light*. At the Brussels International Film Festival of 1935, *A Song of Ceylon* won first place in the documentary class, and the 'Prix du Gouvernement' for the best film in all classes.

7 The videos held in the UN Web TV archive date the films to 1935, but Wright's company was not formed until 1936; in Seán Lester's biography *The Guardian of a Small Flickering Light*, it is mentioned that Lester took part in making the film in what must have been 1936/37 (149).

8 League of Nations official document, 'Technical Concentration of the Activities of the League of Nations and Rationalisation of the Services of the Secretariat and the International Labour Office. A.10.1933.X. Report by the Supervisory Commission to the Assembly', 20 July 1933, LoNA, 7-8.

9 E.g. Potter: 'League Publicity', 406.

10 Today, about 30 old League films are available through the UN Audio-Visual Library. 93 titles were listed as transferred to New York following the Second World War. Folder (1948): *Regarding League of Nations: Films*, GIIB/3/1/25 R1569 LoNA.

11 Information Section of the League of Nations: *Monthly Summary of the League of Nations*, March 1927, LoNA, last page.

12 Information Section: 'Report of the Information Section to the 8th Assembly, 1927', *File concerning Report of the Information Section to the 8th Assembly*, 1927, dossier 62097, R1354, LoNA, 5.

13 Unknown author: 'Films on the League', Confidential note, 16 September 1936, P192 (Adrianus Pelt Papers), LoNA, 1-2.

14 Information Section: *The Monthly Summary of the League of Nations*, September 1927, LoNA 321; Tournès: 'La philanthropie américaine'.

15 Allen: 'International exhibitionism', 91-116. The increased emphasis on technical cooperation should be seen in the context of Patricia Clavin's demonstration that these activities were increasingly seen by the organisation to be its *raison d'être*, replacing its original purpose of peacekeeping through collective security. Clavin: *Securing the World Economy*.

BIBLIOGRAPHY

Unpublished material from United Nations Archives at Geneva:

Folder (1948), 'Regarding League of Nations: Films', GIIB/3/1/25 - R1569.

Information Section of the League of Nations: *Monthly Summary of the League of Nations*, March 1927, League of Nations Archives (LoNA).

Information Section: 'Report of the Information Section to the 8th Assembly, 1927', *File concerning Report of the Information Section to the 8th Assembly*, 1927, dossier 62097, R1354, LoNA.

Unknown author: 'Films on the League', Confidential note, 16 September 1936, P192 (Adrianus Pelt Papers), LoNA.

'Technical Concentration of the Activities of the League of Nations and Rationalisation of the Services of the Secretariat and the International Labour Office. A.10.1933.X. Report by the Supervisory Commission to the Assembly', 20 July 1933, LNA, 7-8.

Published material

Aitken, Ian: blogpost at BFI Screen online; *Night Mail* (1936), http://www.screenonline.org.uk/film/id/530415/ (02.01.2018).

Aitken, Ian: *The Documentary Film Movement: An Anthology*, Edinburgh: Edinburgh University Press, 1998.

Allen, David: 'International exhibitionism – The League of Nations at the New York World's Fair, 1939-1940'. In Jonas Brendebach, Martin Herzer and Heidi Tworek (eds): *International organizations and the Media in the Nineteenth and Twentieth Centuries. Exhorbitant Expectations*, London: Routledge, 2018, 91-116.

Akami, Tomoko: 'The Limits of Peace Propaganda: The Information Section of the League of Nations and its Tokyo Office'. In Jonas Brendebach, Martin Herzer and Heidi Tworek (eds): *International organizations and the Media in the Nineteenth and Twentieth Centuries. Exhorbitant Expectations*, London: Routledge, 2018, 70-90.

Fosse, Marit and John Fox: *The Guardian of a Small Flickering Light*, Lanham, Hamilton Books, 2016.

Holste, Timo: 'Tourists at the League of Nations: Conceptions of Internationalism around the Palais des Nations, 1925-1946', *New Global Studies* 10 (3), 2016, 307-344.

McKernan, Luke: 'A History of the British Newsreal', British Universities Film & Video Council; History; British newsreels (02.01.2018).

Nugent, Frank S.: 'The Life of Emile Zola', *The New York Times*, 12 August 1937.

Potter, Pitman: 'League Publicity: Cause or Effect of League Failure?', *The Public Opinion Quarterly* 2 (3), 1938, 399-412.

The League at Work, Reel 1 and 2. Available online at UN Web TV (02.01.2018).

Tworek, Heidi: 'Peace through Truth – The Press and Moral Disarmament through the League of Nations', *Medien und Zeit* 25 (4), 2010, 16-28.

Benjamin Auberer

MURDER, INTRIGUE, SEX AND INTERNATIONALISM

Novels about the League of Nations

In 1929, a German journalist pointed out that no place seemed more suitable for the setting of a world-class novel than the League of Nations in Geneva. With its sentimental tragedies, intrigues and pseudo-diplomatic comedy, he described the League and its surroundings as a "politico-social panopticon on the international stage".[1] Representing a profound innovation in international relations, the League of Nations stimulated cultural production in the 1920s and 1930s in manifold ways. There were numerous poems, songs, comics and even musicals featuring the League. In 1938, for instance, George Bernard Shaw published his drama *Geneva. Another Political Extravaganza*, a piercing satire of the organisation.[2] But these expressions of the cultural dimension of internationalism are almost forgotten. The disappearance of the League of Nations novels from collective memory is a telling example of the transformation of the commemoration of the League. And though recent scholarship is interested in how the League portrays and narrates itself, as the chapters of Helle Strandgaard Jensen, Nikolai Schulz and Emil Eiby Seidenfaden in this volume show, the cultural history of the League of Nations in a broader context remains a rich and yet understudied field of research.[3]

This chapter tries to redeem this lack of scholarly interest by focusing on novels about the organisation. As will be shown, each and every literary expression of the League must be understood as a result of a specific socio-political context. Investigating the literary transformations of the League helps establish what the League as an international organisation meant. The reintroduction of fiction into the history of the League of Nations provides us not only with a more complete picture of the League of Nations, but also with an insight into the manifold international imaginaries the League of Nations stimulated. The central motifs of the literary field that emerged around this new international creature reflect hopes for the capacities of the newly founded organisation and frustrations about the limits and setbacks of the League's diplomacy, but also the mystical allure of a new kind of diplomatic site. In the following, three main themes are identified: the literary production of officials working in the League; novels on the League during the time of its existence; and the literary afterlife of the world organisation. This chapter thus aims at a multidimensional perspective on the League as a literary subject.

This picture is taken from the 2012 adaption of *Belle the Seigneur*, directed by Glenia Bonder. It depicts Under-Secretary-General Solal de Solace and his lover the Genevese Ariane d'Auble. Self-confident and proud, Ariane challenges Solal inside of the League's most sacred rooms: the Council Chamber. The scene is an impressive example of how the League's structure provided women with access to the central institutions of inter-war diplomacy.

THE DEATH OF A DIPLOMAT – INTERNATIONAL CIVIL SERVANTS AS AUTHORS

Though international civil servants were officially prohibited from participating in public or political activities, during the time of its existence, the League of Nations inspired a couple of its employees to process their experiences in literary form. The majority of these novels were published in the late 1920s and the early 1930s, and they portray the League as an important innovation in international relations.

One of the best-known writers in this field is British journalist and author Vernon Bartlett, who led the League's London Office before he joined the BBC. In 1927, he teamed up with his colleague from the Economic and Financial Section of the League, Per Jacobsson, a Swede who later became Managing Director of the International Monetary Fund. Bartlett mentioned to Jacobsson his difficulties in writing commercially successful detective stories, and after being dared by Jacobsson's wife to create such a story,[4] the two published *The Death of a Diplomat* (1928) under the joint pseudonym Peter Oldfeld.[5]

In the book, the diplomatic milieu around the League provides the context for an entangled crime story. A diamond disappears, a secret treaty is stolen, a German diplomat murdered: nothing less than peace in Europe is hanging in the balance. With neither the police of Geneva nor other diplomats able to solve the case, only the two protagonists can prevent a diplomatic crisis: a British servant of the League of Nations and a smart American 'newspaper girl'. The two characters represent the core innovations of the League of Nations: an independent international administration and the inclusion of modern mass media.

The book was a success. It was subsequently translated into eight languages, and made into a silent film entitled *The Man with the Limp*;[6] a second book, *The Alchemy Murder*, similarly set in an international milieu, followed in 1929.[7] Despite their publishers' best efforts,

Jacobsson and Bartlett decided against giving up the 'real' League to pursue fictional writing full-time, and their third book, *Murder on the Golf Course*, was never published.

Within the Secretariat, there were other authors with a much higher literary output. Hilary Aidar St. George Saunders, for instance, who worked as a translator and précis writer for the League of Nations before he became a World War II chronicler, left an extensive body of fiction. He published the fantasy novel *The Devil and the X.Y.Z.* in 1930, writing with Geoffrey Dennis, the head of the League's Translation Services, under the pseudonym Barum Browne.[8] Together with his colleague in the Secretariat, John Leslie Palmer, however, he wrote about forty books (under their joint pseudonym of Francis Beeding).

Most of these spy novels feature a fictitious head of the British Secret Service as protagonist, and most of them rely on a League of Nations background. 'Francis Beeding's' 1928 novel *The Six Proud Walkers* features an evil cabal, which tries to manipulate world events in order to fulfil its ruthless aims. The murder of Italian workers in Albania by men disguised as Serbian soldiers triggers a series of events that provoke a capricious Italian dictator named 'Caffarelli' to declare war.[9] According to one reviewer, the novel displayed how important the League was in order to "restrain these dangerous forces".[10]

In another novel, *The One Sane Man*,[11] the antagonist, a wealthy financier, tries to use the power provided by a weather manipulation machine to gain control of the League of Nations. His ultimate goal is to abolish national rivalry and initiate a commission composed of international experts, which would guarantee justice and equality throughout the world. Of course, he is stopped by the protagonist – but the plot draws heavily on contemporary discourse on internationalism, the global role of economic entanglements, the role of experts and specialists and the aim of overcoming national resentments.

These examples might suggest that fictional writing was above all an activity of men of the higher ranks of the Secretariat. But there is at least one female author from the League's lower ranking staff who wrote such stories. Alice Ritchie worked for the League's Registry from 1921 to 1923 as a clerical assistant, before she was fired for insubordination.[12] Roughly five years after she left the League, in 1928, Ritchie published a novel about the Secretariat entitled *The Peacemakers*.[13] Ritchie wrote about the lives of her colleagues from the second division of League employees: typists, clerks and other minor officials – many of them women. A central motif of the book is the boredom of both office and everyday life in the small town of Geneva – as part of an isolated international community – and how the League's servants coped with this situation.

German actress Christa Tordy played the American journalist Betty Marshall in the 1928 silent movie *The Man with a Limp*, directed by Willy Reiber and Franz Seitz. The adaption of the English League of Nations novel for a German audience is a manifestation of the importance of the Spirit of Locarno in the discourse on international relations two years after Germany entered the League.

Clearly, the first generation of international civil servants attracted quite a few successful authors, who transformed their experiences as part of the 'Great Experiment in International Administration'[14] into literary works. Ranshofen-Wertheimer noted that the League directorate "looked benevolently upon such honorable efforts or hobbies".[15] This is quite telling regarding the social significance of such novels: research in the cultural dimension of 'traditional' diplomacy has reminded us that fiction writing is a well-established practice of diplomats.[16] This research indicates that there is a stable connection between the social, cultural, educational and professional skills of diplomats and the prerequisites of being a successful novelist. Novel-writing allowed diplomats living in foreign countries to keep in touch with the societies of their home countries by transmitting their own experiences. The authors of the League of Nations followed an already established practice of professionals active in international relations by communicating their Genevese experiences to a global readership.

MYSTERY AT GENEVA: NOVELS ABOUT THE LEAGUE OF NATIONS

Of course, numerous books were also written by authors who had not worked in the League, but were, nonetheless, drawn to its cosmopolitan environment. As a rule of thumb, these publications were usually rather critical about the world organisation.

The very first novel written about the League was probably *Mystery at Geneva. An Improbable Tale of Singular Happenings* (1922).[17] Its well-known author, Rose Macaulay was an ardent supporter of the League and the feminist movement; she attended the General Assembly in 1921 as a special reporter for the *Daily Chronicle*, which inspired her book. Her protagonist, Miss Montana, was introduced to the world of diplomacy at the "heaven of secretaries", the Paris Peace Conference in 1919, but was dismissed for making the sloppy mistake of spelling 'parliament' with a small 'p'.[18] A couple of years later she disguises herself as her bedridden lover, the journalist Henry Beechtree, in order to attend the League's annual conference. Clearly, the novel makes a statement about the failure to accept women in international relations.[19] The League's Covenant with its revolutionary article 7 was a big step forward in terms of gender equality in the field, but, as Myriam Piquet shows in her chapter in this volume, it was a "revolution with its ups and downs". Macaulay's book is a highly intricate international mystery novel: an evil conspirator captures one delegate to the Geneva Assembly after another. Most of the characters are skilled spoofs of people from the League milieu. For example, British delegate Arnold Inglis, who is lured into a trap by the fascinating language of a Greek woman, is a barely masked parody of British internationalist Gilbert Murray, Regius Professor of Greek at Oxford.

The lyrics of the musical piece *At the League of Nation's Ball* describe a celebration at the White House in Washington D.C. which all nations peacefully attend. The song was published in the United States in May 1919, months before the League of Nations was actually established. It reminds us how strongly the mere notion of the League of Nations, as a new form of peaceful world organisation, influenced all levels of popular culture.

Swiss author, journalist and gastronomist Marcel Rouff never actually worked for the League of Nations, but he lived in Geneva during the interwar years. He was the editor of the local socialist newspaper *Tribune de Genève*. In 1926, he published the novel *Les Temps Révolus. Sur le quai Wilson*, which represents a fierce literary left-wing attack on the League.[20] Even in the preface, the book is labelled an

"histoire d'une disillusion": The protagonist, Morchaud, is a smart and idealistic young man who works as a personal secretary at the League of Nations in the early 1920s. The immediate context is the Geneva Protocol for the Pacific Settlement of International Disputes of 1924. For Morchaud, the protocol is a symbol for the potential of collective peacekeeping efforts. When the ratification of the protocol fails after the British Government withdraws its support, Morchaud's disillusionment begins. He realises that for the national diplomats, the League is just another stage for their imperialistic power plays.

In a similar vein, Swiss crime author Friedrich Glauser, who was a patient in a psychiatric institution in Geneva during the First World War, noticed how the arrival of the League changed the social composition of the city. His first crime novel *Tee der drei alten Damen* [The Tea of the Three Old Ladies] explores the deep transformation of the quiet city caused by the arrival of the League institutions.[21] Again, Geneva is seen as a stage for the imperial powers, rather than a democratic assembly of equal states.

Many authors used literary means to express their utter disappointment with the League and its failure as a platform for collective peacekeeping. Hans Habe, who was Geneva correspondent for a Czech newspaper, wrote a novel entitled *Tödlicher Friede – ein Liebesroman mit politischem Hintergrund* [Deadly Peace – A Romance with a Political Background].[22] The context of the story is the turbulence in Geneva at the time of the Munich Agreement of 1938. He depicts Geneva in unrest, with the Swiss already preparing for the outbreak of war. The newly inaugurated Palais des Nations is considered by the locals to be a marble beacon guiding enemy bombers, rather than a symbol of world peace. The publication of Habe's book provoked a scandal: after a complaint from the German embassy, the Swiss government confiscated the book, and Habe was forced to re-publish it in the United States – where it was a success and subsequently translated into 16 languages.

These novels all reflect a critical evaluation of the public standing of the League of Nations during the time of its existence. In the 1920s the League was considered a potent expansion of international relations. Novelists acknowledged the idealistic potential of the League and expressed their fears that its new and public diplomacy could be misused and destroyed by corrupt and reckless enemies of world peace. As the history of the 1930s demonstrated the weaknesses of the League system, the authors found their concerns confirmed: the novels of the late 1930s in particular portrayed the system of the League as a corrupt tool of imperialistic power plays. They transformed the political discourses of the failure of the League of Nations as an institution of liberal internationalism into the literary imaginary.

GRAND DAYS: LEAGUE NOVELS AFTER THE LEAGUE

Literary interest in the League dwindled after the organisation dissolved in 1946, and the Cold War soon provided a new background for novels. This is particularly visible in Ian Fleming, the writer of the James Bond novels. Fleming, who studied at the University of Geneva, worked at the League Secretariat in the summer of 1930 while preparing for the Foreign Office entrance exam. He was deeply disappointed by his experiences in the Secretariat, and considered the League a waste of money and paper.[23] Though none of his later novels were situated in a League of Nations context, they regularly played out in Swiss settings. In Fleming's 1959 novel *Goldfinger*, James Bond visits the small Alsatian Brasserie Bavaria in Geneva and reflects on how the restaurant used to be frequented by diplomats, journalists and international civil servants during the time of the League of Nations.[24]

There were, however, two notable League novels published after its dissolution. Though the first two volumes of Swiss international civil servant-turned-author Albert Cohen's Solal tetralogy (*Solal* (1930) and *Manceclous* (1938)) were published in the 1930s, his best-known work, *Belle du Seigneur*, appeared in 1968, long after the League's dissolution.[25] Protagonist Solal, who had already joined the League, is by the third volume Under-Secretary-General. He witnesses how the rise of fascism and antisemitism profoundly changes life in Europe. Solal, who is of Jewish descent, finally resigns, deeply wounded by the League's passivity. In *Belle de Seigneur*, the rapid decline and failure of the League is not caused merely by forces beyond its control, but also because the institution itself is defective and degenerate. This sharp portrayal of the League in Cohen's work must be seen as continuous with the pessimistic novels of the 1930s. This clearly reflects the disappointment of the first generation of international civil servants with the League of Nations.

Probably the most famous books on the League within the community of historians are the volumes of the 'Edith trilogy' by Australian author Frank Moorhouse, which feature the life of fictitious Australian League of Nations civil servant Edith Campbell Berry: *Grand Days* (1993), *Dark Palace* (2000) and *Cold Light* (2011).[26] One of the main reasons for their popularity among historians is their meticulous composition.[27] In the research for his books, Moorhouse not only talked to numerous contemporaries such as Canadian League of Nations civil servant Mary McGeachy, on whom Edith Campbell Berry is loosely modelled, but also worked in a multitude of archives and libraries around the world, including, of course, the League's archives in Geneva. The result is three extremely well-researched novels and, as Susan Pedersen puts it, "surely the only work of fiction to explain the League's filing system".[28]

The trilogy follows the life cycle of the League, from early optimism (*Grand Days*), to the gloomier days of fascism and nationalism (*Dark Palace*). In *Cold Light*, the seasoned League veteran Berry returns to Australia in the 1940s, where she supports the establishment of the Australian diplomatic service. Thus, Berry's experience with the League plays a key role in the process of Australia becoming an independent international actor. The publication of these three massive volumes, and the decoration of *Dark Palace* with one of Australia's most important literary awards, shows that the League of Nations still bears historical significance.

CONCLUSION

Novels were a medium through which broader discourses on the League penetrated everyday culture. At the beginning of the League's existence, most of these books are characterized not only by curiosity but by hope and belief in the world organisation. This changes profoundly over time. As many chapters in this volume confirm, the League of the 1920s differed distinctly from the League of the 1930s. The diplomatic crisis of the late 1920s and 1930s manifested itself in novels, as the League of Nations is increasingly portrayed as a helpless pawn in the hands of imperialistic and fascist powers.

Although literature has become very quiet on the League, Moorhouse's novels demonstrate the literary potency that the League setting still wields. The twenty-first-century demand for orientation in the face of international challenges has already stimulated the revival of the League as a scholarly topic. One can only hope that this will be followed by new novels, too.

NOTES

1 Gynt: 'Diplomaten, Delegierte, Sekretäre', 633-645.
2 Shaw: *Geneva*, 9-176.
3 Albeit there are a couple of notable exceptions that take the socio-cultural dimension of interwar internationalism seriously. See for example Brendenbach, Herzer and Tworek (eds): *International Organizations and the Media*; Scaglia: 'Branding Internationalism', 79-100.
4 Jucker-Fleetwood: 'The Per Jacobsson Literary Inheritance', 724-731.
5 Oldfeld: *The Death of a Diplomat*.
6 Its original title is *Das Geheimnis von Genf*.
7 Oldfeld: *The Alchemy Murder*.
8 Browne: *The Devil and the X.Y.Z.*
9 Beeding: *The Six Proud Walkers*.
10 'New Novels', *The Times Literary Supplement*, 11 October 1928, 730.
11 Beeding: *The One Sane Man*.
12 Personnel File – Alice Ritchie, *League of Nations Archive Geneva* (LoNA) S 867.
13 Ritchie: *The Peacemakers*.
14 Ranshofen-Wertheimer: *The International Secretariat*.
15 Ranshofen-Wertheimer: *The International Secretariat*, 409.
16 Baldi and Pasquale: *Through the Dipomatic Looking Glass*.
17 Macaulay: *Mystery at Geneva*.
18 Macaulay: *Mystery at Geneva*, 250.
19 Römhild: 'Mentally', 78.
20 Rouff: *Les Temps révolus*.
21 Glauser: *Der Tee der drei alten Damen*.
22 Habe: *Tödlicher Friede*.
23 Lycett: *Ian Fleming*, 35.
24 Fleming: *Goldfinger*, 230.
25 Cohen: *Le Belle du Seigneur*.
26 Moorhouse: *Grand Days*; Moorhouse: *Dark Palace*; Moorhouse: *Cold Light*.
27 For a genre discussion, see Murphy and Howe: 'Oral Sex and the League of Nations'.
28 Pedersen: 'Back to the League of Nations', 1115.

BIBLIOGRAPHY

Unpublished material

Personnel File – Alice Ritchie, *League of Nations Archive Geneva* (LoNA) S 867.

Published material

Baldi, Stefano and Pasquale Baldocci: *Through the Dipomatic Looking Glass*, Rome: Diplo Foundation, 2007.

Beeding, Francis: *The Six Proud Walkers*, London: Hodder & Stoughton, 1928.

Beeding, Francis: *The One Sane Man*, London: Hodder & Stoughton, 1934.

Brendenbach, Jonas, Martin Herzer and Heidi J.S. Tworek (eds): *International Organizations and the Media in the Nineteenth and Twentieth Centuries: Exorbitant Expectations*, New York: Routledge, 2018.

Browne, Barum: *The Devil and the X.Y.Z.*, New York: Victor Gollancz, 1931.

Cohen, Albert: *Le Belle du Seigneur*, Paris: Galimard, 1968.

Fleming, Ian: *Goldfinger*, London: Jonathan Cape, 1959.

Glauser, Friedrich: *Der Tee der drei alten Damen*, Zurich: Arche Verlag, 1996.

Gynt, Per: 'Diplomaten, Delegierte, Sekretäre: Querschnitt durch den Völkerbund', *Der Querschnitt* 9 (9), 1929, 633-645.

Habe, Hans: *Tödlicher Friede – ein Liebesroman mit politischem Hintergrund*, Zurich: Europa-Verlag Emil Oprecht, 1939.

Jucker-Fleetwood, Erin E.: 'The Per Jacobsson Literary Inheritance', *Kyklos* 19 (4), 1966, 724-731.

Lycett, Andrew: *Ian Fleming*, London: St. Martin's Press, 1995.

Macaulay, Rose: *Mystery at Geneva: An improbable tale of singular happenings*, London: Collins, 1922.

Moorhouse, Frank: *Grand Days*, Sydney: Picador, 1993.

Moorhouse, Frank: *Dark Palace*, Sydney: Knopf Australia, 2000.

Moorhouse, Frank: *Cold Light*, Sydney: Knopf Australia, 2012.

Murphy, Ffion and Renate Howe: 'Oral Sex and the League of Nations: The Genre of Faction in Grand Days and Dark Palace', *Journal of Australian Studies* 25 (71), 2009.

'New Novels', *The Times Literary Supplement*, 11 October 1928, 730.

Oldfeld, Peter: *The Death of a Diplomat*, London: Constable & Co, 1928.

Oldfeld, Peter: *The Alchemy Murder*, London: Constable & Co, 1929.

Pedersen, Susan: 'Back to the League of Nations', *The American Historical Review* 112 (4), 2007, 1091-1117.

Ranshofen-Wertheimer, Egon F.: *The International Secretariat: A Great Experiment in International Administration*, Washington: Carnegie, 1947.

Ritchie, Alice: *The Peacemakers*, London: Hogarth Press, 1928.

Römhild, Julia: 'Mentally Neutral – An Improbable Tale of Singular Happenings in Geneva'. In K. Macdonald (ed.): *Rose Macaulay – In Light of the Readers*, London: Taylor & Francis, 2017, 75-86.

Rouff, Marcel: *Les Temps révolus. Sur le quai Wilson*, Paris: Émile-Paul, 1926.

Scaglia, Ilaria: 'Branding Internationalism: Displaying Art and International Cooperation in the Interwar Period'. In C. Viktorin, J.C.E. Gienow-Hecht, M. Will and A. Estner (eds): *Nation Branding in Modern History*, New York: Berghahn, 2018, 79-100.

Shaw, George B.: 'Geneva. Another Political Extravaganza'. In *The Bodley Head Bernard Shaw Collected Plays with their Prefaces*, London: Max Reinhardt, 1947, 9-176.

Paul Reef

IMAGINING THE LEAGUE OF NATIONS

Cartoons as a Prism for Perceptions of International Politics and Organisations

Like the European Union or the United Nations today, the League of Nations frequently found itself satirised or criticised for its actions – or lack thereof – in international politics, the difference being that the League was the first international organisation set up to govern, as well as maintain peace and collective security globally. How did contemporaries narrate this new actor on the international stage, or frame a League in crisis in the 1930s? This chapter explores these contemporary frames and narratives as a prism for understanding representations of the League and perceptions of the international system across borders.

This chapter applies a new cultural lens to uncover contemporary perceptions and feelings regarding the League based on circa 150 British, French, Dutch and German political cartoons. Recently, historians have begun to examine how the League itself perceived and attempted to influence public opinion.[1] However, the media history and perceptions of the League beyond Geneva remain rich yet relatively uncharted territories.[2] This chapter analyses two dominant transnational and national frames: that of a new actor in the 1920s and that of failure in the 1930s. It argues that there are striking cross-border commonalities in how the League was framed as being at odds with the traditional diplomatic system: initially positively as a female embodiment of peace and justice, but later as powerless bureaucrats amidst political crisis.

Different national perspectives display the surprisingly gendered and emotional ways in which contemporaries tried to make sense of interwar international relations.[3]

AT THE ACADEMY OF NATIONS.
THE LEAGUE. "AND TO THINK THAT I ONCE POSED FOR THAT!"

AN INSIGHTFUL SOURCE

Following the 'cultural turn', historians have discovered the value of cartoons for analysing contemporary perceptions of a variety of topics, but international organisations remain underexplored.[4] As a source, they can provide insights into contemporary attitudes, values and emotions regarding an issue in ways written sources cannot. This is because cartoons metaphorically and emotionally frame complex events or issues in a comprehensible narrative that newspaper readers can apprehend in one glance. Cartoonists embed their drawings in existing visual and semiotic repertoires, using concepts and narratives that resonate with readers' knowledge of politics. Thus, cartoons provide a particularly intriguing angle for discovering how contemporaries made sense of, and, crucially, *felt* about issues ranging from corruption and elections to gender and international relations.[5]

Strong framing is part and parcel of cartoons. Cartoons tend to portray issues either very negatively or very positively in order to ensure that their arguments are quickly grasped.[6] However, in doing so they also engender a biased sample of perceptions and feelings. After all, they lend themselves more to satirical criticism and negative emotions, rather than happiness or praise, and moreover tend only to cover issues that are hotly discussed in politics and society. Nevertheless, because of these strong frames, cartoons can reveal how cartoonists in different countries sought to contrast a novel, idealist League of Nations with traditional power politics.

NARRATIVES FROM THE 1920S: A NEW ACTRESS ON THE INTERNATIONAL STAGE

Continuing a nineteenth-century tradition, most cartoonists tried to characterise the League as a novel diplomatic actor within their existing semiotic repertoire of national personifications or allegories to represent international politics.[7] Cartoonists predominantly represented the League as Lady Justice, a positive female embodiment of international peace and order.[8] German cartoonists also depicted it as such, but more frequently opted for the French Marianne, in order to frame the League as an explicitly French and Allied extension of the *Versailles Diktat*.

The symbolical representation of the League as a female harbinger of peace and justice *vis-à-vis* cynical diplomats demonstrates that cartoonists perceived it as an idealist force in international politics. Representations of the League as a female judge further underline how the League became enmeshed with idealist conceptions of international law ending war. This becomes especially clear when 'she' becomes a focal point of fears of failure and broken promises towards the late 1920s.

The framing of the League's female personification gives insight into the perception of it as an actor. Three frames or metaphors are recurrent transnationally. First is that of the strong and powerful Lady Justice or Peace who, despite hardships, is depicted as an independent actor working for the common good. The second metaphor is that of the schoolteacher, judge or disciplining mother. British and French cartoons – but tellingly no German ones – showed the League as an impartial arbiter disciplining unruly boys, representing the revanchist powers of Europe.[9] Conversely, cartoons from after the Sino-Japanese conflict of 1932 portray the League as failing in disciplining China and Japan. The third variety presents the League as a weak-willed woman who is dependent on male Great Powers. It depicts a tarnished and

At the 'Academy of Nations', the lofty ideal of the League as a fair arbiter between nations had begun to disintegrate by 1936. This cartoon visualises a narrative of failure with a 'fallen' woman longing for her former standing and beauty. However, this popular narrative remains silent about how many internationalists and governments continued to support the League. Behind the scenes, League-led global humanitarian and technical efforts continued until 1946.

weak Lady Justice, at times beleaguered in court, a sick or dead League or, in one extreme case, a woman about to be violated by Mussolini. However, these cartoons do not blame 'her', but rather the male politicians who failed the League.

When cartoonists sought to represent international politics revolving around Geneva, they were more inclined to draw male protagonists rather than an independently acting 'Lady League'. Several cartoons even personify the League as a man, although a rather unmanly one. It is a weak man incapable of action, or an overburdened bureaucrat or judge losing control. Tellingly, it is often German cartoonists that use such male personifications.

These representations of the League are clearly connected to the wider historical context. It is no coincidence that the League was frequently personified as a woman. Like the League, women were new on the 'public stage' in an era of women's rights, suffrage and an increased female presence in society and politics following the war. Furthermore, the League's covenant enshrined gender equality and it could count on massive support by women's organisations from all over the world.[10] After the economic crash of 1929 and the ensuing political crises, the League was increasingly represented as a weak woman or a frail old man, both standing no chance against national, masculine figures. These changed gendered frames are imbued with fascist and authoritarian idealisations of virile manliness and actions versus lazy deliberation and pacifist idealism.[11] Cartoons about the League thus became a canvas for all sorts of criticisms of the weak-willed liberal-democratic Versailles order and the lost ideals of the early 1920s.

Drawn a few days after the remilitarisation of the Rhineland, this cartoon signals the literal defeat of League-orchestrated arbitration. On a deeper level, it connects the League to a broader liberal-democratic internationalist cosmos. Plans for a new *Palais des Nations* are enmeshed with the existing Peace Palace and Permanent Court of International Justice in The Hague. Moreover, Lady Justice represents a post-war order of law and compromise rather than the virile right of the strongest.

A LEAGUE UNDER FIRE: CRISIS AND FAILURE IN THE 1930s

In a wider context of international tensions, it is striking how often the League was not the centerpiece of attention, but rather a stage for others to make politics. In the 1920s, criticism was focused on a League that favoured the Great Powers, particularly France and Great Britain. German artists chose French and British caricatures to represent the

League, but British and French cartoonists were not blind to the entanglement of their national interests with those of the League either.

After 1930, however, the common depiction of the League in international relations was that of a mere material stage for the Great Powers, foregrounding the League's impotence.[12] Moreover, the identification of the Geneva system with the Versailles order became a recurrent theme, particularly for cartoonists who criticised those who failed to uphold it. For example, British and Dutch cartoonists drew Mussolini and Hitler undermining the League, while the Allied powers stood by, passively. In a way, these cartoons represent contemporary perceptions of a return to the 'Old Diplomacy' of *Realpolitik* and bilateralism, bypassing Geneva.[13]

SQUABBLING DIPLOMATS AND APATHETIC TECHNOCRATS

Another common transnational frame represents the League mimetically, as a congregation of white, male diplomats in tailored suits. Ironically, this mode of representation is one of the most scathing cartoon comments on the League's functioning. A general theme of such 'realist' depictions is that of a League being 'all talk and no action': a group of generic diplomats endlessly discussing disarmament, yet nothing comes of it. It is a critique both of a new, technocratic order *and* of a return to an old order of selfish national prerogatives that paralysed the League.

It is salient that criticisms of the League as an ineffective gentleman's club were made by cartoonists working for German national socialist magazines as well as Dutch and British liberal outlets. Even a liberal and staunch anti-Nazi cartoonist like Erich Schairer negatively portrayed the Geneva organisation as aged technocrats who continue their work obnoxiously while war rages in China. This is a multifaceted critique of the League that appeals to a demand for strong, personal action in a context of indecisive, flaky liberal democracies versus the allure of decisive and manly authoritarianism – a demand visible in Weimar Germany, but also the Netherlands.[14] Beyond these transnational commonalities, there are clear national differences in narratives of a League in crisis during the 1930s.

France's waning influence in Europe fuelled its frustration over a prostrated League. After 1918, the French forged alliances with the new democratic states of Central Europe to contain German revanchism beyond League multilateralism. However, by the 1930s, most of these states had become autocracies. An increasingly isolated France feared that rapprochement with the growing power of neighbouring Germany and Italy would be far more alluring for these states than French promises of military support.

A LEAGUE IN DESPAIR: FRENCH AND GERMAN PERSPECTIVES

In France, the unravelling of the Versailles order caused security fears.[15] Whereas German cartoons identified Geneva with Marianne, French cartoonists portrayed either a cold and distant League or an organisation begging an isolated France for help. Frequently, caricatures oozed both despair and fear over the fact that France stood alone in upholding the Treaty of Versailles. One cartoon shows a fearful Marianne begging a condescending, dark-clad and indifferent League to impose sanctions,

while Britain's John Bull remains aloof.

German cartoonists, on the other hand, almost gleefully portrayed a France in despair. One cartoon depicts Marianne glaring at a smug-looking German diplomat leaving the Palais des Nations while she mutters "Outrageous, even though I have promised him contractual disarmament for over fourteen years, he still does not want to believe it!" – a cynical jab at France's extreme reluctance either to disarm or to allow German rearmament. Recurrently, cartoons highlighted French and English frustration and anxiety over Germany no longer abiding by the rules of Versailles.[16]

The League forms a focal point for pride or joy in Germany regaining equality outside of the Geneva system. One cartoon in the national socialist *Die Brennessel* nearly mimetically represents the League as condescending diplomats who had chained Germany to a torture chair. Poignantly, they act surprised when their 'equal' breaks free from the chains of Versailles. There are clear continuities in German cartoonists' criticisms of the League and its relation to Allied interests in strongly emotional frames. The openly hostile and at times martial frames in which the liberal Versailles order is shown under fire, however, constitute a new development from the failed World Disarmament Conference of 1932-34 and the shift to Nazi rule onwards.[17]

SMALL STATE AND IDEALIST PERCEPTIONS

Dutch and British cartoons evoked rather different emotions. Paradoxically, several Dutch cartoonists criticised the League's response – or rather, the lack thereof – to crisis by portraying it as *emotionless*, represented by apathetic diplomats. Although French cartoonists also depict the League as an indifferent diplomat, this specific and recurrent representation of a League machinery apathetic to the atrocities and plights of 'lesser' powers can be regarded as a specific 'small state' perspective on the international system of the 1930s. Furthermore, cartoons about the organisation's precarious position in defending smaller states from belligerent powers invoke strong emotions. Often, a fearful Lady League sees herself confronted with or humiliated by menacing-looking Japanese, or Mussolini, usually reinforced with a light-dark contrast.[18]

British cartoonists likewise employ the frame of humiliation, but also that of regret, to represent the failures of League idealism. Time and again the League was portrayed as a dejected, timid and badly-dressed woman who stands alone, abandoned by politicians. The New Zealand-born cartoonist David Low in particular used his cartoons to frame the betrayal or failure of internationalism and idealism. His drawings convey a deep sense of regret, showing politicians visiting Lady League's sickbed or even grave after having failed to support her.

In the 1930s, earlier caricatures of 'egghead' League intellectuals morphed into a broader critique of liberal compromise and multilateralism. This was not unique to the inter-war years: by their nature, international organisations are paradoxical creatures. On the one hand, their technocratic nature makes them prone to criticism for lacking political legitimacy. On the other, it is precisely this self-effacing, apolitical expertise that lends them the legitimacy to tackle cross-border issues.

However, following the League's failures in the face of Italian, German and Japanese aggression, as well as in coordinating an international response to the economic crisis, Low's idealist perspective on the League as a beacon of internationalism had become an outlier during the 1930s.[19] Whether positively or negatively, the League came to signify the failure of international co-operation in the face of nationalism and revanchism, although often the Great Powers rather than the League itself were blamed. The League's subsequent shift towards social, economic and technical work was not lauded – on the contrary, cartoonists vehemently criticised the technocratic nature of the organisation, and its failure to take, let alone defend, a political stance.[20] These narratives

of failure not only had an impact on the international role the League could or still wanted to play in the 1930s, but moreover cast their shadow on its legacy for decades to come.[21]

CONCLUSION

Cartoons provide a prism for studying how contemporaries tried to interpret the League's role within the interwar international system. The League was invariably depicted as being out of touch with the traditional diplomacy of Great Powers and *Realpolitik*, either because of its apparent failure to deal with them in the 1930s or because of its idealism.

Intriguingly, cartoonists from different countries used a very gendered and emotional semiotic reservoir to represent the League and international politics, which *inter alia* overlaps and collides with contemporary perceptions of masculine, authoritarian leadership.

This survey of the specific ways in which international organisations are narrated and framed in cartoons hopes to inspire further research into how narratives of IOs are articulated. In particular, it investigates to what extent these narratives discursively co-construct the actual space within which international organisations had to pursue policies and legitimise themselves, as well as deal with rival organisations and reluctant member states. How did the articulations of these images and narratives shape the self-perceptions of international organisations, as well as limit and shape what they could do on the international stage?

NOTES

1 Akami: 'Peace Propaganda'; Wertheim: 'Public Opinion'.
2 Tworek: 'Peace'; Holste: 'Tourists'.
3 Finney: 'Narratives and Bodies', 621.
4 E.g. Leenders and Gijsenbergh: 'Public Visualization'; Jones: *Europa*; cf. Gilmartin and Brunn: 'Representation'.
5 Palmeri: 'The Image'; Greenberg: 'Framing'; Kemnitz: 'The Cartoon'.
6 Bush: 'Rhetorical Constructs', 68-70.
7 Kemnitz: 'The Cartoon', 83-84; Williams: 'The Shadow'.
8 Wertheim: 'International Law'.
9 Wertheim: 'International Law'.
10 Sluga: 'Women', 67-75.
11 Föllmer: 'Führung'.
12 Carr: *Twenty Years' Crisis*.
13 Mazower: *Governing the World*, 116-128, 141-142.
14 Gijsenbergh and Kaal: 'Kritiek'; Gijsenbergh: 'Complaints'.
15 Steiner: *International History*, 610.
16 Steiner: *International History*, 755-796.
17 Mazower: *Dark Continent*, 84-86; Mazower: *Governing the World*, 180-187.
18 Van Diepen: *Volkenbond*, 193-240.
19 Sluga: *Internationalism*, 74-78.
20 Clavin: *Securing*, 124-128, 162-172.
21 Pedersen: 'Back to'.

BIBLIOGRAPHY

Akami, Tomoko: 'The Limits of Peace Propaganda. The Information Section of the League of Nations and its Tokyo Office'. In Jonas Brendebach, Martin Herzer and Heidi Tworek (eds): *International Organizations and the Media in the Nineteenth and Twentieth Centuries. Exorbitant Expectations*, New York: Routledge, 2018, 70-90.

Bush, Larry: 'More than Words: Rhetorical Constructs in American Political Cartoons', *Studies in American Humor* 3 (27), 2013, 63-91.

Carr, E.H.: *The Twenty Years' Crisis 1919-1939*, London: Macmillan, 1939.

Clavin, Patricia: *Securing the World Economy. The Reinvention of the League of Nations, 1920-1946*, Oxford: Oxford University Press, 2013.

Diepen, Remco van: *Voor Volkenbond en vrede. Nederland en het streven naar een nieuwe wereldorde 1919-1946*, Amsterdam: Prometheus, 1999.

Finney, Patrick: 'Narratives and Bodies: Culture Beyond the Cultural Turn', *The International History Review* 40 (3), 2018, 609-630.

Föllmer, Moritz: 'Führung und Demokratie in Europa'. In Tim B. Müller and Adam Tooze (eds): *Normalität und Fragilität. Demokratie nach dem Ersten Weltkrieg*, Hamburg: Hamburger Edition, 2015, 177-197.

Gijsenbergh, Joris: 'Contrasting Complaints about Parliamentarism in Western Europe (1918-1939)'. In Kari Palonen and José María Rosales (eds): *Parliamentarism and Democratic Theory: Historical and Contemporary Perspectives*, Opladen, Berlin, and Toronto: Verlag Barbara Budrich, 2015, 117-139.

Gilmartin, Patricia and Stanley D. Brunn: 'The Representation of Women in Political Cartoons of the 1995 World Conference on Women', *Women's Studies International Forum* 21 (5), 1998, 535-549.

Greenberg, Josh: 'Framing and Temporality in Political Cartoons: A Critical Analysis of Visual News Discourse', *Canadian Review of Sociology* 39 (2), 2002, 181-198.

Holste, Timo: 'Tourists at the League of Nations. Conceptions of Internationalism around the Palais des Nations, 1925-1946', *New Global Studies* 10 (3), 2016, 307-344.

Jones, Priska: *Europa in der Karikatur. Deutsche und britische Darstellungen im 20. Jahrhundert*, Frankfurt am Main: Campus Verlag, 2009.

Kemnitz, Thomas M.: 'The Cartoon as Historical Source', *The Journal of Interdisciplinary History* 4 (1), 1973, 81-93.

Leenders, Marij and Joris Gijsenbergh: 'The Image of Prime Minister Colijn: Public Visualization of Political Leadership in the 1930s'. In Harm Kaal and Daniëlle Slootjes (eds): *Repertoires of Representation: New Perspectives on Power from Ancient History to Present Day*, Brill: Leiden, in press 2019.

Mazower, Mark: *Dark Continent. Europe's Twentieth Century*, London: Penguin Press, 1999.

Mazower, Mark: *Governing the World. The History of an Idea*, London: Penguin Press, 2012.

Palmeri, Frank: 'The Cartoon: The Image as Critique'. In Sarah Barber and Corinne M. Pennist-Bird (eds): *History Beyond the Text. A Student's Guide to Approaching Alternative Sources*, London and New York: Routledge, 2009, 70-98.

Pedersen, Susan: 'Back to the League of Nations', *The American Historical Review* 112 (4), 2007, 1091-1117.

Sluga, Glenda: *Internationalism in the Age of Nationalism*, Philadelphia: University of Pennsylvania Press, 2015.

Sluga, Glenda: 'Women, Feminisms and Twentieth-Century Internationalisms'. In Glenda Sluga and Patricia Clavin (eds): *Internationalisms. A Twentieth-Century History*, Cambridge: Cambridge University Press, 2016, 61-84.

Steiner, Zara: *The Lights that Failed. European International History 1919-1933*, Oxford: Oxford University Press, 2005.

Tworek, Heidi: 'Peace through Truth? The Press and Moral Disarmament through the League of Nations', *Medien & Zeit* 25 (4), 2010, 16-28.

Wertheim, Stephan: 'Reading the International Mind: International Public Opinion in Early Twentieth Century Anglo-American Thought'. In Nicolas Guilhot and Daniel Bessner (eds): *The Decisionist Imagination: Sovereignty, Social Science and Democracy in the Twentieth Century*, New York: Berghahn, 2019, 27-63.

Wertheim, Stephan: 'The League of Nations: A Retreat from International Law?', *Journal of Global History* 7, 2012, 210-232.

Williams, Chris: '"The Shadow in the East": Representations of the Russo-Japanese War in Newspaper Cartoons', *Media History* 23 (3/4), 2017, 312-329.

Karen Gram-Skjoldager

'A GREAT EXPERIMENT'

Professional Self-Perceptions and Working Conditions in the Secretariat

In April 1945, just as the war was drawing to a close, a hefty 500-page volume called *The League of Nations Secretariat – a Great Experiment in International Administration* was published by the Carnegie Endowment for International Peace.[1] The book was written by the former League official Egon Ranshofen-Wertheimer and was based on a combination of conventional historical research and his own extensive personal experiences from the Secretariat's Information (1930-1933), Economic and Financial (1933-1934) and Social Questions and Opium Traffic (1934-1940) Sections. To this day, Ranshofen-Wertheimer's book remains the most comprehensive and authoritative work on the League of Nations Secretariat.

The subtitle of the book is noteworthy. Ranshofen-Wertheimer's description of the Secretariat as "a great experiment" spoke to a widespread understanding of the Secretariat's institutional nature among former League officials. As Ranshofen-Wertheimer noted, one of the Secretariat's defining features was that it had no clear institutional precedents and experiences to draw on. With the creation of the League, the very concept of an international civil service with a multinational staff that held undivided loyalty to an international organisation saw the light of day for the first time. As Ranshofen-Wertheimer pointed out, the first Secretary-General, Sir Eric Drummond, embarked on "a uniquely adventurous journey into unexplored territory [...] with no familiar landmarks, mapped charts of itineraries to direct the traveller".[2]

In embarking on this journey, he was not able to garner much help from the political leaders who created the League. Lacking any clear vision of the actual scope and tasks that the new Secretariat was to cover, they had left the institutional design of the Secretariat to him; during the interwar years, the Secretariat continuously lacked clearly defined directions from the League's policy-making organs. As the former Director of the Information Section Adrianus Pelt noted, "The League, taken as a political entity, was in itself such an experiment that the Council and the Assembly hardly ever found themselves capable of giving clear directives to the Secretary-General."[3] In combination with Drummond's personal preference for pragmatism and improvisation,[4] this made the Secretariat a peculiarly agile and dynamic bureaucratic organisation that grew and changed as new and different tasks fell to it throughout the interwar years. In this chapter, we will take a look at the professional self-perception that characterised the Secretariat and consider the material consequences of working for an organisation that never stood still.

BUREAUCRATIC ADVENTURERS

When Ranshofen-Wertheimer and other former League officials reflected back on their experiences in the Secretariat, the trope of the 'Secretariat as experiment' was usually embedded in a larger narrative of adventure and internationalist heroism. When former League officials, including Ranshofen-Wertheimer, gathered in 1943 to discuss their experiences and reflect on the possible lessons that could be learned from them, the early Secretariat leadership was cast as a "a group of lay missionaries of a forward idea"[5] who had "joined in a spirit of adventure [...] attracted as they were by the political philosophy of the Covenant".[6]

Part of the adventure, according to the former League officials, was being extremely busy. Raymond B. Fosdick, who was Under Secretary-General for a brief stint during the Secretariat's first months of existence, thus noted how the early staff "worked with feverish haste, trying to organize the Secretariat".[7] Eleven years later, when the

Secretariat's original staff of three people had expanded to almost 700, the pace, apparently, was still the same. In the opening paragraph of his book, Ranshofen-Wertheimer vividly describes his first day in the Secretariat in 1930:

> Hardly had I set foot in the office on the third floor of the old Palais des Nations [Palais Wilson] on an unforgettable May day in 1930 when a flood of files and mimeographed papers arrived, as if by magic, on a tray reserved for "incoming mail and documents." The reflection of the early afternoon sun in Lake Geneva in front of my office filled my room with a light that was painful in its intensity. I sat down at the supersized desk which indicated that I had been appointed to an important post. Before I had time to recover my breath the telephone began to ring. I was caught in a machine which did not release me until I left the Secretariat exactly ten years later.[8]

However, there was also a material, practical side to the Secretariat's improvised nature that these writers rarely touched upon: the crowded and insufficient working conditions that the majority of the staff worked under as they tried to keep up with the unpredictable and expanding demands for their services. Thus, when Ranshofen-Wertheimer noted how he was seated at a "supersized desk" overlooking Lake Geneva it was a rare exception that reflected his high-ranking position as a member of the First Division in the prestigious Information Section. For most of the League's staff, daily working life was a lot less glamorous. It is to this material side of the 'great experiment' that we now turn.

DR. LÉON WEBER-BAULER'S REPORT

When tourists visit Geneva today, many go to see the Palais des Nations. The former headquarters of the League of Nations is a stunning construction that sits on the outskirts of the city, in Ariana Park, with beautiful views of Lake Geneva and the French Alps. The Palais was the first major purpose-built headquarters of an international organisation, and at the time of its creation, the second-largest building in Europe, superseded only by Versailles.[9]

The Palais Wilson was originally designed as a luxury hotel by Genevan architect Jacques-Elisée Goss (1839-1921). However, constructing a large building on the unstable terrain of the embankment proved extremely costly and the hotel went bankrupt just two years after it opened, in 1877. When Drummond acquired the building, a hotel magnate from the Côte d'Azur had begun renovating the derelict construction and his architects were now put in charge of transforming the hotel into an office building.

However, the construction of the Palais des Nations was not completed until 1936. Throughout the League's rapid expansion in the 1920s, the Secretariat held much more modest quarters in the former Hôtel National in the northern part of Geneva. Constructed in 1873-1875, this five-storey, 225-room hotel by the lake was essentially the only building in Geneva big enough to accommodate the new international organisation. The old hotel – renamed Palais Wilson in 1924 – was not particularly well-suited for administrative functions to begin with, and as the League's work picked up pace, the leadership of the Secretariat tried to fit the growing number of staff, meetings and conferences into the impracticable building, as well as a number of improvised extensions and private homes around the old hotel. In February 1930, six months before Ranshofen-Wertheimer took a seat behind his supersized desk, the League's medical adviser, Dr. Léon Weber-Bauler, inspected the building. His report allows a rare glimpse into the material realities of working in the Secretariat at its pinnacle, just before the world economic crisis and the political disintegration of the 1930s hit.[10]

The interior of the Palais Wilson today. After the 1992 Earth Summit in Rio de Janeiro, the Swiss Federal Council bought the building as part of Switzerland's (unsuccessful) bid to host the world's main environmental organisations under one roof. Rather than renovate the building, it was decided that it should be restored to its old splendour as a luxury hotel in 1875. In the picture we see the original main staircase with its skylight, recreated flower-stencilled walls, and light fixtures reproduced based on old images.

A TOUR OF PALAIS WILSON

If we were to follow in the footsteps of Dr. Weber-Bauler, we would enter the Palais Wilson through the lobby on the ground floor and start by ascending to the offices on the first to third floors at the front of the main building, facing Lake Geneva. These offices were the old hotel's most luxurious rooms. They were spacious and well-lit with sinks and lavatories, as well as soundproof double doors. Nearly all rooms had fireplaces, which provided ventilation. These hotel rooms-turned-offices were occupied by higher League officials, such as Ranshofen-Wertheimer, and their clerical staff.

However, even here, in the spacious quarters of the highest echelons of the League, it was apparent that the old hotel was short on space. On the first floor, for instance, a little closet by the service lift was occupied by two short-hand typists, and in the lobby the main switchboard had been fitted into a small room at the end of a narrow, wooden spiral staircase. Dr. Weber-Bauler describes how "in this low, cramped, gloomy and ill ventilated inferno they do work which is both physical and mental in a manner that astounds the visitor", reminding the reader that "[s]uch psycho-physical acrobatics should be performed in an airy, well-lit and spacious room".

In the wings of the Palais, the rooms were still of decent quality, but smaller, darker and sometimes overcrowded. Officials in the Health and Information Section in particular occupied "very small rooms in which nearly all the space is taken up by tables, cupboards and shelves".

However, this was nothing compared to the offices in the attics. Here rooms were very small, badly lit and so overcrowded that in one of them staff "can hardly find room for their work-tables". The rooms were accessed by a wooden staircase, which was also the only escape route in case of a fire, and they were positioned directly under a zinc roof, making them "excessively hot" during summer and cold during winter. Working here could be downright dangerous. One room faced "a chimney one meter away from the window, and the kitchen chimney sends its combustion gases into the room when the windows are open". Because of this, one former employee, according to Weber-Bauler, "developed specific anaemia, probably due to chronic carbon monoxide poisoning".

Weber-Bauler also inspected the basement, which he deemed even more unsafe than the attic. It was occupied by the kitchen, a restaurant, a library, a warehouse for documents, the dispatch service and a storeroom.

> Incongruently, an engine-room with its stocks of wood and coal, placed in the middle of the passage, spreads heat, dust and noxious gases all around [...]. Its gaping boilers belch forth the gases from the clinkers taken out of its furnaces, straight into the main corridor on which all the rooms already mentioned open, including the restaurant!

The room where documents for the storeroom were received was particularly badly hit by the fumes from the engine room, while in the library storeroom "fumes, probably from the sewers, fill this cellar with odours which are sometimes unbearable to those who work there". With few offices in the basement having windows, it resembled, according to

Weber-Bauler, the inside of "an ill-designed and ill-constructed ship; it is the worst place of the whole building".

Odours were also an issue on the mezzanine that was attached to the back of the Palais, home to the League's verbatim reporters. Here rooms were not only small and crowded – during Assemblies five people were working in each room – but the lavatories were also poorly ventilated, allowing unpleasant smells to filter into the corridors.

If we were to leave the Palais Wilson and walk through the garden, away from the lake and through the streets behind the former hotel, we would encounter four different buildings that served as extra League office sites. One building, in the Rue des Paquis, just opposite the Palais, was in good condition with light and spacious rooms. The same could not be said for an apartment building in Rue Rothschild, where the League's typing pool was located. A cheap house built for small families of modest means, the rooms here were small and dark and most of them were overcrowded and noisy. Working conditions for most of the typists there were "by no means satisfactory", Weber-Bauler dryly observed.

The last two houses inhabited by the League were two villas accommodating the internal, administrative services of the Secretariat. In one of them, the head of the services, H.R. Huston, and his three assistants had decent offices with good lighting. However, the adjacent offices were crowded, holding up to 12 persons, with the air unbearably thick with cigarette smoke. Both villas were rundown and in critical need of repair. The villa that accommodated Huston and his staff was a "dilapidated building, the ground floor of which has never been repaired, and which still has wallpaper and paint dating from the middle of the last century; it is quite impossible to keep the place clean".

What Weber-Bauler saw, in other words, was an organisation bursting at its seams. While the higher officials and their staff were housed under decent conditions, chiefly in the front of the main building, almost all other members of staff had been squeezed into insufficient office spaces at the margins of the main building or in cheap, run-down buildings in nearby streets. The staff of the middle and lower grades, situated in the wings of the old hotel building and in the apartment building in Rue Rothschild, worked in poor conditions, while staff of

similar rank in the villas, the attics and the basement of the main building were working under downright unhygienic and dangerous circumstances.

FROM PALAIS WILSON TO THE PALAIS DES NATIONS

Dr. Weber-Bauler was preaching to the converted: by 1926, the League Assembly had decided that new headquarters were needed. However, due to problems with the Swiss planning authorities and disagreements about who should design the new building, it took a full ten years before the new Palais des Nations was completed.[11]

It is one of the many ironies of the League of Nations that by the time the new, spacious Palais des Nations was finished, it was not really needed. Due to the global economic crisis and increasing political tensions, funding for the League diminished throughout the 1930s; by the end of the decade, the staff had been reduced to around 400. During the Second World War only around 100 people inhabited the enormous new building. However, after the Second World War the Palais des Nations re-emerged as the busy international hub it had been designed to be, as it became home to the UN's European office. Today it is the second largest of the four UN office sites with 1600 employees, 8000 annual meetings, many conferences and events and 100,000 visitors.[12]

Today the Palais des Nations is home to the UN's European office. The buildings are open to visitors, who can get a brief glimpse of what goes on behind the scenes at one the largest organisations in the world. Tours are conducted in 12 different languages and each year 120,000 tourists, students and schoolchildren visit the Human Rights Room, the Salle des Pas Perdus, the Assembly Hall and the Council Chamber.

The Palais Wilson itself has also made a comeback as an international organisation headquarters. In the decades after the League moved out, the old building fell into serious disrepair; after two fires in the mid-1980s, the Swiss authorities decided to restore it and once again turn it into the headquarters of an international organisation. After its renovation, the building was made available at a preferential rent to the UN and today it is home to the Office of the High Commissioner for Human Rights (OHCHR). It is another small irony that the staff of the OHCHR soon outgrew the Palais Wilson, so that today some of its 700 employees are housed in the Palais des Nations.[13] Apparently, even after 100 years of experience, international administration is still a volatile profession that is difficult to predict and plan.

CONCLUSION

When former League officials looked back on their work in Geneva, they often called it 'a great experiment'. As this article has shown, there was much truth to this characterisation. Due to the lack of institutional precedents to build on and the absence of clear political directions from the League's governing bodies, the Secretariat became a peculiarly agile and dynamic bureaucratic organisation. While former League officials liked to frame their work as a heroic internationalist enterprise, this chapter has pointed to the harsh material consequences of working for an organisation that was continuously understaffed and overburdened with ever-expanding and changing tasks on a shoestring budget.

NOTES

1 Ranshofen-Wertheimer: *The International Secretariat*.

2 Ranshofen-Wertheimer: *The International Secretariat*, 81; cf. also Pelt: 'Peculiar Characteristics', 108-114.

3 Pelt: 'Peculiar Characteristics', 109.

4 Ranshofen-Wertheimer: *The International Secretariat*, 81; Pelt: 'Peculiar Characteristics', 109.

5 Carnegie Endowment for International Peace (CEIP): Uncensored transcript of *Proceedings*.

6 CEIP, Uncensored transcript of *Proceedings*; for more on these discussions, see Auberer: 'Digesting the League of Nations'.

7 Fosdick: *The League*, 23-24 (quotation on 24).

8 Ranshofen Wertheimer: *The International Secretariat*, ix.

9 Seán Lesters' Papers, 'The League Building', Information Section, March 1937.

10 Commission 13: 'Report by the Medical Adviser on the Hygienic Conditions of Work in the Secretariat of the League of Nations', signed L. Weber-Bauler, 14 February 1930. Unless otherwise indicated, the following paragraphs are based on this report.

11 See Marco Ninno's contribution to this volume.

12 http://www.geneve-int.ch/en/palace-nations-monument-peace (07.10.2018), http://www.un.org/en/sections/resources/visitors/ (07.10.2018).

13 http://www.geneve-int.ch/palais-wilson-memory-and-hostage-geneva (07.10.2018); http://www.ohchr.org/EN/ABOUTUS/Pages/Headquarters.aspx (07.10.2018).

BIBLIOGRAPHY

Unpublished material

Columbia Rare Books and Manuscripts. Carnegie Endowment for International Peace – New York and Washington Offices Records, 1910-1954 – Division of International Law - Series V. Conferences and Institutes – Box 210-211: Uncensored transcript of *Proceedings of the Conference on Experience in International Administration Held at Washington on January 30, 1943, under the Auspices of the Carnegie Endowment for International Peace*, Washington: Carnegie Endowment for International Peace, 1943.

League of Nations Archives, Geneva: Commission of 13, 1930, Com. 13/16-32: 'Report by the Medical Adviser on the Hygienic Conditions of Work in the Secretariat of the League of Nations', signed L. Weber-Bauler, 14 February 1930.

University College Dublin: Seán Lester's Papers, folder 203/67: 'The League Building', Information Section, March 1937.

Published material

Auberer, Benjamin: 'Digesting the League of Nations: Planning the International Secretariat of the Future, 1941-1944', *New Global Studies* 10 (3), 2016, 393-426.

Fosdick, Raymond B.: *The League and the United Nations after Fifty Years*, Newtown, Connecticut, published by the author, 1972.

Pelt, Adrianus: 'Peculiar Characteristics of an International Administration', *Public Administration Review* 6 (2), 1946, 108-114.

Ranshofen-Wertheimer, Egon F.: *The International Secretariat. A Great Experiment in International Administration*, Washington: Carnegie Endowment for International Peace, 1945.

Online sources

http://www.geneve-int.ch/en/palace-nations-monument-peace (07.10.2018).

http://www.un.org/en/sections/resources/visitors/ (07.10.2018).

http://www.geneve-int.ch/palais-wilson-memory-and-hostage-geneva (07.10.2018).

http://www.ohchr.org/EN/ABOUTUS/Pages/Headquarters.aspx (07.10.2018).

Marco Ninno

A MODERNIST IN GENEVA

Le Corbusier and the Competition for the Palais des Nations

This chapter will investigate the construction of the headquarters of the League of Nations – the *Palais des Nations* in Geneva. Is it a valuable prism through which to examine the complex bureaucracy of the League, or to understand its desire to express the new model of peaceful international collaboration? Having disclosed an intriguing and little-known story of the involvement of the notorious architect Le Corbusier, can we detect a more 'classic', Eurocentric view on architecture prevailing over a contemporary one? Did an older style of secret diplomacy prevail in the new model of international relations that the League was supposed to represent in the twentieth century?

As we will see, Le Corbusier was de facto the victim of a double snub. First, the hard-core modernist was weeded out in the prestigious architect competition the League arranged, as the competition jury emphasised the traditional traits of a palace structure.

Second, after a compelled reopening of the competition – following a major debacle about the building site – Le Corbusier was cheated again. The jury's preferred project had been inspired by Le Corbusier's drawings to a suspicious degree. As with so many other aspects of the League, however, the story continued into the postwar years, as Le Corbusier became one of the key architects behind the new United Nations building in New York.

Acknowledging the scarcity of secondary sources on this subject, this article will make use of the existent Italian and French literature – in translations that are entirely mine – upheld by extensive use of primary sources from the Archives of the League of Nations.

THE IMPORTANCE OF SEMANTICS

Since the time of the Roman emperors, the term 'palace' has been used to indicate the physical seat of power. As is often the case in Western history, the proclaimed greatness of the Roman Empire inspired subsequent societies, and the term *palatium*, or palace, never lost its ideological charge, becoming instead a part of the vocabulary of every modern European language. A simple image search on Google for 'palace' shows how this term is linked with images of Greco-Roman architecture and monuments of power and prestige. It was this history of the word 'palace' that would cause so much trouble for the modernist architect Le Corbusier.

In its early days in Geneva, the League of Nations Secretariat was quartered at the Hôtel National. As Karen Gram-Skjoldager has illustrated in the previous chapter, it was clear from the beginning that the hotel was ill-suited as an administrative building. Therefore, when the Swiss authorities offered it a site for a new conference hall, the Secretariat seized the opportunity. In 1924, the League Assembly asked for a building which was not only to "perform fully and adequately the essential function and purposes of an Assembly Hall of the League of Nations",[1] but which could also host all the main bodies of the League, serving as the permanent centre for the new international diplomacy. The League opted for an international competition, with guidelines drawn up by an international jury in order to clarify and emphasise the great ideological and symbolic importance of the construction of the first world parliament.

The jury believed that "it was the idea of the League of Nations which had to inspire the construction of the building, and that it was from an understanding of the world based on brotherhood that the architectural realization had to be emanated".[2] This idea seemed to crave modernity: a modernity expressed through a new architectural concept for the physical seat of power – which is why so many modernist architects took part in the competition with great enthusiasm.

Despite the fact that this was to be the headquarters of an organisation that sought to break with the past of secret diplomacy and fleeting alliances, the jury, having referred to the building as a Conference or Assembly Hall, decided in the official guidance for the competition to opt for the history-laden term "the Palace".[3]

Arguably, through this semantic alteration, the jury implicitly foresaw the League headquarters as a site of traditional power and diplomacy, akin to the Palace of Versailles – where the League was born. The case of the exclusion of the modernist architect Le Corbusier confirmed and underlined the traditionalist inclination of the jury.

The layout of Corbusier's League headquarters, machine-printed and not hand-drawn. The project proposed by Le Corbusier and Jeanneret represented cutting-edge modern architecture in the 1920s. It introduced entirely new technical solutions: ad hoc designed office spaces, a large acoustic assembly room, horizontal and vertical circulation, heating and ventilation, etc. Another ground-breaking innovation was the use of reinforced concrete for the construction of a palace.

THE CASE OF LE CORBUSIER

By the deadline of the competition in January 1926, 377 different projects had reached Geneva. Due to the overwhelming response, and differing views within the jury, the verdict was not an easy one. An additional challenge for the judges was that an overwhelming majority of the projects had ignored the rules set up by the jury. For instance, most projects exceeded the 13 million francs budget limit stipulated by the jury, some of them reaching estimates of 50 million francs.

The jury overcame these challenges by recommending not a single winner, but 27 different ones – a decision that was heavily criticised. The jury was accused of having neglected its own budget limits, nominating projects estimated to cost more than 13 million francs, and to have ignored the fundamental premise of the competition by nominating 27 different 'winners'. Thus, a Committee of Five, consisting of seasoned diplomats, was nominated to resolve the impasse. The Committee promptly deemed the procedure hitherto as irregular but necessary, since none of the projects respected the conditions of the competition. For this reason – even though it selected the project of the French architect H.P. Nénot as the one that came closest to meeting the aesthetic and functional needs of the Palace – the Committee requested a new

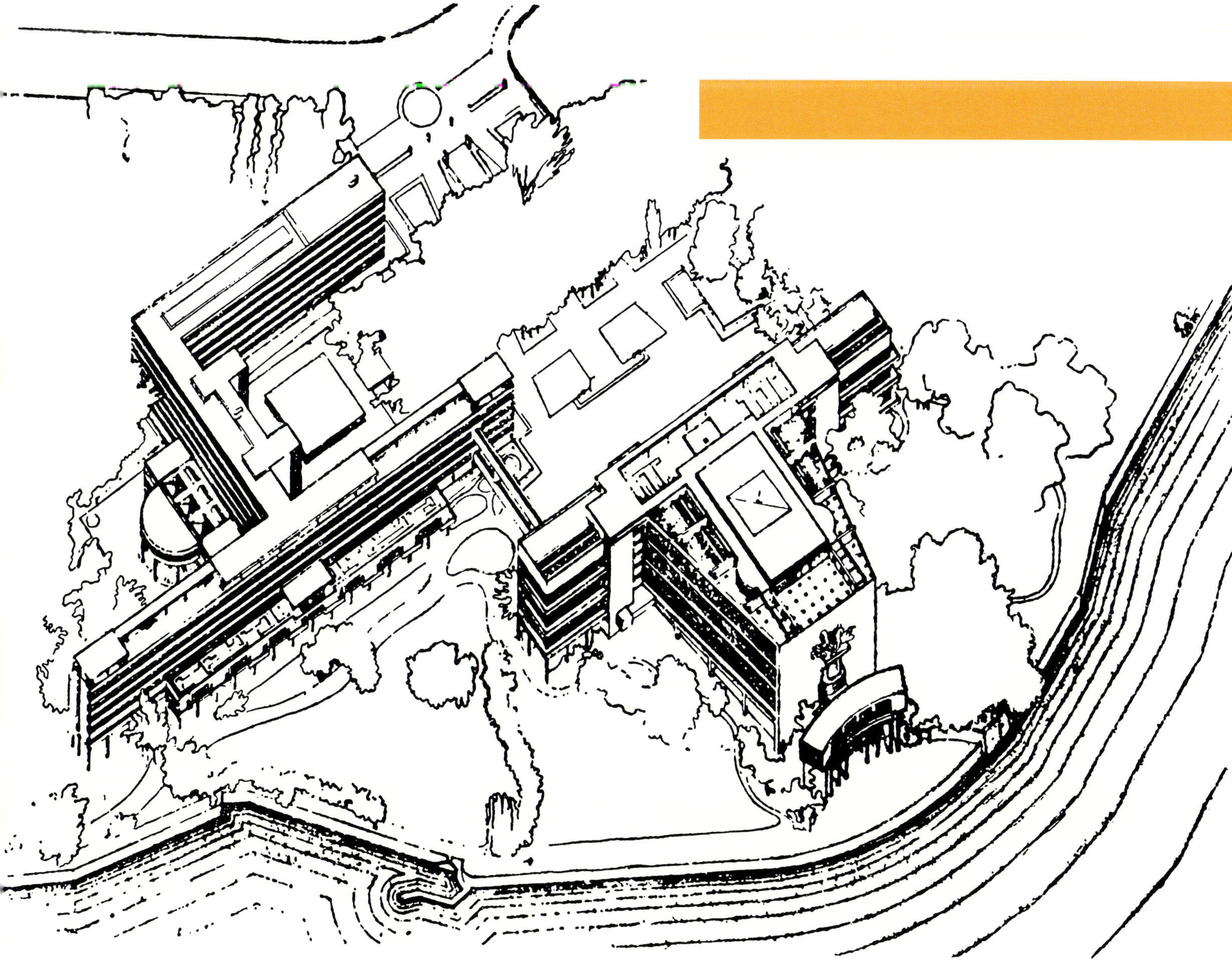

project to be submitted by Nénot, developed together with three other architects whose projects had been awarded in the previous nomination round: Broggi, Lefèvre and Vago.

This decision was soon questioned, however, by part of the specialised public opinion; the architects, architectural critics and journalists who were following the competition started gathering around one project that scrupulously respected the regulation. The architects Le Corbusier and Pierre Jeanneret – one of the 27 winners – had, as it turned out, presented a project which fulfilled all the criteria of the competition, with an estimated expenditure of 12,500,000 million francs.

The jury, on the other hand, proving itself intent on avoiding a modernist winner, clung to a minor deviation in the project presented by Le Corbusier: its prospects were machine-printed and not hand-drawn as the regulations required. Critics argued, however, that the real problem was that Le Corbusier's proposed building broke with the traditional notions of a 'Palace'.

This was certainly true: Le Corbusier and Jeanneret presented a ground-breaking building, which had nothing in common with the palaces of the past. On the contrary, it resembled a modern office building where actual work could be carried out in a convenient way. In laying out this plan, the architects did not conceal the ideological charge of their project. In the competition record annexed to the project, in fact, they addressed the jury directly:

> if the intentions of the League of Nations [to represent the pacific glory of the 20th century] are sincere, then it is not possible to constrain such an innovative social organization to the straitjacket of traditional architecture. No colonnaded hall for bored sovereigns, but salubrious working rooms for the busy representatives of the various peoples. No dark corridors for the intrigues of diplomacy, but open, glazed spaces for public negotiations carried by honest men.[4]

After the jury had commissioned a new joint project by Nénot, Broggi, Lefévre and Vago, many proposed an entirely new competition. This proposal was well timed, as John D. Rockefeller Jr had recently offered

Sketch of The United Nations Permanent Headquarters in New York. This modernist, iconic glass slab represents a synthesis between the project of Le Corbusier and that of Brazilian architect Oscar Niemeyer. The present building has a distinctive General Assembly building, a long low horizontal block housing the other meeting rooms and a tall tower for the Secretariat.

to pay for the construction of a library adequate to the new building. Such an important addition to the Palace would substantially change the parameters of the building. Despite these considerations, the Committee of Five – resolute in avoiding a second round – declared themselves bound, by mandate, to choose between one of the nominated projects.

Determined not to fall victim to diplomatic trickery, Le Corbusier decided to address an extensive plea to the Council of the League, in which he urged them to reject the decision of the Committee of Five and to "adopt a solution [...] respectful of the principles which are at the basis of the organization of the competition and which inspired the mandate entrusted to the Committee of Five".[5]

Despite the unassailable evidence presented in Le Corbusier's plea – impeccably drafted by André Prudhomme, at the time one of Paris' top lawyers – the Council did not include it on its agenda. As a result, the resolution of the Committee of Five was passed by the Council on 6 March 1928, officially endorsing the controversial results of the competition.[6]

Months later, the Secretariat of the League explained that the reason the petition was not presented to the Council was that no private citizen could directly appeal to the organs of the League.[7] It is worth noticing though that on 6 March 1928, the president of the Council, to whom the plea was addressed, was none other than Dr. Francisco J. Urruita, the Colombian member of the Committee of Five. Moreover, Japan was represented at that meeting of the Council by M. Mineitcirô Adatci, president of the Committee of Five.[8]

THE NEW PROJECT FOR THE ARIANA PARK AND THE ALLEGED PLAGIARISM

Still, diplomacy could not change the fact that if the library sponsored by Rockefeller was to be built, a bigger site for the Palace was needed. Weeks after Le Corbusier had presented his plea, the League, with the help of the Swiss authorities, managed to appropriate a new site – known as Ariana Park – where the Palace would eventually find its final seat. This park, however, had been donated to the city of Geneva by the late Gustave Revilliod, and his heir, Hélène de Mandrot Revilliod, had the final say on the use of the site. Unfortunately for the Jury, the Committee of Five and the Secretariat, Mme de Mandrot had followed the case of Le Corbusier and favoured his project. Therefore, in exchange

A view of the Court of Honour of the Palais des Nations. The grandiose open court fills the space between the Assembly Hall, the Library wing and the Council wing, looking down to Ariana Park, Lac Léman and the French Alps. In his plea, Le Corbusier lamented how he had been the only one to propose an open courtyard, while the others opted for a courtyard surrounded by walls, and thus denounced how the symbolic openness of his project was improperly 'borrowed'.

for her consent, she asked that all the architects awarded with a first prize in the competition would be allowed to present a new project for the Ariana site. Being short on time, the Secretariat accepted the conditions and agreed to present the new solution when the Assembly reunited in September 1928. Against this background, on 25 September, the Assembly approved the choice of the Ariana Park as the new site of the Palace and conferred to the Committee of Five all the necessary powers to head a quick and smooth process.[9]

With Mme de Mandrot's conditions, Le Corbusier's project was back in the game. The League and the Committee of Five, however, had no difficulties in untying the strings attached to the Ariana Park site. While Le Corbusier was invited to present a new project – which he did in April 1929 – the League had already signed the contract with the architects backed by the Committee of Five the previous month.

Thus, the project recommended by the Committee of Five won out. However, that was not the end of the controversy. In 1931, Le Corbusier filed a plagiarism complaint against Nénot and the other architects of the project underway. Once confronted with the definitive project, Le Corbusier noticed that the general concept – the blueprints, the distribution of the different premises, but especially the absence of a central courtyard – were inspired by the original conceptions present in his project. Furthermore, he argued that the final project presented for the Palace had only a few similarities with the first projects presented by the architects entrusted with the construction of the building. If we compare the buildings as they are presented in Le Corbusier's plea, his point is clear.

Despite strong evidence of plagiarism, the League rejected the second plea on the same grounds as the first. Thus, the works for the Palace were set to start on 1 March 1931.

CONCLUSION: LE CORBUSIER'S 'REVENGE'

As regards Le Corbusier, we can reassure the reader that he had his own personal compensation. With the dissolution of the League of Nations in 1946, its successor, the United Nations, needed a new home far from Geneva and the air of failure surrounding the Palais. A new modern

Conscious of the controversy triggered by the international competition held by the League of Nations, delegates decided that the United Nations home should be the result of a joint project between leading architects from many countries, nominated by governments. Wallace K. Harrison of the United States was appointed chief architect with the title of Director of Planning and a ten-member Board of Design Consultants, which included Le Corbusier, was selected to assist him.

building, a glazed skyscraper in the middle of New York City, would serve this purpose; its realisation was entrusted to a team of architects, including one familiar name. The name of an architect whose reputation had no ties to the League, and whose enthusiasm for modernity the deceased organisation had rejected: Le Corbusier.

NOTES

1 Special Supplement 23/156 (1924), League of Nations Official Journal, League of Nations' Archives (hereafter LoNA).

2 Minutes of the second session of the works of the jury (January 1926), 31-33, 32/49424/28594, LoNA in Delizia, Mangone: *Architettura e Politica*, 26.

3 Programme et Règlement du Concours d'Architecture pour l'édification d'un Palais de la Société des Nation à Genève, 17 April 1926, LoNA.

4 See competition report in Wittwer: *Hans Wittwer*, 28-29.

5 Requête adressée par Mm. Le Corbusier et P. Jeanneret à M. le President et à Mm. les Membres du Conseil de la Société des Nation, Paris, February 28 1928, in Anzivino: *Il Concorso*, 96-99.

6 League of Nations Official Journal, 9/383 (1928), LoNA.

7 Le Corbusier, *Une Maison-Un Palais* (Paris 1928) in Anzivino: *Il Concorso*, 101.

8 League of Nations Official Journal, 9/367 (1928), LoNA.

9 League of Nations Official Journal – Special Supplement, 64/163 (1928), LoNA.

BIBLIOGRAPHY

Unpublished material

Minutes of the Directors' meetings, Directors' Meeting papers (1921-1935), League of Nations Archives, United Nations Archives at Geneva.

Seán Lester's private papers, P203/48 University College Dublin.

Published material

Anzivino, Ciro Luigi: *Ginevra 1927: il concorso per il Palazzo della Societa delle nazioni e il caso Le Corbusier*, Firenze: Modulo Editore, 1979.

Cheronnet, Louis: *The palace of the League of Nations*, Paris: L'illustration, 1938.

Delizia, Ilda and Fabian Mangone: *Architettura e politica : Ginevra e la Società delle nazioni, 1925-1929*, Roma: Officina edizioni, 1992.

League of Nations Official Journal, Special Supplement 195v. (London, England: Harrison & Sons, 1920-1946), HeinOnline United Nations Law Collection.

League of Nations Official Journal, Vols. 1-21 (1920-1940), HeinOnline United Nations Law Collection.

Pallas, Jean-Claude: *Histoire et architecture du Palais des Nations (1924-2001): l'Art déco au service des relations internationals*, New York: United Nations publication, 2001.

Wittwer, Hans-Jakob: *Hans Wittwer 1894-1953*, Zurich: gta Verlag, 1988.

Torsten Kahlert

'THE LEAGUE IS DEAD, LONG LIVE THE UNITED NATIONS'

The Liquidation of the League and the Transfer of Assets to the UN

International organisations never die. But the League of Nations did.

The League is one of the very few large-scale international organisations that have been dissolved and closed down entirely. But when exactly did it cease to exist? How was the diplomatic and administrative process conducted, and which actors were involved with what kind of interests and agency?

This chapter narrates the final, irrevocable end of the League: the physical liquidation and the transfer of its material assets and properties to the United Nations after the United Nations Conference on International Organization in San Francisco in 1945, where the League leadership were "guests at their own funeral",[1] and then after the League's final Assembly in April 1946. As will be argued, the negotiations between the League of Nations and the United Nations were not a neutral process of "handing over" assets to the UN, as one League publication suggested, nor was there really a neat distinction between the two negotiating parties.[2] Rather, the League's liquidation clearly demonstrates two complicating factors. First, that the UN sought to distance itself from the League to avoid being tainted by its failure, while the League itself sought to retain a minimum of dignity. Second, that the UN officials negotiating the League's final act where overwhelmingly old League officials. Thus, the liquidation of the League was its last administrative act, with League officials active on both sides, as a reminder that International Organizations rarely cease to exist – they only change form.

When visiting the League Archives in Geneva, searching for information about the careers of the Secretariat's personnel after the dissolution of the organisation, I came across a pile of documents concerning the transition phase of 1946/47 and the transfer of the League of Nations' property to the newly-founded United Nations. The documents list the properties of the League of Nations (the Palais des Nations being the main estate), the furniture, the typewriters, the publications, the library and the funds the League owned. They also contain detailed correspondence on how to estimate the value of each of these assets. These records document the final administrative efforts involved in the transition of the League of Nations to the UN. While the lists and administrative documents concerning the properties and assets were produced by League officials, the records were already filed in the UN section in the archive in Geneva, reflecting the transition even on an archival level.

DISSOLUTION AND LIQUIDATION

For a short period, from 1945 to 1947, the League of Nations and the United Nations existed side by side. In June 1945, the Charter of the United Nations was adopted. This is usually seen as the birth of the United Nations. The League of Nations did not cease to exist before the final League Assembly in 1946, and liquidation in 1947.

During the period 1945-1947 a complicated negotiation process played out, involving various institutional actors from both organisations. All in all, a machinery of six main bodies and a number of commissions and committees were involved in the transfer and liquidation process (which will be described in more detail below). Besides the League Secretariat and the Supervisory Commission of the League, the Board of Liquidation set up by the League – consisting of nine League representatives, from Bolivia, China, Czechoslovakia, France, India, Norway,

The signing of the documents that enabled the transfer of what remained of the League, its huge building and other assets, to the UN. While Seán Lester (on the left) went back to Ireland and never held a position in an international organisation again, Wlodzimierz Moderow became the first Director of the European Office of the United Nations and thus became the personal successor of Lester in the Palais des Nations.

South Africa, Switzerland and the United Kingdom – was responsible for the formal liquidation. In Geneva, the UN operated with a Secretariat, the UN Geneva office, which transmitted the reports and agreements to the respective organs of the United Nations in New York.[3]

The period is divided into at least two distinct phases: 1) the negotiation and planning phase from the San Francisco Conference in April/June 1945 to the last League Assembly in April 1946, in which the so-called "Common Plan", the main document which laid down the main lines of the transfer was negotiated; and 2) the subsequent period of the actual administrative transfer, which managed all the details of the transfer and the dissolution after the League as an organisation had officially ceased to exist.

The UN position for the takeover was developed in the Preparatory Commission, which had representatives of all 51 UN member states and held its meetings in London in the second half of 1945. In February 1946, the UN held its first General Assembly in London. Part of the agenda was how to deal with the League of Nations, especially the transfer of functions, property and assets. All such matters were gathered in the so-called "Common Plan", which had been negotiated and worked out by the Supervisory Commission of the League and the United Nations Committee, and was approved by the General Assemblies of both organisations. Apart from officially confirming the dissolution of the League of Nations, the Common Plan stipulated a mutual agreement on the transfer of material assets.[4]

Negotiations on which assets would be transferred, which would be sold and which would be returned to their original owners started in March 1946. With this settled, the UN Geneva office, the Liquidation Board of the League of Nations and the remaining staff around Seán Lester, the League's last Secretary General, dealt with the valuation of the assets, property, publications (e.g. the treaty series and the library) and the different funds the League owned, from April 1946 to July 1947. Former League officials helped the UN by providing information about the inner administration, and acted as intermediates between the two organisations. For example, the former League official Egon Ranshofen-Wertheimer, who was appointed as chief of the UN Overseas Division in 1946, was sent to Geneva on behalf of the UN to report in detail on possible functions and assets to be transferred.[5]

DISRESPECT AND DIGNITY

It is a well-established fact that the UN was keen to distance itself from the League. This was because of the failure of the League to prevent the outbreak of a new war, as well as the exclusion of the USSR in 1939.[6] At the same time, however, the UN was keenly interested in acquiring the physical remnants of the League. The last League officials were interested in retaining the organisation's dignity and expected to be treated as on a par with UN officials. As the following anecdote indicates, this did not always lead to an amicable liquidation process.

While the last Assembly, initiated by the British Foreign Office, was deliberately held to give the League a dignified end, UN officials working on its liquidation could not wait that long. Indeed, Seán Lester was surprised by UN officials on 10 April 1946, around a week before the last League Assembly. The officials informed him that they wanted to inspect "the grounds of La Pelouse and the house itself" – his private home and grounds. Bemused by the surprise visit, Lester decided to let them visit the grounds, but refused access to his private residence "on such short notice", as he wrote to Wlodzimierz Moderow, Chairman of the UN Negotiating Committee and the highest-ranking UN official in Geneva. Moderow replied that Lester's Director of Personnel and Internal Administration, Valentin Stencek, had been notified on 9 April but added that the "inspection tour [was] completed" anyway, and that they would "certainly not disturb [him] at [his] private residence during the few hours of rest which [he] enjoy[ed] at present".[7]

This short anecdote tells us a lot about the relationship between the new and the old organisation. Instead of respectfully apologising for the short notification and the disturbance, Moderow simply referred to bureaucratic procedure, claiming that one day's notice was enough. The scene is illustrative of the League's dwindling importance, but perhaps even more of Lester's marginalised role in international politics by the end of the war. Moderow avoided confrontation by side-stepping to bureaucratic procedures, but actually referred very clearly to the end of Lester's role in Geneva. It is also striking that UN officials were entitled at this time to access the private quarters of the League's highest officials. Of course, the League had been officially dissolved with the last Assembly two days before, but Lester was officially the Secretary-General of a Secretariat that was still authorised to handle the administrative dissolution. One cannot help but read a bit of sarcasm into Moderow's last sentence, though this might not have been the intent. Certainly, if

Aerial photo of the League building including the surrounding Ariana Park, an area by Lake Geneva, which had been donated to the city by Gustave Revilliod in 1890. Since the 1940s, the complex has been substantially expanded. Part of the *'Nations'* quarter of Geneva, the Palais is flanked by the headquarters of many other international organisations such as the WHO, ILO and the Red Cross.

all Lester had to do was to hand over the remains of the League, then he should have had plenty of time for inspections. Lester's firm but futile stance, moreover, captures his attempt, perhaps also on behalf of the League as such, to retain control and dignity to the very end.

Though the example above implies a passive League responding to the demands of a new and potent world organisation, Moderow, and the UN more generally, were very much dependent on the League officials to finalise the liquidation. In July 1946, Moderow asked for an expert to come to Geneva in order to evaluate the lists of properties prepared by the League itself, and to verify their estimated value. Zdenek Smetacek,

from the Czech Foreign Ministry, was called, and he stayed in Geneva evaluating the lists of properties and prices for almost a month. In a joint meeting between League and UN staff, the procedure was laid out, and it was decided that his examination should be limited to the verification of "furniture, fittings, typewriters etc., and stocks of stationary, printing paper, office supplies and equipment". Smetacek concluded that the lists were "as correct as they may be expected to be in the circumstances and can be relied upon in determining the valuation of items transferred to the United Nations by the League of Nations on August 1st, 1946".[8] Though the procedure clearly indicates an asymmetric relationship between the two organisations – one doing the grunt work, the other supervising – it also shows that League officials were instrumental in settling the estates.

THE LEAGUE ON BOTH SIDES

In fact, League officials and former League officials played key roles on both sides of the table, as the final act of the story of the League played out.

On the UN side, there were at least four former officials of the League Secretariat involved. Moderow himself, a lawyer by training with a background in Polish administration, had worked for the League's Permanent Committee for Transit and Communication. Adrian Pelt, the assistant of the first UN Secretary-General Trygve Lie and deeply involved in the transfer and liquidation, had worked for the League Secretariat for twenty years, first as a member (1920) and then as head (1934) of the Information Section.[9] Egon Ranshofen-Wertheimer, assisting the UN as an expert of the structure and functioning of the League's Secretariat, had worked since 1930 in three different sections of the League Secretariat.[10] Last, Thanassis Aghnides, whose road to the Secretariat Haakon A. Ikonomou explores in this edited volume, functioned as Rapporteur of the report on the transfer of assets of the Fifth Committee of the UN in December 1946. There was one man who, while not directly involved in the transfer of assets, was an important hub in the network of former League officials: Arthur Sweetser, an American, who had worked as a high official in the Information Section and had been the main contact point for the Americans – who never joined the League as a member state – and headed the United Nations Information Office (UNIO) from 1942.[11]

The First Assembly of the UN held its first meeting in London's Westminster Central Hall, near Westminster Palace, in January 1946. It was the last General Assembly on European ground, before the UN crossed the Atlantic to hold the second meeting of the first session in the future hometown of its new headquarters: New York. Formally the UN headquarter is extraterritorial and belongs the United Nations, not the US government.

CONCLUSION

Though Robert Cecil, one of the most important founding figures of the League, famously proclaimed "The League is dead, long live the United Nations" in his opening speech at the last Assembly of the League, in April 1946, this was not entirely true. The remaining officials still had to demonstrate the administrative abilities of the League one last time. More significantly, it was former League officials who drove the process of liquidation on the UN side. This might indicate a wish on the former League officials' part to send the organisation off in a dignified way, but it was also a question of competence. The UN depended on the know-how and contacts of former League officials to complete its shutdown – another chapter in the interwoven stories of the two world organisations.

The ambivalent and intertwined process of liquidation on the one hand and transition on the other is evident in these stories. In this sense the two international organisations are different but the same – separate but connected. The Palais des Nations, the most important asset of the League, still serves today as the European headquarters of the UN. Not surprisingly, its interior shows many material signs of both world organisations.

The liquidation process and its handling from both sides is also a poignant illustration of how international organisations develop institutional identities that affect the personal identities of the people who run them, entailing emotional qualities such as the need for dignity and respect, face-saving, pride and shame.

The closing event of the last chapter of the League of Nations was a cocktail party, held for the remaining League officials and the staff of the UN Geneva headquarters. It was more expensive than expected. It was now up to the new organisation to pick up the tab for the old one.[12]

NOTES

1 Clavin: *Securing the World Economy*, 341.

2 League of Nations, 'The League Hands Over'.

3 For details on the procedure and commissions involved: Myers: 'Liquidation of League of Nations Functions', 320-354.

4 General Report of the Finance Committee to the Assembly (Second Committee), Twenty-first ordinary Session of the Assembly, Geneva, 18 April 1946, 12.

5 Egon Ranshofen-Wertheimer (1894-1957), a journalist of Austrian origin, had joined the League Secretariat in 1930 and stayed in different functions until 1940. He published a book on the Secretariat of the League in 1945 with the support of the Carnegie foundation. Ranshofen-Wertheimer: *The International Secretariat*.

6 There were many reasons for this, which are discussed first in Goodrich: 'From League of Nations to United Nations', 3-21. For a broader view on the foundation of the UN, see Mazower: *No Enchanted Palace*.

7 LoNA, G1, 4/1 (23): Transfer Assets, Function and Staff.

8 LoNA, G1, 4/4 (26): 'Report by Zdenek Smetacek, 8 August 1946' in Transfer of Assets, Functions and Staff. Valuations of Assets.

9 A short biography of Pelt is to be found at the Dutch Huygens Institute: http://resources.huygens.knaw.nl/bwn1880-2000/lemmata/bwn2/pelt (13.07.2018).

10 Entry: 'Egon Ranshofen-Wertheimer'.

11 Herren and Löhr: 'Being international', 535-552.

12 LoNA, G1, 4: Cocktail Party on termination of League activities.

BIBLIOGRAPHY

Unpublished material

LoNA, G1, 4: Cocktail Party on termination of League activities.

LoNA, G1, 4/1 (23): Transfer Assets, Function and Staff.

LoNA, G1, 4/4 (26): 'Report by Zdenek Smetacek, 8 August 1946' in Transfer of Assets, Functions and Staff. Valuations of Assets.

Published material

Clavin, Patricia: *Securing the World Economy: The Reinvention of the League of Nations, 1920-1946*, Oxford: Oxford University Press, 2013.

General Report of the Finance Committee to the Assembly (Second Committee), Twenty-first ordinary Session of the Assembly, Geneva, 18 April 1946, 12.

Goodrich, Leland M.: 'From League of Nations to United Nations', *International Organization* 1 (1), 1947, 3-21.

Herren, Madeleine and Isabelle Löhr: 'Being international in times of war: Arthur Sweetser and the shifting of the League of Nations to the United Nations', *European Review of History* 25 (3-4), 2018.

Mazower, Mark: *No Enchanted Palace: The End of Empire and the Ideological Origins of the United Nations*, Princeton: Princeton University Press, 2009.

Myers, Denys P.: 'Liquidation of League of Nations Functions', *The American Journal of International Law* 42 (2), 1948, 320-354.

Ranshofen-Wertheimer, Egon: *The International Secretariat: A great Experiment in International Administration* (Studies in the Administration of International Law and Organization 3), Washington: Carnegie Endowment for International Peace, 1945.

Online sources

Pelt, Adrianus, Dutch Huygens Institute: http://resources.huygens.knaw.nl/bwn1880-2000/lemmata/bwn2/pelt (13.07.2018).

'Ranshofen-Wertheimer, Egon': Entry in: Lonsea/League of Nations Search Engine (13.07.2018).

Patrick Finney

'A LIVING THING IS BORN'

The League of Nations and the Contemporary World

On 14 February 1919, addressing the third plenary session of the Paris Peace Conference, US President Woodrow Wilson read out the draft League of Nations Covenant and famously declared: "a living thing is born". The Covenant, Wilson explained, was of necessity a relatively brief framework document, since it had not been possible "to foresee the variety of circumstances with which this League would have to deal" or to prescribe in detail "all the machinery that might be necessary to meet differing and unexpected contingencies". Yet for Wilson this was a prime virtue rather than a vice; it meant the League was endowed with flexibility in responding to emerging issues and crises, and would have the capacity to evolve and mature in pursuit of its core goal of the "guarantee of peace".[1]

For several decades after the end of the Second World War, conventional historiographical opinion damned Wilson's view as naïvely optimistic. The League's failure in a succession of collective security crises seemed to have demonstrated that the Covenant's vaunted flexibility in fact amounted to a fatal lack of precision, rigour and automaticity. Moreover, far from adapting and growing into a "vital thing", as Wilson had on another occasion prescribed, the League seemed to lapse into senescent impotence long before its existence was formally terminated in 1946.[2]

The new historiography this collection both showcases and advances has, of course, challenged these judgements through multiple acts of reframing. It has supplanted the narrative of the League as simply an experiment in failure, moving beyond narrowly realist interpretations focused solely on collective security to consider the full range and enduring legacy of the League's endeavours, especially in technical and humanitarian fields.[3] In reconstructing the work of ardent internationalists pushing up against the prerogatives of state sovereignty as they struggled to protect the rights of ethnic minorities, combat people trafficking and forced labour and promote global health, we seem to encounter recognisably modern forebears. Hence the League has been resurrected as an object of contemporary concern and a site for meditation upon the political and ethical problems of the present: far from a dusty irrelevance, the attentions of the new historiography have infused the League with life.

One of the crucial moves involved here is the resituating of the League within a larger normative internationalist project. Rather than conceiving of it as a discrete endeavour rooted in the specific contingencies of the interwar period, it is being reconsidered as part of wider and ongoing intellectual and institutional attempts to transcend the primacy of nation states and to develop global civil society.[4] On the one hand, this entails locating the League as part of a thicker landscape of internationalist institution-building and activism in the interwar years: the League drew strength from and animated a dense and complex network (or perhaps, "force field", to adapt Susan Pedersen's term)[5] of other individuals and organisations interested in cooperating to resolve technical and political problems and improve the

Fortunino Matania's iconic 1919 painting 'President Woodrow Wilson Announcing the Birth of the League of Nations'. Matania had become renowned for graphic depictions of trench warfare; in the inter-war years he specialised in historical illustrations, recreating images from the ancient world for diverse periodicals as well as advertisements. Here, Wilson's sweeping hand gesture consigns the chaotic destruction of war to the past as he proclaims his vision of transforming international politics.

human condition.[6] On the other hand, it is to place the League within a longer chronology stretching from the late nineteenth century, when international organisations and transnational entanglements began to proliferate, through to a post-Cold War present in which non-state actors and globalising flows of capital, people and ideas have loomed so large that they triggered a transnational turn in historical studies (of which this writing on the League is one manifestation).[7] This in turn contributes to sustaining the core argument of the new historiographers, "that internationalisms were central to the major political questions and themes of the twentieth century: war and peace, imperialism and nationalism, states and state-building".[8]

The synchronic and diachronic dimensions of this move can both be illustrated by a case study focusing on my own place of work, the Department of International Politics at Aberystwyth University. In their contributions, Søren Friis, Hagen Schulz-Forberg and Tomoko Akami have discussed other institutional developments linked to the League, specifically the more systematic development of academic thinking about international relations. However, the founding of my Department – which will celebrate its centenary in 2019 in parallel with the League – was certainly another crucial step in the establishment of the discipline of International Relations (IR).[9] It occurred when industrialist and philanthropist David Davies of Llandinam, together with his sisters Gwendoline and Margaret, endowed a Chair at the (then) University College of Wales, Aberystwyth in 1919. The Chair was eventually named after Woodrow Wilson, and from the beginning the link between the Department and the League was explicit. Repulsed by what he had witnessed serving on the Western Front, Davies intended the Chair "in memory of the fallen students of our University for the study of those related problems of law and politics, of ethics and economics, which are raised by the prospect of a League of Nations and for the truer understanding of civilizations other than our own".[10]

Thereafter, through the interwar years this small West Wales seaside town became a vibrant if unlikely hub for internationalist thinking. Successive holders of the Wilson Chair lectured and wrote on the League and international politics; one landmark publication was *The League of*

Nations in Theory and Practice, co-authored in 1933 by Charles Webster and the Department's junior lecturer Sydney Herbert.[11] Davies himself was a tireless and generous campaigner for League causes and a major figure in the British League of Nations Union. In 1926, at his initiative, Aberystwyth hosted the annual congress of the International Federation of League of Nations Societies. Over two hundred delegates – their travel and subsistence expenses personally underwritten by Davies – spent a week in receptions, lectures, debates and excursions to local sites of historic interest; there was even an opportunity to watch the League-produced 1925 documentary film "on the evils of war and the benefits of the League", *Star of Hope*, at the Imperial Cinema. Local people participated avidly in the proceedings and University staff served as guides and interpreters, though the atmosphere of international amity was slightly soured when a member of the audience at a public meeting heckled the German delegate, Count Bernstorff – "What about the *Lusitania*? ... You dirty dog. You dirty German!" – and had to be removed from the University Hall by the local police.[12]

The academic work of the Department was also hallmarked by contestation over the League project. As the 1920s wore on, Davies developed very distinct ideas – set out at length in his 1930 book *The Problem of the Twentieth Century* – about the need to strengthen the League and to establish an international police force with monopoly possession of the most powerful weapons to swiftly punish delinquent aggressors.[13] He was therefore dismayed when successive Wilson Professors evinced considerable scepticism about the viability of collective security. This culminated in the 1940s with a vitriolic campaign against E.H. Carr – Wilson Professor from 1936 and author in 1939 of *The Twenty Years' Crisis*, often viewed as a canonical realist text[14] – that only concluded with Davies' death in 1944. His efforts to sustain and develop the League, Davies wrote with fury in June 1942, "have been hindered rather than helped by the holders of the Wilson Chair".[15]

Despite this gloomy verdict, the Department clearly deserves a place in the thicker history of interwar internationalist endeavour intertwined with the League that has begun to emerge. Engagement with the League experiment was also very important to the evolution of the

Old College, Aberystwyth University. From its founding in 1919 to 1964, the Department of International Politics was housed in 1-2 New Promenade, the white Georgian villas immediately to the left of Old College. This site is currently the focus of an ambitious restoration project – 'New Life for Old College' – supported by the Heritage Lottery Fund; the New Promenade properties are to be incorporated into what will be one of the most significant cultural and community centres in Wales.

intellectual project of IR as a whole, even if it is too simplistic to see the interwar period as simply consisting of a "great debate" between idealism and realism, as was once commonly thought.[16] Moreover, although conceptual debates in IR have of course moved on considerably since, the discipline has nonetheless continued to wrestle with issues around the prerogatives of the state, the anarchical nature of the international system and the causes of war, all of which the League also confronted. Hence it is legitimate to conceive of IR as one of the longitudinal strands within the larger internationalist enterprise of which the League was also a part. In Aberystwyth, too, the preoccupations of the Department have ebbed and flowed over the decades amidst personnel changes and larger intellectual shifts. Yet as it celebrates its centenary, it remains hallmarked by the normative rationale that underpinned its founding: "understanding the diverse facets of world politics (politics, law, economics, ethics) in order to mitigate organised violence".[17]

The second process – related but distinct – that has lent the League new contemporary relevance is the rethinking of its role in the longer history of modern global governance. In one sense, this is a matter of institutional continuities. The founders of the United Nations (UN) took pains to distance it from "its purportedly 'failed' predecessor" in an "act of diplomatic theatre"; dramatising the rupture, and presenting 1945 as an entirely fresh start, was intended to enhance the new organisation's legitimacy. Subsequent generations of historians all too often endorsed the trope of the League "as a salutary failure, the indispensable political counterpoint and analytical premise of the UN's rise".[18] Yet while the UN was undoubtedly shaped in some ways by the negative exemplar of the League experience, recent work has uncovered myriad continuities in personnel, organisation and approach between the older body and the new, especially in technical and humanitarian fields. This historiography constitutes a powerful corrective to the view of the League as a dead-end wrong turn – rather, it reinscribes it as an intrinsic element in "the genealogy of our [...] present".[19]

As well as resuscitating the League as an object of attention, this development raises important interpretive questions about the nature of global governance in the present and the past. Mark Mazower's *tour de force* history, *Governing the World*, underlined the implication of the network of post-1945 international organisations with both US power and the emergence of neoliberalism, confounding any simplistic coding of internationalism as an inherently progressive force. Moreover, as Mazower writes the League into the pre-history of the UN system, that body also becomes implicated as an avatar of neoliberalism (as is explored in a very literal sense by Hagen Schulz-Forberg here).[20]

There is an understandable temptation – as Susan Pedersen has remarked – for "a history aimed at recovery" to fall into a "celebratory" mode.[21] Historians engaged in any revisionist historiographical enterprise, rescuing their subjects from the damnation or condescending neglect of posterity, can become fondly protective of them. In this instance it is extremely easy to portray figures such as the young internationalist idealists of the League Secretariat as tragic heroes, fighting an ultimately vain but noble battle to transcend the constraints of sovereign power, preserve peace and protect human dignity as the world descended into the catastrophe of the Second World War. Yet it is vitally important to resist such urges – as the authors in this volume do – in order to mount a critical appraisal of the politics and legacy of the League experiment.

Such an appraisal must take account of the myriad varieties of internationalism that swirled around and through the League of Nations project in the interwar period. It is not just that there were fascist and communist internationalisms that rubbed up against liberal internationalism – that latter ideological project was itself fractured and fissiparous, with statist, reformist, radical and pacifist variants. (This point is readily demonstrated by Marco Moraes' analysis of the affinities between Secretary-General Joseph Avenol's vision for a technocratic League and fascist internationalism.) Moreover, it would also be fruitful to widen our perspective further, to take fuller account of internationalist visions generated at the "peripheries" by non-Western or otherwise "subaltern" actors.[22]

It is also necessary to gauge the ambiguities – even the dark sides – of many of the League's activities. Here the entangling, or perhaps the co-implication, of internationalist and transformative aspirations with older currents of imperialist, civilisational and power political thinking loom large. This is most obviously evident in the mandates system, at once a powerful mechanism for the generation of proto-decolonising norms and a fig leaf for refurbished racist colonial domination (the latter point underlined vigorously in Florian Wagner's chapter and in the acerbic criticisms of Israel Zangwill related in Laura Almagor's).[23] By the same token, while the League valorised the production of objective knowledge as a means to overcome political and social problems and promote peace, the work of its experts was never ideologically innocent, not least because it was shot through with hierarchical Eurocentric assumptions, as Quincy Cloet demonstrates in his chapter. (It should be noted, moreover, that recent scholarship has underlined that the nascent social science of IR was also shaped and tainted by pernicious racial thinking.[24]) Equally, while noting positively the continuities between the League's global health work and that carried out under

Mural in the Council Chamber of the Palais des Nations, Geneva, opened in 1936. The Catalan artist Josep Maria Sert decorated the Chamber with a number of fine murals illustrating human progress through the advance of health, technology, freedom and peace. It is an irony that the grandiose Palais was inaugurated just as the League's influence in global politics was in serious decline; another is that Sert later became an ardent supporter of General Francisco Franco.

the UN, Niels Brimnes also underlines how the former was profoundly shaped and limited by colonial power relations.

The League minority protection system was also problematic. Whilst undoubtedly an ambitious and unprecedented attempt to protect the rights of racial, religious and linguistic minorities, paternalistic thinking ensured that the great imperial powers imposed obligations upon the new states of Europe that they would not assume themselves. Moreover, the architects of the system were primarily animated by the conviction that minorities constituted a problem in relation to the stability of the Versailles territorial and political order, rather than by revulsion at their oppression or sympathy for their political and cultural aspirations. Indeed, British and French policy-makers ultimately wished minority "problems" to be resolved by assimilation and often exhibited a strong antipathy to the minorities' "difference".[25] Similar criticisms could be made of the League's complicity in the Greco-Turkish population exchange, the full extent of which is uncovered in Mads Drange's chapter: while welfare considerations were not totally absent, the League's actions involved treating hundreds of thousands of individuals in a brutally instrumental manner.

Turning to the League's role in postwar economic reconstruction, success in stabilising the economies of several Central and Eastern European countries was a noteworthy achievement. But there were significant imperialist overtones to the way in which the League assumed oversight of their economies and imposed budgetary discipline; there is a lineage here through to "IMF stabilization schemes after 1945" and "European Central Bank schemes to achieve stability in credit-crunched Europe" in the very recent past.[26] From a different angle, other great powers looked askance at the role of the Bank of England in these reconstruction schemes, seeing them as a mechanism to establish the "veritable financial domination" of Britain.[27] Collectively, the rest of the League's functional work, which often involved similarly intrusive interventions, is also vulnerable to the recent critiques that have uncovered the dark sides of international humanitarianism.[28]

The further probing and untangling of these complexities is one of the most important tasks for ongoing historiographical work on the League. This is essential not only to enhance our understanding of the League and interwar internationalism themselves, but also to help us gain a firmer purchase on the intractable political and ethical problems of global governance in the present. The contributions in Part 2 of this collection point to multiple productive avenues down which that research might proceed.

More generally, this collection *in toto* demonstrates how the League of Nations has become a site for international historians to deploy cutting-edge techniques in transnational and cultural history, and to work through innovative preoccupations. Part 1 underscores the fruitfully multi-faceted nature of the new scholarship. Locating the League within thicker and broader networks of internationalist activism in the interwar years or the longer history of global governance does sometimes tend to blur the sense of it as a distinctive agent in its own right. Yet simultaneously a different strand in this historiographical enterprise is subjecting the League as an institution to close examination. The rich studies included here offer sociological and prosopographical insights into the personnel of the Secretariat and thought-provoking analyses of the League's bureaucratic practices, in line with the very best contemporary work on the social and cultural history of diplomacy.[29]

This is not simply a matter of recuperating mundane biographical detail or tedious administrative minutiae. So, Karen Gram-Skjoldager's study of the Supervisory Commission sheds vital light on the power relations between small and great powers and between the institution of the League and its constituent members. Similarly, Haakon A. Ikonomou's analysis of the Translation and Interpretation Service unpicks the profound practical and symbolic significance of an ostensibly merely technical apparatus: facilitating international understanding was, after all, central to the League's transformative ambitions. Moreover, read carefully, the microscale work in this vein does in fact link back to the other historiographical strands previously discussed. For instance, Myriam Piguet underlines how the practical matter of gender balance in the Secretariat was intimately intertwined with the transnational feminist activism that made a significant contribution to interwar internationalism. Equally, Torsten Kahlert and Karen Gram-Skjoldager reveal more details about the continuities in personnel that were an important component of the larger story of the evolution of global governance, as the League gave way to the UN.

The contributions in Part 3 similarly demonstrate how the new scholarship on the League is squarely located in the vanguard of contemporary international history practice. It manifestly speaks – as the editors point out in their introduction – to the two core concerns I have identified elsewhere as "narratives" and "bodies".[30] On the first count, scholars in international history and IR have lately become much more interested in how international actors present themselves through narratives, in terms of both identity projection and contestation over particular interests and issues.[31] The essays in the first section of Part 3 enfold the League into this endeavour on several different levels.

Helle Strandgaard Jensen, Nikolai Schulz and Emil Eiby Seidenfaden analyse how the Information Section explicitly sought to tell a positive story about the League in the mid-1930s, even as its political power was in steep decline. Seidenfaden also explores the League's efforts – more negatively – to constrain the proliferation of false information through networking with media organisations and journalists. This again casts new light on the League's perception of the power of both "objective truth" and global public opinion. Benjamin Auberer's essay on novels about the League deploys the interpretive device of narrative in a different but complementary sense. His contribution expands our understanding of the diverse significances attributed to the League and reveals its afterlife in fiction.

The essays in the second section take up the rubric of "bodies", which is here shorthand for concern with the material. The recent "material turn" within international history comprises diverse strands, but some of the most productive involve gauging the political implications of lived experience, the sensory and the material environment. These are, for example, central themes within a major ongoing research project based at Nottingham University entitled "Conferencing the International", which examines diverse forms of interwar internationalism as they were "manifested in their conferencing spaces". Focusing on certain key interwar conferences – including the League-sponsored International Studies Conference – the project explores how their geographical locations influenced their proceedings, how they were experienced ("how were spaces created and policed ... and how can we recreate their multi-sensory character by reference to their sounds, smells, tastes and associated social intimacies?") and how their environments were created (in terms of venues and equipment, the training of staff and how "interactions between speakers and audiences" were "facilitated, reported and received").[32]

Such innovative approaches have enormous potential to reframe and deepen our understanding of internationalism, and they are also on display in the contributions in this section. Gram-Skjoldager's study of working conditions in the Palais Wilson is suggestive of how the physical environment in which the Secretariat operated shaped the lives of

The Secretariat Building at the United Nations Headquarters, New York. The UN complex was designed collaboratively, with the lead architects being the Swiss-French Le Corbusier and the Brazilian Oscar Niemeyer. The striking modernist form of this 154-metre-high skyscraper, opened in 1952, was one among many symbolic moves intended to instantiate a break between the UN and its tainted predecessor, the League, and to help conceal the substantial continuities between the two.

its members and perhaps constrained the achievements of the League. By the same token, Marco Ninno's account of the architectural competitions that led to the construction of the Palais des Nations reveals how the League sought symbolically to incarnate its internationalist ideals in concrete form; in recalling the slightly grubby episode of how Le Corbusier's path-breaking modernist visions were sidelined, it also casts fresh light on how the League remained hidebound by certain traditional modes of thought.

As League historians expand the possibilities of all these innovative approaches and preoccupations, they are not only fruitfully expanding our understanding of the League and interwar internationalism; they are also providing inspiration for historians of other international organisations and for international history as a whole. This is yet another way in which we can discern, a hundred years since its birth and over seventy years since its death, that the League in fact lives on.

NOTES

1 Wilson: 'Address'.

2 Wilson: 'Vital Thing' (the text of a speech given in Paris on 25 January 1919).

3 The indispensable starting point for consideration of these reframings is Pedersen: 'Back'.

4 See, for example, Sluga and Clavin (eds): *Internationalisms*.

5 Pedersen: *Guardians*, 5. Other ways of expressing this include the "Greater League of Nations" referred to by Emil Eiby Seidenfaden and Hagen Schulz-Forberg's notion of the League as a "dot connector". Similarly, Simon Jackson and Alanna O'Malley have referred to the League and the UN "not as unified actors, but as 'platforms' for both formalizing and splintering political ideas and international norms, and as laboratories and toolkits of legal and technical procedures", 'Rocking', 9.

6 Laqua (ed.): *Internationalism Reconfigured*.

7 On the turn to transnational history in general, see for example Saunier: *Transnational History*.

8 Sluga and Clavin: 'Rethinking', 6.

9 For some time, the creation of the Wilson Chair was proclaimed – and not just by those with a vested interest in Aberystwyth – as the single key moment in the establishment of the discipline. This claim is no longer sustainable in the light of recent disciplinary historiography, which has drawn attention to longer-term intellectual antecedents and prefiguring developments elsewhere in the world. See, for example, de Carvalho, Leira and Hobson: 'Big Bangs'. It was, nonetheless, a very significant development in disciplinary history.

10 John, Wright and Garnett: 'International Politics at Aberystwyth', 86.

11 Webster and Herbert: *Theory and Practice*.

12 Davies: 'International Peace Congress'.

13 Davies: *Problem*.

14 Carr: *Twenty Years' Crisis*.

15 Porter: 'E. H. Carr', 36-67, quotation on 55.

16 There were in reality no coherent and homogeneous 'idealist' or 'realist' positions: moreover, "rather than being driven by metaphysical concepts such as realism or idealism, the debates of the time were dominated by more prosaic and pragmatic concerns linked to the immediate problems of international affairs". Ashworth: *International Thought*, 171, and more broadly 134-180.

17 Department of International Politics: 'Centenary'. Anecdotally, I can confirm that the League remains a very palpable presence in Aberystwyth during this centenary year, and not only among the undergraduate students taking my optional module on 'The Dream of Internationalism: The League of Nations and its Legacies'.

18 Jackson and O'Malley: 'Rocking', 1-2. Issues of continuity from the League to the UN are also discussed in Torsten Kahlert's chapter.

19 Pedersen: 'Foreword', xi.

20 Mazower: *Governing*.

21 Pedersen: 'Foreword', xi.

22 This is a core aim of Jackson and O'Malley (eds): *Institution*; note also the recent large-scale research project, *The Reluctant Internationalists*, led by Jessica Reinisch at Birkbeck College, University of London, http://www.bbk.ac.uk/reluctantinternationalists/.

23 Pedersen: *Guardians*.

24 For example, Vitalis: *White World Order*.

25 I sketched out this view in an early contribution to the new historiography: 'Evil'.

26 Clavin: 'Austrian Hunger Crisis', 277-278.

27 Mazower: *Governing*, 151, quoting the Governor of the Bank of France, Emile Moreau.

28 Hilton et al.: 'History and Humanitarianism'.

29 See, for example, the work associated with the research network on *New Diplomatic History*.

30 Finney: 'Narratives and Bodies'.

31 For example, Miskimmon, O'Loughlin and Roselle: *Strategic Narratives*.

32 Quotations from the homepage of the *Conferencing the International: A Cultural and Historical Geography of the Origins of Internationalism, 1919-1939* project, https://www.nottingham.ac.uk/research/groups/interwarconf/home.aspx.

BIBLIOGRAPHY

Ashworth, Lucian M.: *A History of International Thought: From the Origins of the Modern State to Academic International Relations*, London: Routledge, 2014.

Carr, E.H.: *The Twenty Years' Crisis 1919-1939: An Introduction to the Study of International Relations*, Houndmills: Palgrave, 2001 (rev. edn, edited by Michael Cox).

de Carvalho, Benjamin, Halvard Leira and John M. Hobson: 'The Big Bangs of IR: The Myths That Your Teachers Still Tell You about 1648 and 1919', *Millennium* 39 (3), 2011, 735-758.

Clavin, Patricia: 'The Austrian Hunger Crisis and the Genesis of International Organization after the First World War', *International Affairs* 90 (2), 2014, 265-278.

Conferencing the International: A Cultural and Historical Geography of the Origins of Internationalism, 1919-1939, (08.01.2019).

Davies, David: *The Problem of the Twentieth Century: A Study in International Relationships*, London: Ernest Benn, 1930.

Davies, Elgan: 'When Aberystwyth Hosted an International Peace Congress', *Wales for Peace*, 2016 (08.01.2019).

Department of International Politics, Aberystwyth University: 'International Politics Centenary' (08.01.2019).

Finney, Patrick: 'Narratives and Bodies: Culture Beyond the Cultural Turn', *International History Review* 40 (3), 2018, 609-630.

Finney, Patrick B.: '"An Evil for All Concerned": Great Britain and Minority Protection after 1919', *Journal of Contemporary History* 30, 1995, 533-551.

Hilton, Matthew et al.: 'History and Humanitarianism: A Conversation', *Past and Present* 241, 2018.

Jackson, Simon and Alanna O'Malley (eds): *The Institution of International Order: From the League of Nations to the United Nations*, London, Routledge, 2018.

Jackson, Simon and Alanna O'Malley: 'Rocking on its Hinges: The League of Nations, the United Nations and the New History of Internationalism in the Twentieth Century'. In Simon Jackson and Alanna O'Malley (eds): *The Institution of International Order: From the League of Nations to the United Nations*, London, Routledge, 2018, 1-21.

John, Ieuan, Moorhead Wright and John Garnett: 'International Politics at Aberystwyth, 1919-1969'. In Brian Porter (ed.): *The Aberystwyth Papers: International Politics, 1919-1969*, London: Oxford University Press, 1972, 86-102.

Laqua, Daniel (ed.): *Internationalism Reconfigured: Transnational Ideas and Movements between the World Wars*, London: IB Tauris, 2011.

Mazower, Mark: *Governing the World: The History of an Idea*, London: Allen Lane, 2012.

Miskimmon, Alister, Ben O'Loughlin and Laura Roselle: *Strategic Narratives: Communication, Power and the New World Order*, London: Routledge, 2013.

New Diplomatic History, https://newdiplomatichistory.org/ (08.01.2019).

Pedersen, Susan: 'Back to the League of Nations', *American Historical Review* 112 (4), 2007, 1091-1117.

Pedersen, Susan: 'Foreword: From the League of Nations to the United Nations'. In Simon Jackson and Alanna O'Malley (eds): *The Institution of International Order: From the League of Nations to the United Nations*, London: Routledge, 2018, ix-xvi.

Pedersen, Susan: *The Guardians: The League of Nations and the Crisis of Empire*, Oxford: Oxford University Press, 2015.

Porter, Brian: 'E. H. Carr – the Aberystwyth Years, 1936-1947'. In Michael Cox (ed.): *E. H. Carr: A Critical Appraisal*, Houndmills: Palgrave, 2000, 36-67.

Saunier, Pierre-Yves: *Transnational History*, Houndmills: Palgrave, 2013.

Sluga, Glenda and Patricia Clavin (eds): *Internationalisms: A Twentieth Century History*, Cambridge: Cambridge University Press, 2017.

Sluga, Glenda and Patricia Clavin: 'Rethinking the History of Internationalism'. In Glenda Sluga and Patricia Clavin (eds): *Internationalisms: A Twentieth Century History*, Cambridge: Cambridge University Press, 2017, 3-14.

The Reluctant Internationalists, http://www.bbk.ac.uk/reluctantinternationalists/ (08.01.2019).

Vitalis, Robert: *White World Order, Black Power Politics: The Birth of American International Relations*, Ithaca, NY: Cornell University Press, 2015.

Webster, Charles K. and Sydney Herbert: *The League of Nations in Theory and Practice*, London: Allen and Unwin, 1933.

Wilson, Woodrow: 'Address at the Third Plenary Session of the Peace Conference in Paris', *The American Presidency Project* (08.01.2019).

Wilson, Woodrow: 'Make this League of Nations a Vital Thing', *International Organization* 10 (4), 1956, 525-528.

PHOTO CREDITS

Cover	League of Nations Archives, Geneva
Page 21	The Print Collector/Heritage Images/Science Photo Library/Ritzau Scanpix
Page 22	Egon Ranshofen-Wertheimer: *The International Secretariat. A Great Experiment in International Administration*, Washington, 1945
Page 27	League of Nations Archives, Geneva
Page 33	League of Nations Archives, Geneva
Page 35	UN Photo/ARA
Page 36	UN Photo/MB
Page 43	League of Nations Archives, Geneva
Page 45	League of Nations Archives, Geneva
Page 46	League of Nations Archives, Geneva
Page 53	League of Nations Archives, Geneva
Page 54	UN Photo
Page 56	League of Nations Archives, Geneva
Page 66	Chicago Daily Tribune, 29 April 1919
Page 67	League of Nations Archives, Geneva
Page 68	League of Nations Archives, Geneva
Page 82	Bildarchiv der Deutschen Kolonialgesell-schaft, Universitätsbibliothek Frankfurt am Main/082-2990-114
Page 83	Bildarchiv der Deutschen Kolonialgesell-schaft, Universitätsbibliothek Frankfurt am Main/002-1001-05
Page 85	UN Photo/Andrea Brizzi
Page 86	UN Photo
Page 91	Library of Congress, Prints & Photographs Division, J.E.Purdy, Boston
Page 92	University of Iowa. Libraries. Special Collections Department
Page 94	Library of Congress, Prints & Photographs Division, LC-DIG-ppmsca-13291
Page 97	Library of Congress, Prints & Photographs Division, LC-DIG-matpc-02284
Page 105	Library of Congress, Prints & Photographs Division, WWI Posters, LC-DIG-ppmsca-50553
Page 106	League of Nations Archives, Geneva
Page 107	Still picture from "From both sides of the Aegean: Expulsion and Exchange of Populations Turkey-Greece 1922-1924", directed by Maria Iliou
Page 109	Photographic Archive, Centre for Asia Minor Studies, Athens, Greece
Page 115	With special thanks to the Anatolia College Archives & Special Collections
Page 116	With special thanks to the Anatolia College Archives & Special Collections
Page 118	Photographic Archive, Centre for Asia Minor Studies, Athens, Greece
Page 124	Martin Grandjean: *Les réseaux de la coopération intellectuelle. La Société des Nations comme actrice des échanges scientifiques et culturels dans l'entre-deux-guerres*, Lausanne: Université de Lausanne, 2018, 600
Page 126	Det Kgl. Bibliotek
Page 129	Topfoto/Ritzau Scanpix
Page 138	League of Nations Archives, Geneva
Page 142	UN Photo/Eskinder Debebe
Page 145	Martin Grandjean: 'Complex structures and International Organizations' in *Memoria e Ricerca* (2), 2017, 371-393

Page 153 League of Nations Archives, Geneva
Page 154 Leonard Raven-Hall/The Granger Collection/Ritzau Scanpix
Page 157 Science Source/Ritzau Scanpix
Page 163 League of Nations Archives, Geneva
Page 164 League of Nations Archives, Geneva
Page 168 Nakaoka, Tetsurō: *Kindai Nihon shisō taikei vol. 28: Tosaka Jun shū*, Tokyo: Chikuma shobō, 1976
Page 174 UN Photo/Sean Sprague
Page 176 UN Photo/Pernaca Sudhakaran
Page 178 UN Photo/Yutaka Nagata
Page 190 League of Nations Archives, Geneva
Page 193 League of Nations Archives, Geneva
Page 194 League of Nations Archives, Geneva
Page 203 UN Photo
Page 204 League of Nations Archives, Geneva
Page 206 UN Photo/Cliff Watts
Page 213 UN Photo/Pierre Albouy
Page 214 Ullstein Bild-Atelier Binder/Ritzau Scanpix
Page 217 Library of Congress, Music Division, M1646.B
Page 224 Topfoto/Ritzau Scanpix
Page 227 League of Nations Archives, Geneva
Page 229 Bogislas/Ritzau Scanpix
Page 231 The Granger Collection/Ritzau Scanpix & Mary Evans Picture Library/Ritzau Scanpix
Page 238 League of Nations Archives, Geneva
Page 239 FIPOI©luca fascini
Page 242 UN Photo/Violaine Martin
Page 249 Sigfried Giedion: *Space, Time and Architecture. The Growth of a New Tradition.* Cambridge, Massachusetts, Harvard University Press, 1969
Page 251 UN Photo
Page 252 UN Photo/Violaine Martin
Page 254 UN Photo/MB
Page 258 League of Nations Archives, Geneva
Page 261 League of Nations Archives, Geneva
Page 262 League of Nations Archives, Geneva
Page 268 Unknown/Ritzau Scanpix
Page 270 Aberystwyth University
Page 274 UN Photo
Page 278 UN Photo/JG

The League of Nations – Perspectives from the Present

Contributors: see www.unipress.dk
Publishing editor: Peter Bejder
Cover illustration: League of Nations Archives, Geneva
Cover, layout and typesetting: Jørgen Sparre
This book is typeset in Walbaum and Gill
Printed on 130 g Arctic Volume White by Narayana Press, Denmark
Printed in Denmark 2019
1st edition, 1st impression

ISBN: 978 87 7184 620 1
Aarhus University Press
Finlandsgade 29
DK-8200 Aarhus N
Denmark
www.unipress.dk

Published with the financial support of
Aarhus University Research Foundation
Danish National Research Council (grant no. DFF – 4180-00147)

International distributors:

Oxbow Books Ltd.	ISD
The Old Music Hall	70 Enterprise Drive, Suite 2
106–108 Cowley Road	Bristol, CT 06010
Oxford, OX4 1JE	USA
United Kingdom	www.isdistribution.com
www.oxbowbooks.com	

PEER REVIEWED

MIX
Paper from responsible sources
FSC® C010651